Strange Fate

An Extraordinary True Story of Paranormal Discovery

Graham Phillips and Jodi Russell

ISBN (PB): 979-8-9880684-0-2
ISBN (E): 979-8-9880684-1-9

Visit our website: StrangeFate.Net.

Contents

Introduction

What follows began as a historical investigation into a Victorian secret society and its strange esoteric beliefs. However, it soon became an extraordinary adventure of discovery and the search for a mysterious artifact believed to hold tremendous power. Throughout this remarkable quest, we encountered some of the most bizarre phenomena imaginable, forcing us to question what we thought we knew about reality itself. Occurring amid central England's rolling hills and lush green landscapes, this astonishing true story is way beyond what would typically be called paranormal. The account you are about to read will no doubt sound unbelievable, seeming to defy logic and challenge the very concepts of existence. But—we assure you—it is based entirely on actual events.

Concerning our writing style. As this book was written by two of us and involved us both directly, we decided to write in the third person. The narrative has been abridged or modified for clarity, and names have been changed.

Graham Phillips and Jodi Russell. Birmingham and Los Angeles, 2023.

-Prologue-
The Meonia Mystery

During the second half of the nineteenth century, the Victorian mansion of Biddulph Grange, just north of the city of Stoke-on-Trent in Staffordshire, central England, was home to a mysterious secret society called the Order of Meonia (pronounced *me-on-eye-a*: "a" as in cat). This was the period of the Gothic Revival when anything paranormal, supernatural, or mystical was the height of fashion. It was an age that saw the birth of spiritualism, psychical research, and a deep fascination with the occult. Many organizations emerged in Europe and the USA, purporting to practice various forms of ancient mysticism and study esoteric traditions worldwide. For example, the Hermetic Order of the Golden Dawn explored a medieval Judaic tradition called Kabbalah; the Theosophical Society, which absorbed an amalgam of age-old Asiatic beliefs; and Druid revivalists who sought to rediscover the shamanic customs of the early Celts. The Order of Meonia, which seems to have combined diverse strands of ancient knowledge, was founded in 1851 by Maria Bateman, the lady of Biddulph Grange. Having inherited a fortune and his father's banking business, her husband James was free to pursue his passion for botany, becoming head of the prestigious Royal Horticultural Society's plant exploration committee. After building the mansion on the site of an old rectory he acquired in 1840, James Bateman decided to surround the house with splendid gardens to display flowers, shrubs, and trees from around the world and spent much of the next thirty years traveling the globe collecting a wealth of exotic plants for the purpose. During the 1850s, Maria remained behind to design and oversee the building of several unusual shrines in the gardens, including a Chinese sanctuary, a Celtic glen, and a mock Egyptian tomb, where the Order of Meonia is said to have held meetings, performed strange ceremonies, and conducted mysterious rites.

Little is known concerning the Order of Meonia. Still, a fascinating insight is revealed in a short commemorative pamphlet prepared for a private memorial event on May 4, 1897, a copy of which survived with the descendants of those who once lived at Biddulph Grange. The event was in remembrance of one Mary Ann Heath, who died 25 years earlier at 28. Mary came to live at Biddulph Grange in 1871 after the Batemans moved to London and her father, Robert Heath, bought the property. A neighbor and life-long friend of the Batemans, Heath was a wealthy industrialist, local councilor, and later a Member of Parliament, who continued to live at the nearby family home of Clough Hall, leaving Mary to run the Grange alone. Although Mary Heath was only the lady of Biddulph Grange for just over a year, dying of typhoid on a trip to London on October 13, 1872, she left a great impression on those around her. The commemorative pamphlet contains brief epitaphs by various friends and relatives, from which we learn that Mary had been the Order of Meonia's leader, evidently succeeding Maria Bateman sometime around 1865. It also reveals that she was regarded in high esteem as a clairvoyant and spirit medium, even as a child, and that the order was founded after she discovered a lost relic when she was only seven years old. This mysterious, unspecified, ancient artifact, believed by the group to harness extraordinary mystical power, was referred to only by its enigmatic name, the "Heart of the Rose."

After Mary's death, her brother Robert Heath Jr. took over the estate, while his wife Laura became the third lady of the Grange, succeeding Mary as the Meonia group's new leader. The society continued until 1897 when, on January 16, a mysterious fire swept through the mansion, gutting much of the building. Although no one was harmed, so much of their occult paraphernalia was lost in the blaze that the group could no longer continue. According to the pamphlet, Laura disbanded the Order of Meonia and ensured the safety of their prized possession, the Heart of the Rose, but whether she hid it or handed it on to someone else is not disclosed. Laura Heath died of tuberculosis on May 5 that same year, just one day after the memorial event, and her husband Robert Jr., owner of the estate since his father's death in 1893, had the place rebuilt. Following the First World War, the Heath family faced bankruptcy. Biddulph Grange was sold to become a hospital, its scenic gardens abandoned to the elements, its discarded shrines left to decay.

In 1981, British author and historical researcher Graham Phillips first visited Biddulph Grange to investigate occultism during the Gothic Revival of the 1800s. He was fascinated by the story of the Order of Meonia and Mary Heath, the charismatic young lady who seems to have inspired the secret society's founding. However, other than local rumors concerning strange ceremonies on the estate in the late nineteenth century, Graham found no further record regarding the Order of Meonia or its mystical beliefs. At least, not *that* Order of Meonia. Intriguingly, an earlier secret society of the same name, thought to have been founded by the Elizabethan astrologer Dr. John Dee, existed in the late sixteenth and early seventeenth centuries. However, that organization met some 90 miles south of Biddulph, at Canons Ashby House in the county of Northamptonshire, and had disbanded almost three centuries before. Graham learned that this Elizabethan order took its name from a location regarded as the birthplace of Western occultism: "Meonia," also spelled "Maeonia," an ancient kingdom in what is now Turkey, later known as Lydia. Presumably, Graham reasoned, the Victorian Order of Meonia had also associated themselves with the occult traditions of this ancient land.

Having exhausted his historical investigations, in 1982, Graham visited Biddulph Grange accompanied by Jenny Blackwood, a spiritualist medium whose "psychic impressions," as she called them, had proved uncannily accurate. On occasions, she even helped police locate missing persons. With nothing else to go on, and on the off chance that she might shed further light on the Grange, he took Jenny to the replica Egyptian tomb, the only garden shrine not wholly overgrown. Inside the cold, dank, dilapidated structure, the medium appeared to fall into a trance, and Graham recorded the few words she spoke.

Find the stone carved with the letter B. Only then will your quest to understand the Order of Meonia and your search to discover the Heart of the Rose truly begin.

Curiously, she failed to elaborate. When Jenny awoke from the trance, she claimed to have no recall of her brief and cryptic pronouncement. Graham was amazed. He had told her about the Victorian secret society but *nothing* concerning the Heart of the Rose. There was seemingly no way she could have known anything about it. At the time, Graham and his colleagues investigating the mysteries of Biddulph Grange had not yet discovered the memorial pamphlet revealing that the Heart of the Rose had been an ancient relic. The name, however, had been mentioned by descendants of people connected with Biddulph Grange, who recollected talk of something called the Heart of the Rose, having held great importance to the Heath family. Strangely, no one admitted to knowing what it was except for one lady whose grandmother had worked at the mansion during the time of the Heaths. She thought it might have been a secret location, perhaps a site the Meonia group considered sacred.

Jenny listened carefully as Graham told her of the Heart of the Rose and what, at the time, it was thought to have been. "If it *is* a place," he suggested, "going by what you said, could it be marked with the stone carved with a letter B?"

Jenny remained deep in thought for a moment before answering. "No. I can't explain how, but I get the impression that the stone—let's call it the B Stone—is not where the Heart of the Rose is to be found but where your quest will begin. However, I have a feeling that won't be for a while. When the time is right."

Graham was puzzled. He had not even considered searching for the Heart of the Rose, let alone embarking on a quest.

Jenny said she had no idea who had spoken through her, and further attempts to repeat the apparent channeling failed. The only additional information Jenny could offer was that she had the strong feeling that the Heart of the Rose was not to be found on the Biddulph estate. Sadly, she died shortly after, and no further psychics, researchers, or local historians could elaborate on what she had said.

Strange Fate

Because of Jenny's intriguing words concerning the Heart of the Rose, the fact that she could seemingly have known nothing about it through normal means, and that it was the only aspect of the Meonia mystery she mentioned during her trance, Graham was resolved to find it. However, even though he later learned that it had been a relic of some kind rather than a place, he discovered nothing else concerning the artifact. Not *what* it was or was meant to do, *where* it originated, or *why* it had been considered so important by the Order of Meonia. Neither did he find the enigmatic stone carved with the letter B. And there, his investigation ceased. In 1988, the National Trust (the UK's largest organization for heritage conservation) took ownership of the Biddulph estate; most of the house was converted into private apartments while its gardens were renovated and opened to the public. Until recently, however, large areas of the estate remained overgrown, but they are now fully restored. When Graham eventually returned to Biddulph Grange, he was accompanied by American researcher and long-time friend Jodi Russell. From the start, it seemed almost as if fate had decided it was time for the investigation to resume.

-1-
Biddulph Grange

Two stone sphinxes, the size of living lions, faced each other from three-tiered plinths, one to either side of the entrance to what the Biddulph Grange guidebook called the Egyptian temple. Despite its name, it was more a tomb recreation than a temple. Above the portal was painted a winged disk, the symbol of the ancient Egyptian sun god, and on top of the structure was a pyramid formed from an intricately-trimmed yew bush. Inside, a long, narrow passageway, its stone walls painted red, its atmosphere heavy with the musty smell of age, led to a small chamber where a further stone statue—an ugly, human-sized, dog-headed baboon—squatted on a concrete plinth.

"Aani, also known as the Ape of Thoth, was the Egyptian spirit of botany." A guide explained the statute to a group of around ten students crammed into the chamber as Jodi Russell and Graham Phillips waited for them to leave. "James Bateman and his wife Maria, who designed the Grange's wonderful 15-acre gardens in the mid-1800s, considered it an appropriate image to represent their love of nature."

"What was this place used for?" asked one of the boys.

"It was purely ornamental," the guide said, "a decorative park or garden building called a folly. The Batemans built two other features to augment the worldwide collection of plants, shrubs, and trees they planted here: the Chinese sanctuary and the Celtic glen. The three constructions are collectively known as shrines."

This was Jodi's first visit to Biddulph Grange. "Could that have been all this was?" she asked Graham as the party moved on. "Ornamental?"

Graham had given Jodi only a brief outline of what he had discovered about Biddulph Grange, the Bateman and Heath families, the Order of Meonia, and the Heart of the Rose. "That's the official line," he said. "But my research suggests otherwise. Beside the memorial pamphlet, there's a series of articles in a gardening magazine from the 1860s relating how the Batemans held ceremonial events here. Neither provides details, but several elderly people in the 1980s recalled rumors that there had been strange gatherings at the shrines during Victorian times when the owners and their guests would dress up in robes."

"Simple pageantry?" Jodi suggested.

Graham paced as he talked, his footsteps echoing through the mock Egyptian tomb. "Although I've found few historical references to the Order of Meonia, I *have* uncovered much to suggest that the Batemans and Heaths had more than a casual interest in the occult. James's preoccupation with horticulture led him to travel the world, during which time he developed a deep fascination with ancient mysticism, which his wife Maria shared. Both later joined the mystical Theosophical Society, and James became a member of the Society for Psychical Research and joined a lodge of nineteenth-century Druids. Then there's Laura, Mary Heath's sister-in-law, who assumed leadership of the Meonia group after Mary's death. She had a keen interest in all things esoteric and paranormal."

"And Mary herself?"

Graham sighed. "Little is known of her apart from what's in the memorial pamphlet. Referring to her affectionately as Mary Ann, we are told how much she was admired, that she was a respected clairvoyant, and that she discovered the Heart of the Rose that somehow led to the founding of the Order of Meonia."

"But we're not told what exactly it was, how she found it, or how it led to the group being founded?"

"No." Graham stopped pacing. "Household records concerning her time running the estate between 1871 and 1872, and a few passing references to her as a child—that's all we know of Mary Heath."

That had Jodi thinking. "Why was *she* left to manage Biddulph Grange? She had brothers, right? In the misogynistic Victorian Era, wasn't that unusual—a woman estate manager?"

"It is, but not unheard of. Mary's parents continued to reside at the much grander family home of Clough Hall, just a few miles away, and her brothers were either too young or married and lived elsewhere. However, there was probably more to it. If Mary's father had been part of the Meonia group, he might have appointed her to run the Grange because she was the society's leader."

"That's another thing," Jodi said. "A female head of a secret society? Weren't such groups an exclusively male thing?"

Graham explained what he knew. "Fraternal lodges, like the Freemasons, certainly were. But these were generally social, financial, or charitable organizations. Some incorporated ritual activities, but these were largely symbolic. The *occult* secret societies genuinely believed in the supernatural, immersing themselves in clairvoyance, mediumship, and ritualistic practices. Their ceremonies were performed to enhance psychic abilities, commune with spirits, and control supernatural forces. They accepted both men and women equally, and the women excelled. The Meonia group's leaders were women: Maria, Mary, and Laura. Other such mystical groups founded in Victorian times also had female leaders. For example, the Russian-born author Helena Blavatsky established the Theosophical Society in 1875, and the British actress Florence Farr was the leader of the Hermetic Order of the Golden Dawn in the 1890s."

"But the Meonia group included men," Jodi said. "And they had no problem following a female leader?"

"Not that I can tell. Take James Bateman's son, Robert, for example. He was certainly a group member until the end, as he composed an epitaph for the memorial pamphlet. He remained at Biddulph when his parents moved to London, renting a property on the Grange estate to assist Mary in managing the place and presumably help her run the Meonia group."

"Were Robert and Mary an item?" Jodi asked.

"Possibly. They'd been childhood friends. Although Mary married an army surgeon named James Heffernan in the late 1860s, she and her husband spent little time together as he was stationed in India; she also continued using her birth name—Mary Heath. It was probably an arranged marriage of convenience. Her family had money, and he had aristocratic connections. It may also be significant that Robert—just two years older than Mary—didn't marry until eleven years after her death."

A breeze blew along the dark passageway, ruffling Jodi's hair. "Besides the memorial pamphlet, you say you've found no additional evidence regarding Mary's involvement with the occult. What about Robert?"

Graham related what he had learned. "Robert Bateman was a relatively famous painter. Through his association with the Pre-Raphaelite artist movement in London, where he spent half his time, he became close friends with various well-known occultists. They included Florence Farr, whom I've already mentioned, the author A. E. Waite, and the poet W. B. Yeats, all members of the Golden Dawn. All three were prolific writers on the subject. And Robert's artistic mentor, the painter Edward Burne-Jones, was a noted authority on the history of sorcery, mysticism, and magic, and was a member of the same Druid order to which Robert's father, James Bateman belonged."

"And they all visited Biddulph Grange?"

"Frequently."

"So, they were probably members of the group. Anyone else?"

"There are several close acquaintances of the Heath and Bateman families who shared a fascination with the occult and the paranormal that are very likely to have been involved with the Order of Meonia. Firstly, Jane Morris, a Pre-Raphaelite model and leading interior designer of the late 1800s. She was a close friend of Laura Heath and a frequent visitor to the Grange, while her daughter May was besties with Florence Farr. Furthermore, her husband William, a Pre-Raphaelite painter and textile artist, was a lifelong friend and collaborator with Edward Burne-Jones. Then there's textile designer Elizabeth Wardle from the nearby town of Leek. As well as she and Laura belonging to the same women's rights society, their husbands were involved in a joint business venture. The three women spent considerable time together at Biddulph Grange while their partners busied themselves with their Leek-based dye-manufacturing company. Perhaps the most interesting is the Pre-Raphaelite artist, educationalist, and writer Barbara Bodichon, who came from nearby Alfreton in the Peak District, the hilly region north of Biddulph. She was introduced to the Batemans by Edward Burne-Jones and, during the early 1850s, became an in-house tutor to the young Robert Bateman and his sister Katherine. Consequently, she lived at Biddulph Grange in 1851 when the Order of Meonia began."

"So, she might even have been involved in establishing the group," Jodi said.

"Almost certainly. At the time, she was keenly interested in the new spiritualist craze of seances, table-turning, and mediumship. Anything supernatural or mystical was right up her street. As she was right there at the time of the Meonia group's inception, she was likely one of the order's founding members. What clinches it for me is that she painted the only known depiction of what seems to have been a Meonia ritual. Sadly, few of her pictures survive, but one, a watercolor titled The Hooded Procession, shows a group of hooded, white-robed figures—seemingly both men and women—making their way along an isolated tree-lined valley in the dim, eerie light of a damp and misty dawn. The lead figure is reading from a large book, and another holds a triangular banner depicting a skull on a black background.

Jodi frowned. "Pretty morbid."

"Not really. The skull was an ancient symbol of time, fate, and fortune."

"How do we know the painting depicted the Order of Meonia? It might have been a group of Druids. Bateman and Burne-Jones were into that."

"True. However, although the picture is undated, it is widely thought to have been painted in the summer of 1851, precisely when the Meonia group came into being."

A small bird briefly fluttered along the corridor towards them, seemed to realize it had taken a wrong turn, and flew back outside. "Sounds like there were a lot of Pre-Raphaelites involved. Who exactly were they?" Jodi asked.

"They were an alliance of English artists founded in 1848 by students from the Royal Academy of Arts, led by the painter Gabriel Rossetti. They wanted to return to the more romantic style of art prominent before the time of the Renaissance painter Raphael in the early 1500s. Hence their name. As their subject matter often involved classical mythology and medieval legends, such as Greek and Roman epics and the Arthurian saga—usually magical and mystical themes—many Pre-Raphaelite artists developed a fascination with the occult and the esoteric."

Jodi was familiar with Rossetti and had seen some of his paintings. "Was Rossetti a member of the Meonia group?"

Graham smiled. "Unlikely. He was too narcissistic to join anyone else's club."

"So, the Pre-Raphaelites were attracted by the occult. But how would they have known about the Meonia group?"

"To begin with, I'd imagine through the artist Barbara Bodichon."

Jodi was intrigued. "Were there many female artists at the time?"

"Not in the 1850s. At least not that became known or exhibited. Barbara was one of the first. In fact, through her, the Pre-Raphaelite movement ultimately attracted many female artists, and the mold began to break. She was a leading advocate of women's rights; soon after the Meonia group started, she set about writing a book that virtually kick-started modern feminism."

"But is there anything to prove these people were in the Order of Meonia?"

"Household records reveal that they were regular visitors to Biddulph Grange, and other reasons, such as I've outlined, strongly imply their involvement with the group, but no *absolute* proof."

"Why is that?"

"For the same reason that we know so little about Mary Heath. Many of the Grange's records, personal writings, and private correspondence were destroyed during the fire of 1897."

A thought occurred to Jodi. "As I recall, most people you mentioned lived in London, well over 150 miles away. I assume it would have been a long, awkward journey back then?"

Graham shook his head. "Surprisingly, it was probably easier than today. From 1864, Biddulph had a railway station that didn't close until 1927. So, just a few hours by steam train, with only one change, and you were within a short carriage ride of Biddulph Grange."

Jodi paused to get her head around all the names Graham had been reeling off. "You mentioned that Laura Heath was also keenly interested in the paranormal. How do we know?"

Graham smiled. "Far more has survived concerning Laura than Mary, in records found at Robert Bateman's later home of Benthall Hall in Shropshire. Through Robert, Laura became friends with occultists Florence Farr and A. E. Waite. Laura was also a committed spiritualist, spending time with the famous American medium Cora Scott when she visited London in 1874. She was a keen Theosophist, traveling to Bavaria in 1885 to stay with Helena Blavatsky, arguably the most notorious mystic in the world. It's clear Laura was up to her neck in the weird and wonderful."

Jodi held out a booklet she was holding. "Why is that not in the Biddulph Grange guidebook?"

Disappointment showed on Graham's face. "It's the gardens that attract visitors. What the owners got up to in their spare time is of little interest to most people."

"So, go one; why are we here?" Over the years, Jodi had gotten used to Graham keeping his discoveries to himself until he could dramatically reveal them, usually at the locations involved.

"I might reopen the investigation," he said.

Jodi raised her eyebrows. "After four decades?"

"Parts of the estate have been newly renovated and opened to the public for the first time, such as the Celtic glen and additional parts of the Chinese sanctuary. Maybe lost evidence concerning the Order of Meonia has been revealed. Perhaps even clues to lead to the Heart of the Rose." Graham had yet to elaborate on the mysterious relic.

"What exactly *was* the Heart of the Rose?"

Graham leaned against the cold chamber wall. "This is all guesswork, but it might have originated in the land of Meonia in southern Turkey, perhaps explaining why the society called themselves the Order of Meonia. Once a province of the Minoan Empire centered on the Mediterranean island of Crete, Meonia had a legendary queen named Omphale, possibly based on an actual person who lived over 3000 years ago and was said to have fashioned sacred stones. She was supposed to have been a personified demigod, the embodiment of destiny, an ethereal entity who could control fate. So, it was probably a magic stone."

Jodi was skeptical. "You think it had some kind of magic power?"

Graham waited for a new party of tourists to move on. "I doubt it, but the Order of Meonia thought so."

"So how did Mary Heath supposedly find it?"

"We're not told." A young boy and girl ran laughing through the Egyptian temple as a gust of wind swept along the corridor, howling through the building to create a low resonating hum. Graham waited for the noise to subside before continuing. "But she probably found it around 1851 when the Order of Meonia was founded. At least that's when they started building the shrines."

Jodi did a quick calculation in her head. "Mary was born in 1844, as I remember, so she would have only been seven." Her eyes opened wide. "A *seven-year-old* founded an occult order!"

Over the years, Graham had thought long and

hard about this apparent incongruity. "The memorial pamphlet only implies that she *inspired* its founding; it was Maria who started it," he said. "Mary seems to have been regarded as a child psychic, so I assume she located the relic clairvoyantly—at least, as far as the Order of Meonia was concerned. In some way—and before you ask, I have no idea how—either Mary or the relic she found instigated the setting up of the group. I do have some idea *where* she might have discovered it, however. The memorial pamphlet says she found it in a 'sepulcher,' a tomb. We're not told where, but I can hazard a guess. Around 1851, Mary traveled with her parents to visit the classical ruins of Greece. The ancient Greeks possessed various stones they believed had been fashioned by Omphale of Meonia, some of which have been discovered in their tombs. If the Heart of the Rose *is* an Omphale Stone, Mary may have found it while visiting one of these."

A young couple entered the Egyptian temple at the other end of the long corridor and presumably decided the place was somewhat menacing, with Graham and Jodi, dressed in dark colors, standing staring at them on each side of the creepy Ape of Thoth. They abruptly turned and left. Jodi laughed, then said, "If the Heart of the Rose was an Omphale Stone, what would its power have been?"

"The stones were said to have the power to change fate—whatever that might mean—and could bestow what we would now call psychic abilities, such as clairvoyance, telekinesis, and precognition."

"You think it made Mary psychic?"

"The memorial pamphlet suggests she was already psychic before she found it. Maybe they believed the relic amplified her gift. I suppose that would explain her influence over the others at such an early age."

Jodi looked around at the Egyptian temple, imagining a little girl directing her elders to construct it. "How many Omphale stones were there?"

Graham held out his hands. "No one knows. A few dozen, perhaps."

"And one of them could be the Heart of the Rose." Jodi frowned. "If it was finally hidden around 1900, do you think it's still there after all this time?"

"Jenny seemed to think so."

"But that was based on a *psychic* impression, not actual evidence," Jodi frowned. "Anyway, at the time, Jenny thought the Heart of the Rose was a place, didn't she?"

Graham shook his head. "She never actually said *what* it was. Just that it still awaited discovery. At the time, *I* thought it was a place. And true, it *was* just her impression, but I reckon it's worth taking seriously. As far as I know, Jenny had never heard of the Heart of the Rose. So how come she—her spirit guide or whatever—knew about it? By all accounts, Jenny was a remarkable psychic. She once helped police locate a missing girl who turned up alive and living in Germany. There was no way she could have discovered the teenager's whereabouts by normal means. So, yes, I do think the Heart of the Rose might still be hidden somewhere."

Jodi wandered over to the rear entrance of the Egyptian temple that directly adjoined the chamber at right angles to the central passageway. Outside, leading from it, a pathway wound through the picturesque gardens, flanked on either side by tall redwood, cedar, and monkey puzzle trees, all grown from seeds, cuttings, and saplings collected by James Bateman during his excursions around the world. "These gardens are spectacular," she said. "It's astonishing how they managed to create them back then. I have enough trouble looking after my garden with all the modern conveniences."

Seen from the outside, the façade of this side of the Egyptian temple was strangely fashioned in the form of what has been described as a Swiss cottage, and above the entrance was painted a monogram incorporating the initials of Maria and James Bateman, along with the date 1865. Jodi was confused. "You said this place was built during the 1850s, but this suggests it wasn't built until the 1860s."

Graham joined her in the sunshine. "The Swiss cottage façade was added *later*. Probably on the insistence of James. He'd seeded the area with Alpine plants—the path here is called the Alpine pathway—and presumably wanted a complementary feature."

Jodi gazed along the path to where the two children were playing amongst the flowers. "So, you hope to find new clues concerning the Meonia group in these gardens?"

Graham moved returned to the temple, looking back to the rear entrance where Jodi was silhouetted in bright sunlight. "The recent renovations might have revealed something."

"Like what?" Jodi asked, reentering the shrine.

"The stone Jenny said was carved with a letter B."

Jodi gazed at the menacing face of the Ape of Thoth. It reminded her of a snarling bulldog. "So how does this statue come into things? The guide seemed sure that it represented the Batemans' love of gardening."

"If the Batemans wanted an Egyptian representation of botany, they would have chosen Geb, the chief deity of horticulture, usually depicted in majestic human form, rather than this ugly little critter." Graham patted the statue's head. "No offense."

Jodi smiled. "What *does* he represent then?"

"Aani *was* associated with nature, but its wild, chaotic side, not the horticultural order the Batemans cherished. There must have been another reason for them to erect his statue here. Aani was more than your usual demigod. Considered beyond good and evil, and outside space and time, he was the lord of misrule—chaos. He was the trickster of the gods, like Loki in Norse mythology or the Fool in Western tradition. But primarily, he had power over fate and fortune. Associated with one of the supreme deities, Thoth, the god of learning, he also acted as guardian of secret wisdom and gatekeeper to mystic realms."

Jodi cracked a broad smile. "Quite a resumé." She ran her hand along the sculptured gray stone from which the statue was made. "Would the Meonia group have worshiped him?"

"Unlikely. The occult is rarely about worship in the way that religion is. Occult groups sought to gain mystical knowledge, attain enlightenment, and control supernatural forces. They may have believed they could invoke entities referred to as gods, angels, demigods, and spirits. However, most occultists regarded them as custodians of wisdom and power rather than higher beings to be adored."

Jodi looked about her at the mold-stained, featureless walls of the mock Egyptian tomb. "Perhaps there were once inscriptions here, like in real Egyptian tombs, to reveal what went on, which have since been painted over," she suggested.

Graham brushed a hand against the rough red paint. "It would need analytical techniques such as infrared reflectography and X-ray radiography to know for sure, but cursory investigation has suggested not. There's certainly no historical mention of hieroglyphics."

"I noticed that the sphinxes outside have what appear to be hieroglyphics on them."

"Yes, an inscription on both reads 'Begat of Ra, Ruler of Egypt,' which referred to Egyptian pharaohs. There are also paired cartouches—oval designs containing the names of a king and queen—but they're too faded to determine their identities. So, they remain something of a puzzle."

"Appropriate! In mythology, the sphinx set riddles." Jodi recalled.

"So did Aani," Graham added. "The Ape of Thoth was said to reveal knowledge in riddles, which might be what this place was for. It may have been what you could call a riddle shrine."

"That's a weird concept." Jodi stared at the dog-headed baboon statue, realizing its expression was more a mischievous smile than a snarl. "How would Aani make his riddles known?"

Outside, the sun was temporarily obscured by clouds. As Graham explained his take on Egyptian mediumship, the chamber grew darker and noticeably colder. "As in many ancient cultures, the Egyptians imagined that supernatural beings could temporarily inhabit idols made in their likeness, from which they would communicate via an oracle—a medium or channeler if you like. I'd imagine one of the Meonia group would either experience enigmatic visions or fall into a trance and speak on Aani's behalf."

"Maybe it was Aani who spoke through Jenny," Jodi suggested. "What she said was certainly a riddle." She remained silent for a moment as she reconsidered. "The message was in English rather than ancient Egyptian, so I suppose not."

Graham rubbed the back of his neck. "From the occultist's perspective, spirits can talk in any language they want, though it is often irrelevant. The idea is that supernatural beings can overlay their mind on the recipient's, using the medium's brain as a universal translator."

Jodi frowned. "In movies, supernatural entities speak in ancient languages, often Latin."

Graham smiled. "That's fiction. But it *is* said to happen. Some say the spirit wants to prove itself by showing fluency in a language the medium is ignorant of. Latin is relatively common, but that's because, until recently, Latin was a universal language spoken by wealthy, educated people."

Jodi examined an alcove in the wall facing the Alpine pathway exit, in which a bench was set facing out onto the tree-lined pathway. "So, it's likely that Maria, Mary, and Laura, maybe others, acted as oracles to channel Aani's riddles. At least, so they believed."

"Something like that. In this chamber, anyway."

Just to the right of the bench alcove, divided from it by a thick wall, a short gloomy corridor ran to a flight of stone steps leading to a further room directly overhead. The room was large enough to hold a gathering of around a dozen people, lit by leadlight windows to either end, with a fireplace in one of its plain, whitewashed walls. "Local gossip has it that séances were held here during Victorian times. Some people even call it the séance room," Graham said as they entered.

"The fact that there's a fireplace suggests it wasn't just a summerhouse," Jodi observed.

"Implying they used the place in winter."

"Or at night!" Jodi added. "If they did sit around a table, ouija board, or holding hands in a ring, they'd need to keep warm." She gazed out the southern-facing window at the tree-lined path below. "I assume there are plenty of ghost stories here. Gray ladies walking the grounds," she suggested with a smile.

Graham shook his head. "It's odd. Most grand

old estates have at least one ghost story, but I've not tracked down a single account of hauntings anywhere at Biddulph Grange."

"That *is* odd." Jodi examined the small room, imagining the wealthy Victorians holding hands in candlelight, with their sacred relic—a stone or whatever it was—on a table before them. "Why *was* it called the Heart of the Rose?" she said, turning to Graham.

Graham was examining a picture on the wall, showing Biddulph Grange as it was before the fire of 1897. The exterior of the present mansion, rebuilt by Laura's husband Robert, was a close approximation of the original building. "I have no idea. Besides its mention in the memorial pamphlet and the local gossip, I've found no reference to it anywhere."

Jodi's eyes widened. "That's even odder. You know nothing about it yet still want to find it?"

Graham laughed. "It does sound a bit mad. It's the Order of Meonia I'm mainly interested in. But it *would* be fun to search for their lost relic—a real-life treasure hunt. That, and that it was the only aspect of the Meonia mystery Jenny Blackwood mentioned."

They left the séance room and descended a further flight of stone steps that led down behind the Egyptian temple to a narrow, winding gorge, cutting through the hillside to arrive at a small lake, around 40 feet wide and 60 feet long, which was spanned by an ornate, traditional Chinese footbridge at the point where it narrowed at the nearest end. Bamboo plants, and exotic oriental trees, some with amber or russet leaves, surrounded the pool, and the branches of weeping willows hung over the water's edge. This was the Chinese sanctuary, also known as the Chinese garden, with its principal feature, a pagoda painted red and green, at the other end of the lake. Gold dragons and phoenixes reflected the sunlight along its roof while little golden bells hanging on silver chains along the façade chimed pleasantly in the wind. The scene reminded Jodi of the famous blue-and-white Willow Pattern used since the eighteenth century to decorate ceramic wear, except that this was in vibrant, living color.

"Pretty elaborate for a folly," she said.

Graham was looking into the clear waters of the pool, where large, multi-colored fish swam slowly back and forth, every so often bobbing to the surface to gobble food people had thrown for the ducks. "The Victorians did build some elaborate follies. But, as in the Egyptian temple, ceremonial events were performed here. Pity we're not told what they involved." He explained how the same series of articles in the 1860s gardening magazine that mentioned the events held at the Egyptian temple reported similar activities at the other shrines. "Note the phoenix figures on the roof. Once placed all over the gardens, large ornamental bowls were decorated with images of this mythical creature. As the symbol of rebirth and an imagined new age, it may have been the Meonia group's insignia."

Graham led the way along the path, skirting the right side of the pool and into a lawned enclosure with a rectangular stone archway to either end. On the grass were two dragons shaped in the turf and in-filled with red pebbles. "Something here is rather weird." He pointed to a gilded statue of the forequarters of a life-size bull or cow on a wall above the red dragons, facing toward the lake beneath a protective wooden canopy. Between its horns was a large golden disk. "That's an Egyptian icon. They depicted sacred bulls and cows with the sun disk between their horns. The Chinese didn't. So, what's it doing in a Chinese garden? The books say it's a sacred water buffalo, but that's a Hindu concept. Besides, the horns are completely wrong for a buffalo. I think it's more likely Hathor, an Egyptian fertility goddess often depicted as a cow with the sun disk between her horns." Graham reached up and rapped the creature with his knuckle. "It's hollow and made of metal. Bronze, I'd imagine. The gold is just paint."

Jodi was using her phone to search online. "The horns aren't right for Hathor either. Look." She showed Graham various images of statues and tomb paintings she'd found. "Hathor's horns are curved vertically, whereas these are more horizontal." She searched further. "It's more like this, the Apis Bull." This creature, they read, was associated with the Egyptian god Apis, a deity that acted as an intermediary between this world and the next: a guardian to the world of gods. Just as the Ape of Thoth imparted knowledge, the Apis Bull was thought to enable communication with spirits. Moreover, it was venerated in the hope of influencing fortune and fate.

Jodi had traveled widely throughout Asia and visited China several times. As she looked out over the lake, with the bridge at one end and the pagoda to the other, she was struck by the familiarity of the scene. "Apart from the Apis Bull, this layout is similar to Chinese shrines where people float water lanterns," she said. "Paper boats with candles in the middle that hold written messages. These days they're usually wishes, making the shrine ponds the Chinese equivalent of wishing wells. Traditionally, however, the messages were requests sent out to Chang'e, not a goddess so much as the spirit of destiny. It's said that the answers to these requests could be heard as whispers in the wind as it blew through the weeping willows." As if in response to Jodi's words, a light breeze rustled the branches of the trees surrounding the pond.

As Jodi talked, Graham gazed into the pool, imagining delicate paper boats, like floating lanterns, drifting across its surface in the dark. Suddenly, his attention switched to the Apis Bull. He then turned to stare Jodi right in the eyes. "You say Chang'e was the spirit of destiny!"

Jodi was surprised by the intensity in Graham's voice. "Yes," she said tentatively.

"Destiny, as in fate and fortune!".

"Yes."

"Just like the Apis Bull and the Ape of Thoth! Wow! They were all attributed with the power to influence providence. That can't be a coincidence."

An enlightening new perspective was being cast on the mystery of Biddulph Grange.

-2-

Forgotten Secrets

Jodi and Graham crossed the verandah of the Chinese pagoda to enter a tunnel cut into a sandstone outcrop of higher ground at the far end of the lake. A flight of steps led up to an iron gate, behind which was a deep, brick-lined, circular pit that once served as an icehouse. A second dark passage wound its way through the rock before emerging into what could almost be a different country, a hidden dale adorned with colorful bushes and vibrant flowers. To the left, where the land rose steeply, there was an artificial cliff cleverly constructed from irregular-shaped rocks, from which ferns and ivy cascaded in a tumble of greenery. Here, an enticing little spring flowed cheerfully into a tiny pool, from which a tranquil stream snaked its way through the bulrushes and the huge, broad-leaved plants of the newly-reconstructed Celtic glen.

Beside the spring were rough-cut monoliths. Standing stones around 10 feet high reminded Jodi of Stonehenge, except they had no horizontal lintels linking them together. "This looks like a partial recreation of a stone circle," she observed.

Graham strode into the sunlight to examine the stones. "They certainly look like standing stones from Megalithic times."

Jodi listened as he explained how the Megalithic era was a period between approximately 3000 and 1000 BC—named after the word *megalith*, meaning "large stone"—when hundreds of stone circles were erected throughout the prehistoric British Isles. These circles, of which about 1300 still survive, were usually between 20 and 50 feet in diameter, generally made up of 10 and sometimes as many as a hundred stones. The largest had monoliths as much as 20 feet high.

"Stonehenge is the most famous such monument," he concluded, "being the only stone circle with arches."

Jodi made her way to the pool, careful not to slip on the damp moss of its surrounding rockery. "So why a *Celtic* glen?"

"The Celts, originally from the European mainland, arrived in Britain and Ireland around 1000 BC. They had their own sacred sites." Graham indicated to the pool. "Brick-lined basins created below natural springs to form holy wells. And sacred caves or rock chambers called grottos." He pointed to the tunnel from where they had just emerged. Its 6-foot-high, 3-foot-wide, rectangular entrance at the tops of a short flight of flagstone steps was lined with heavy stone blocks, like the portal to some long-forgotten tomb. "Between their arrival and their conquest by the Romans in the first century AD, the British Celts also venerated the stone circles of their predecessors, the Megalithic people; the Celtic priesthood, the Druids, *also* built stone circles and erected individual standing stones. This area of the gardens appears to be an amalgam of all three Celtic shrines: grotto, well, and monoliths."

Jodi surveyed the dale; its exotic flora, at either end of a line of steppingstones that crossed the stream, had the menacing appearance of giant carnivorous rhubarb plants, while the various grasses and wildflowers growing around the spring seemed peaceful and welcoming. "It's marvelous, but what purpose would this place have served?"

"To the ancient Celts, sacred springs and standing stones were places to commune with gods and spirits, whereas grottos, whether artificial creations or natural caves, were considered entrances to mystical realms." Graham returned to the tunnel. "Certain Druids were thought to know how to open these magical portals. In *this* part of Britain, they were said to be guarded by a winged spirit called Bride."

The name was new to Jodi. "Bride? As in a wedding bride?"

"Sounds the same, but no. The word 'bride' comes from 'bridle,' the equipment used to control a horse. In medieval times it signified that a woman was submitting to the charge of her husband, the 'groom.'"

Jodi was horrified. "Like a person who grooms a horse!"

"Exactly. It's strange the terms are still in use.

Anyway, Bride is the British version of Brid, the name of an Irish deity known as Brig or Brigid. In the fifth century, Irish migrants arrived in the part of the country we're in right now, where she was adopted by the local inhabitants who called her Bride.

"You said that Bride had wings; that seems unusual for a goddess."

"It is. But, strictly speaking, Bride wasn't a goddess. She emerged from an amalgamation of two goddesses, the Irish Brid and a native deity called Gwener. Brid was the goddess of the sun and moon, while Gwener was the goddess of Venus and the new light of dawn. Bride not only became associated with all four of these so-called celestial lights, from which her power emanated, but she came to be regarded as a spiritual entity with divine powers known as a 'celeste,' short for celestial being. She was more like an angel than a deity, hence the wings."

"So, what was she the goddess—sorry, celeste—of?"

"Destiny, fate, and fortune." Graham suddenly had a feeling of déjà vu.

"Power over destiny!" Jodi exclaimed. "Aani, the Apis Bull, Chang'e, and now Bride were *all* attributed with that power."

Graham remained silent momentarily, staring at the water babbling from the rocks. "Thinking about it, they had more in common. None were actual deities—they were each regarded as spirits or ethereal beings."

As Graham paced back and forth across the steppingstones considering the implications, Jodi was browsing on her phone. From the look on her face, she was learning something important. "Was Bride associated with rabbits?" she asked.

The question took Graham by surprise. "Yes, she was. Well almost. Hares, to be precise. In Ireland, Brid was believed to have come from a magical land called Tír na nÓg, but in mainland Britain, Bride was said to have lived on the moon. The Celts imagined that dark markings on the moon formed the outline of a squatting hare, as people today think they see the Man in the Moon. As such, the hare was her sacred animal. What made you ask?"

"Because the same applies to Chang'e. I looked her up just now. She was known as the Lady of the Moon because she too was said to have come from the moon, and her sacred animal is the rabbit, for the same reason, except the Chinese regarded the moon shadows as a bunny rather than a hare."

"A remarkable coincidence!"

"No way. Besides the moon, Chang'e was also associated with the other two brightest objects in the sky, the sun and Venus. Like Bride, her power was thought to emanate from them. Furthermore, she was regarded as the bringer of dawn."

Graham was wide-eyed. "It *can't* be a coincidence." Then a bewildered expression crossed his face. "But how on Earth did two completely different cultures on opposite sides of the world, who knew nothing of each other, both imagine an identical spirit being?"

"Perhaps because they didn't *imagine* her!"

"You think she was *real?*"

Jodi shrugged. "Well, maybe not a flying lady from the moon, but a force or energy of some kind. I don't know. But it seems likely that Maria Bateman and the Order of Meonia regarded them as the same. Otherwise, why the two shrines? Is there a rabbit or hare statue anywhere around here?"

"Oh my god! Yes. One of each. Well, there used to be. A stone hare in this glen somewhere and a bronze rabbit in the Chinese sanctuary. When I first came to Biddulph in 1980, I was told they had been stolen after the gardens were neglected."

"I'd say that clinches it." Jodi held up her palms. "The Celtic and Chinese shrines were used for the same purpose. Perhaps the Meonia group was hedging its bets, trying out forms of the same kind of magic from different cultures. There's nothing online to link Aani and the Apis Bull with the celestial lights —the sun, the moon, Venus, and the dawn—but I wouldn't mind betting that the ancient Egyptians attributed them with similar associations, or at least Maria Bateman thought they did."

Graham leaned against one of the megaliths. He needed to. His head was spinning with all these new realizations. "The big question is: What were the Meonia group up to with their occult activities? They must have had an objective.

"Jodi's attention became focused on the dark passage entrance, and she climbed the steps to look inside. She turned back to Graham and said, "You mentioned that such sacred tunnels or caves were considered portals to mystical realms of which Bride was guardian. Almost the same applies to Chang'e. In her case, the passageway she guarded led to a sacred well, affording access to other worlds. A well! A hole in the ground! The first tunnel from the pagoda led to that round pit the guidebook calls an icehouse. It may ultimately have been used as one, but that might not have been its original purpose.

Graham linked his hand above his head as if experiencing an epiphany. "Astonishing! It's all coming together. What the Meonia group was up to. The Chinese, Celtic, and Egyptian shrines were all built as portals to other realms. Egyptian tombs had unusually long passageways deemed necessary for the soul to be transported to the next world. I'd say that Maria Bateman had this in mind when designing the Egyptian shrine."

"The Ape of Thoth sits at the end of the main passageway, the guardian to another world." Jodi conjectured. "Just like Chang'e and Bride."

Graham shook his head, smiling. "Not just another *world* but other *worlds*, at least if Celtic mythology is any indication. They regarded them as other versions of the *physical* world rather than some ethereal spirit realm like heaven or the afterlife. Various legendary heroes, and creatures, such as fairies, goblins, and elves, are said to inhabit them; the authors Tolkien, C. S. Lewis, and J. M. Barrie based their worlds of Middle Earth, Narnia, and Neverland on such Celtic legends. There were believed to be countless such worlds, many inhabited by human beings, some living almost identical lives to humans. I suppose they were thought to be what we might today call the multiverse: parallel worlds or alternate realities."

"So, people from our world were said to travel to these other universes?"

"And vice versa."

"Well, that's what the Meonia group must have been trying to do. Open a portal to another reality. Maybe more than one."

"It all fits." Graham shook his head slowly in disbelief. "It's remarkable," he said. "We've only been here for an hour or two, yet together we have worked out more than I've done alone in forty years."

Jodi was pleased, but a nagging question remained. "We still don't know *why* they were doing it."

* * *

As they moved back towards the main house from the Celtic glen, Jodi flicked through her copy of the official guidebook. She furrowed her brow. "It refers here to the Celtic glen as the *Scottish* glen."

Graham appreciated the confusion. "Foreign tourists, even English visitors, often don't know who the Celts were. As Scotland was a Celtic country, it was simpler to refer to the shrine as Scottish. They could just as easily have used the name of one of the other Celtic countries of the British Isles: Wales and Ireland."

Graham explained how today, Britain refers to England and Wales, Great Britain consists of England, Wales, and Scotland, and the United Kingdom also includes Northern Ireland. In contrast, the British Isles refers to all these areas plus the Irish Republic. The Celts inhabited the entire British Isles until the Germanic Anglo-Saxons—the English—invaded most of what is now England by the late 700s. As it was not until centuries later that the English annexed Wales, Scotland, and Ireland, they remained primarily Celtic countries.

Jodi was unfamiliar with Celtic history. "You keep mentioning the Druids. Who exactly were they?"

"We don't know much about their practices, as the pre-Roman Celts had no form of writing to document their beliefs. That was left to others like the Romans and Greeks."

Graham explained what had been recorded concerning the Druids. Although they existed in other Celtic regions, such as France, classical writers said they originated in the British Isles. Consisting of both men and women of equal standing, they were not only a priesthood but were healers, teachers, advisors, judges, and were respected as sorcerers, mystics, and prophets. They were chosen from among talented children who spent twenty years in training. Because they lived outside the structural constraints of usual society, the Druids acted as a unifying force amongst the British tribes. Consequently, after the Roman conquest of the mid-first century, they were eradicated or driven into Ireland, which the Romans failed to invade. Years later, as the Roman Empire collapsed during the fifth century, Ireland converted to Christianity, and Irish Druids returned to Britain, until the spread of Christianity here initiated their ultimate demise within a few decades.

"Why are the Druids so often portrayed as blood-thirsty maniacs?" Jodi asked.

"All based on Roman and early Christian propaganda. To the contrary, archaeological evidence reveals they were remarkably peaceful."

"So, the Celtic glen is a Druid shrine."

"Yes, or at least an amalgam of such shrines."

When they reached the main house, Jodi perused the gift store while Graham spoke to the lady staffing the counter. Only a tiny part of the Grange remains as it was during the time of Maria Bateman, Mary, and Laura Heath. It originally had kitchens, conservatories, servants' quarters, dozens of bedrooms, recreational, reading, and dining areas, and a ballroom. The place had undergone considerable rebuilding after the fire of 1897 destroyed much of the center of the house. When it was later transformed into a hospital, it was further remodeled. Today, most of the building has been converted into private luxury apartments; only a cafe, a tearoom, and the gift store in the west wing are now open to the public.

"We can't go into the main house, but you can see into its communal area just round here." Graham led Jodi from the gift shop, past the estate office, and out onto a small lawn, at the center of which stood a large, spreading' yew tree. Behind it, windows looked in on a large, wood-paneled hall with doorways leading off to either side. At the opposite end, a magnificent staircase divided left and right between two sturdy marble pillars, where a stained-glass window flooded the scene with multicolored light. "This is one of the few parts of the building to remain much as it was during the nineteenth century."

"Biddulph Grange must have been a stunning place to live." Jodi glanced up to four more stained-glass windows above them on the external wall. "They're unusual," she said, referring to the fact that they were round. The images in the windows, each with a diameter of about 4 feet, could not be discerned from the outside. Still, the guidebook included photographs taken from inside the hall showing that they depicted four women dressed Roman style, representing the classical elements: earth, water, fire, and air.

"They were made by John William Brown of the eminent Victorian stained-glass manufacturers James Powell and Sons," Graham explained. "However, the actual designer is unknown."

"Wouldn't that have been Brown?" Jodi said.

"No, he undertook the commission to turn original, now lost paintings into these stained-glass windows. Both Brown and the Powell company worked closely with various Pre-Raphaelite artists to transfer their creations to glass so that they may be the work of Robert Bateman, perhaps even his more illustrious friend and mentor Edward Burne-Jones. Whoever designed them, they probably have esoteric significance; the four elements are certainly an occult theme."

An idea occurred to Jodi. "Do you think that the

shrines in the garden relate to earth, air, fire, and water?"

Graham raised an eyebrow. "You could be right. The Celtic glen, water—"

"The Chinese sanctuary, fire. It has dragons and phoenixes, both associated with fire and if they did light floating lanterns—"

"And the Egyptian Temple could be air," Graham interjected. "The Ape of Thoth was considered an air spirit. The structure is built so that the prevailing wind howls through it."

"Which leaves earth. Implying that there might have been a fourth shrine."

Graham turned to Jodi with an animated expression. "There *was* a fourth shrine. An underground chamber, the entrance to which was in a conservatory called the Rhododendron House."

"Where was it?"

"Right here." Graham pointed downwards. "Directly below where we're standing. It seems to have stretched from here to just beyond the corner of the house where that tea terrace is now." He motioned to where a group of visitors was seated in an open-air eating area at the end of the path running across the front of the Grange facing the gardens."

"Underground! An *earth* shrine. It makes sense." Jodi bent down to examine a line of old brickwork along the edge of the lawn. "It seems there was something *here*."

"Yes. The underground chamber was filled in after the Rhododendron House, which stood precisely here, was demolished around 1900. The gardeners recently dug a hole where that brickwork is, briefly exposing the steps that would have led down to it."

"Any idea what it contained?"

"Unlike the other shrines, its existence was kept secret. I've only found a single historical reference to it. The series of articles in *The Gardeners' Chronicle and Gazette*, published throughout the summer of 1862 by a landscape gardener named Edward Kemp—the ones describing the three garden shrines—mentions nothing about the chamber. However, the National Trust has Kemp's original draft copies. They are word-for-word the same as the articles, apart from one paragraph that didn't appear in print. A paragraph that *does* refer to the fourth shrine. Referring to it as a catacomb, Kemp writes that it was a replica of an old Roman tomb containing a collection of cremation urns and sarcophagi—stone coffins adorned with sculptures and inscriptions—plus other items he fails to name. Someone seems to have redacted it before publication. Presumably, the Batemans didn't want the chamber's existence known."

Graham looked down at the ground, imagining the chamber beneath, before continuing. "I've located just one item known to have been housed in the chamber: a sarcophagus now kept in the Potteries Museum in Stoke-on-Trent. It's been identified as a Roman stone coffin around 1800 years old and was probably obtained by James Bateman during his travels. It's decorated with the image of the cornucopia. Also known as the Horn of Plenty, the cornucopia was a horn-shaped container overflowing with riches, which symbolized prosperity and was the emblem of the Roman goddess Fortuna. It's been conjectured that the coffin contained the body of a woman who may have been an oracle or priestess of that deity. Fortuna temples were usually built underground and, like later churches, often incorporated sepulchers of the dead. For the mysterious chamber here to have been built underground and contained coffins and cremation urns, I'd say that what Kemp called a catacomb was a temple dedicated to Fortuna."

Jodi pulled a face. "You don't think the sarcophagus still contained a body?"

"I doubt it. Most Roman tombs were plundered by the hostile tribes that repeatedly sacked the Empire after its collapse. The skeleton would likely have been cast aside centuries ago as a heap of useless bones..." Graham fell abruptly silent, struck by a sudden realization. "Fortuna was the goddess of fate and fortune!" he said, almost in awe.

"Like Chang'e, Aani, the Apis Bull, and Bride!"

Graham nodded emphatically. "Her name comes from the Latin *fortuna*, meaning 'fate;' our modern word 'fortune' derives from it. She was usually depicted holding the cornucopia in one hand, signifying her influence over fate, with her other hand guiding a ship's rudder, symbolizing her power to steer destiny." Memories from Graham's past studies were flooding into his mind. "What's more, just like Bride and Chang'e, her power was thought to emanate from the principal celestial lights: the sun, the moon, Venus, and the dawn." Graham realized another remarkable similarity. "Ordinary Romans had figurines of her in little shrines in their homes, hoping that she would open the way for new and better prospects. She was believed to have the power to access gateways to alternative futures!"

"So, in her way, she too was a guardian to other worlds." Jodi shook her head in disbelief. "It's incredible. Not two, but *three* completely different cultures had an almost identical goddess or spirit being. More importantly, all four shrines seemed to be associated with the same thing, opening doorways to alternate realities."

Graham agreed. "That *has* to be what the Meonia group hoped to achieve." He turned to Jodi. "If you hadn't told me about Chang'e, I doubt we'd have put it all together."

Jodi smiled appreciatively. "Well, since you last investigated Biddulph Grange, you've done research for loads of books you've written concerning ancient history. You wouldn't have known enough to work it out back then. Besides this, we now have the internet. I'd say it's a combination of all three."

Jodi stooped down to place a hand on the grass. "Why keep *this* shrine secret?"

Graham had an idea. "Perhaps because it contained the Order of Meonia's most treasured possession—the Heart of the Rose?"

Maybe it's still buried here," Jodi suggested enthusiastically.

Graham frowned. "I hope not. We couldn't persuade the National Trust to dig out the entire underground chamber. No, wherever it's hidden, I doubt it's anywhere at Biddulph Grange. In the memorial pamphlet, Laura says she 'secured its safety.' Leaving it here would not seem particularly safe. Besides which, Jenny said it wasn't to be found on the Biddulph estate."

Jodi was peering through one of the windows into the reception hall, imagining what it had been like in Victorian times, when the mention of the memorial pamphlet clicked something in her mind. "The memorial event of 1897. What exactly was it?"

"Some kind of service to observe the twenty-fifth anniversary of Mary Heath's death?"

"Remind me, what date was it held?"

"May fourth."

"But didn't Mary die on October thirteenth?"

Graham scratched his head. "I've wondered about that myself. Laura was suffering from tuberculosis. She died the very next day. Perhaps they held the memorial early as her death seemed imminent."

Graham noticed that Jodi looked bemused. "What's wrong?"

"Nothing. It's just a strange coincidence. May fourth is my birthday."

Before the end of the day, the coincidences were to get a lot stranger.

* * *

As they left the Grange and made their way across the parking lot, Graham told Jodi what he had learned earlier from the lady in the gift store. "The standing stones in the Celtic glen weren't just replicas; they came from a genuine stone circle. From the research the National Trust carried out to reconstruct the glen, it's been discovered that James Bateman had them moved here from a stone circle called the Bridestones, which stood on the edge of the Biddulph estate."

The Bridestones, Graham explained, was an ancient monument that once included a stone circle consisting of 10, approximately 10-foot-high monoliths in a ring around 27 feet in diameter, which stood some two miles north of Biddulph Grange on the Staffordshire moorlands, at the very edge of the property owned by the Batemans and Heaths.

"Only *some* of these stones still survive at the site," he concluded. "Bateman had the others transported here in May 1851 when creating the first shrine—the Celtic glen."

"The *Bride*-stones!" Jodi realized that Graham had been keeping things back. His dramatic flair again. "I don't suppose they have anything to do with the ethereal Bride we've been discussing?" she said sarcastically.

Graham grinned. "Very likely. The stone circle is considered a Celtic monument where she was venerated. It's one of several ancient Celtic sites incorporating the name Bride in central Britain. It's surely significant that James Bateman moved stones from the Bridestones when recreating a Celtic shrine associated with Bride."

Jodi sighed in exasperation. "You knew about this all along?"

"No. I knew of the Bridestones but had no idea it was so close, let alone that they were in any way connected with Biddulph Grange. The first I knew of it was when the woman in the shop told me. That Bateman moved the stones here has only recently been known."

Jodi quickened her stride. "The Bridestones. Whatever's left of them, let's go."

* * *

They left Biddulph and drove up the winding country road to the moors. Luckily Graham had a small, two-door car, as the lanes narrowed to be almost impassable. After a steep, meandering journey that seemed to take forever, the monument finally stood before them. It overlooked the Grange in the valley below, situated beside a small copse, amongst the fields and pastures lining the North Staffordshire hills at the edge of the Peak District. The sun shone brightly from a clear blue sky and filtered through the tree branches overhanging the ancient, weathered stones but failed to penetrate the tangle of brambles and wild thorn bushes encroaching on the monument from within the wood. What remains to be seen today are two 10-foot standing stones next to the vestige of an ancient burial mound—a rectangular arrangement of long, horizontal megaliths comprised of stones averaging around a foot wide and 5 feet high, creating a chamber with inner dimensions of around 6 by 14 feet, and divided into two equal parts by a broken slab, all once covered with earth and rubble to create an artificial hillock.

"This was originally a tomb mound." Graham gestured to the rectangular arrangement of stones. "The stone circle stood here, right next to it." He gestured toward the lane where they had parked and the small wooden gate through which they had entered the site. "It was one of the last stone circles built in the British Isles. Nevertheless, it's still around 1500 years old."

Jodi examined the two remaining monoliths and the tomb chamber, now empty and open to the sky. Imagining the ring of tall megaliths that once stood beside it, she felt sadness tinged with anger. "Bateman deliberately destroyed a stone circle! A malicious act for a supposedly spiritual man."

Graham wasn't so sure. "He probably thought he was saving the stones. They were being vandalized, with visitors hacking off pieces as souvenirs; worse, a local preacher, considering the stone circle a heathen temple, was coercing his congregation to destroy it. In nineteenth-century England, there was no legal protection for ancient monuments. So, being on his land, Bateman was within his rights to have the stones moved. He presumably felt obligated to protect them."

"But how did the tomb end up like this?" Jodi said, referring to it being empty and open to the sky.

Graham explained how the assembly of horizontal stones that still survived originally enclosed two adjacent chambers, with human remains in one compartment and grave goods, such as personal possessions, jewelry, and precious items, in the other. Once the structure was sealed with capstones to form a roof, the whole thing was covered with a mound of rocks, then earth. The original tomb would have appeared as a grass-covered mound, around 40 feet across and 8 feet high, with a stone-lined entrance gully at one end leading to a heavy slab that sealed the burial chamber. "The rocks were removed by builders for leveling a nearby road in the 1920s, and the capstones ended up over there." Graham pointed to a couple of large flat stones lying amongst the brambles.

Jodi was puzzled. "The lady in the gift store told you all this?"

"Only about the stones being transported to the Biddulph gardens by James Bateman in 1851. I already knew quite a lot about the Bridestones, even that the original circle stones had been moved elsewhere. But it's only since the renovation of the Celtic glen that it's been rediscovered where they ended up. Some websites concerning the Bridestones still erroneously asserted that they were moved to Tunstall Park in nearby Stoke-on-Trent. Until now, I've had no reason to associate this monument with Biddulph Grange. I didn't realize it was quite so close, let alone on the Grange's land."

Jodi noticed how the rectangular, box-like tomb was open at one end. She carefully went inside to see the remains of the slab that had once divided the structure into two equal parts. On the ground, at the other end, a large metal bowl, clearly of recent origin, had been placed, in which there were beads of different colors, garlands of flowers, and sticks tied with ribbons. "Someone still seems to venerate the site," she said.

"Probably many people. Wiccans, Pagans, New Age groups, and even casual visitors often leave offerings at ancient sites."

Jodi ran her fingers over one of the two 10-foot upright stones that flanked the tomb's entrance." "How old are the Bridestones?" she asked.

Graham began by explaining how the site had been wrongly dated. "As it looks today, the Bridestones appear to be the remains of a long barrow. That type of tomb mound is characterized by tall, heavy monoliths at their entrance, as this one now has, and such barrows date from between 3500 and 3000 BC, during the Neolithic age. However, these two monoliths were originally from the stone circle. When archaeologists attempted to restore the site in the 1930s, they re-erected the monoliths in their present positions, wrongly assuming they were restoring the site to its original condition—making it resemble a long barrow. Luckily there survive descriptions of the site as it was in Bateman's time before anyone got to mess around with it too much, and from these, we can determine its more likely date. It was a so-called box tomb, with an adjoining stone circle, identical to monuments built on the east coast of Ireland in the late fifth century and early sixth century, dating this monument to around AD 500."

"You mentioned the Irish coming here before. Why exactly were they in central England?"

"The Romans eradicated the Druids and much of Celtic religion after they invaded Britain in the first century. Later, Britain became a Christian country when the Romans adopted Christianity as the Empire's state religion in the early 300s. At least officially. Most people living outside the Roman towns continued to practice various forms of paganism. So, when the Roman Empire began to collapse, and the Roman armies left Britain in 410, the country descended into anarchy, and Christianity was in turmoil. During the early fifth century, many British Christians escaped the chaos and fled to Ireland, where they rapidly converted the Irish chieftains who expected their subjects to follow suit. Those who didn't convert faced persecution and emigrated to the relative safety of the pagan areas of Britain. By the mid-400s, separate kingdoms had been established around the old Roman towns and cities, leaving the wild upland regions ungoverned. Accordingly, in places like the Peak District, where we are now, the Irish migrants settled, bringing Druidism with them."

"Surely, we're a long way from Ireland."

"Not really. The Mersey estuary that flows into the Irish Sea is less than thirty miles away."

Jodi looked around at the countryside, sloping away to the south, cows grazing lazily amongst the buttercups and daisies of its lush, sunlit meadows. "So, the Irish built the Bridestones stone circle and its tomb."

Graham began filming the area with his phone. "Both the Irish *ana* the native Britons, I'd say. Stone circle building ceased in Britain during the Roman occupation, but the Irish immigrants erected new ones. From its name, we can assume that the Bridestones circle was dedicated to Bride, implying that by the time it was erected, the Irish and local Britons had merged into a single community venerating the amalgamation of the goddesses Gwener and Brid—the celeste, Bride."

"So, who would have been buried in the tomb?"

"As the chief devotees of Bride were women, I'm guessing it was her high priestess or oracle. An important Druidess."

A sudden gust of wind rustled through the overhanging trees as the sun disappeared behind a cloud. Neither Jodi nor Graham had noticed the skies darkening, but they looked up to see a heavy storm cloud directly overhead.

The rain began to fall.

Graham had been filming the tomb, while Jodi had repeatedly looked around at the sunny hillsides, admiring the view. "Where did that come from?" she said. "The sky was clear a moment ago."

"The cloud must have been behind the trees. Although I didn't—" Graham's words were cut short by a flash of lightning, followed by an immediate clap of thunder.

"The wind isn't blowing from that direction," Jodi shouted above the noise of the rain. "It just came from nowhere."

"There were no clouds before!" Graham said, still filming. "The impossible storm," he joked as the rain turned torrential, and he joined Jodi to run for cover.

After just a few moments of sheltering beneath the trees, the storm ceased as abruptly as it began.

As Jodi took pictures of the stones, Graham continued to film as he exited the gate to return to the car. He then saw something they had failed to notice on their arrival. Beside the lane, on the opposite side to the Bridestones, there was a 5-foot wall, at the bottom of which, within an arched recess, stood a rectangular stone, about 2 feet high and a foot square. The top was engraved with an equal-armed cross, and a large letter B was carved at the bottom of one side, around 8 inches high. As Graham looked back across the field, towards the Bridestones, around 30 yards away, a shiver ran down his spine.

When Jodi joined him, he was staring at the stone. "That's odd," she said. "Why build an arch into the wall for a stone? Was it a part of the original Bridestones?"

Graham shook his head. "They're much bigger and a different type of rock." The megaliths were gray, while this stone was sandy brown. It was also more sharply cut than the roughly-hewed monoliths, lacking their centuries of weathering. It seemed to be carved from the same stone as the wall. Other than the niche for the stone, the wall ran uninterrupted along the side of the lane that continued down to the main road, some 50 yards away. "I'm guessing this wall was erected by James Bateman in the 1800s to mark the edge of his estate, so the stone probably dates from then."

Jodi stooped down to examine the letter B. "What do you think that stands for—Bridestones? Biddulph? Bateman? "She looked up at Graham, noticing the strange look on his face. "What's wrong?"

"Remember what I told you Jenny said all those years ago about the B stone." The exact wording was still clear in Graham's memory.

Find the stone carved with the letter B. Only then will your quest to understand the Order of Meonia and your search to discover the Heart of the Rose truly begin.

He crouched down to join Jodi and examine the stone. "I think we just found it."

-3-

The Quest Begins

Back in the bar of Jodi's hotel near Graham's home in Birmingham, the largest city in central England, she and Graham were glued to their phones, examining maps of the Biddulph area as it was in the nineteenth century. They quickly determined that the Grange estate originally encompassed the 15-acre gardens, a further 24 acres of what is now the adjacent Biddulph Country Park, and hilly countryside to the north as far as the Bridestones.

"The B Stone stood on the very edge of the estate," Graham observed.

Jodi found a site that revealed its purpose. It had been customary for such stones to mark district borders. Called boundary stones, they were often inscribed with a region's initials. "The letter B presumably stood for Biddulph, so there's nothing unusual about the stone itself." Jodi looked up from her phone. "But could it be where the Heart of the Rose was hidden?"

"Not if Jenny is to be believed. Although she had no idea where it was hidden, she was adamant that it wasn't near the B Stone. She said the Heart of the Rose wasn't *anywhere* on the Biddulph estate."

Jodi spread her hands. "If her impressions are right, and the Biddulph boundary stone is the B Stone she referred to, then new insights concerning the Meonia mystery might now unfold."

Graham pondered for a moment. "They may already have. We visit Biddulph Grange, prompted by the recent restorations, where we learn that the Celtic glen megaliths came from the Bridestones, and that leads us to find a stone carved with the letter B. One hell of a coincidence."

"Synchronicity?" Jodi said, referring to the expression for apparently meaningful coincidences— chance and timely events where the influence of fate or some unexplained directive seems to be at work.

Graham agreed. "As Sherlock Holmes would say, 'the game's afoot.' And I assume it will involve the two of us."

Jodi was taken aback. "*Both* of us?"

"The B Stone was only found after we visited Biddulph *together*."

Jodi had long been fascinated by mysteries and had investigated some strange paranormal events during her life. She had even had psychic and clairvoyant experiences: vivid dreams of incidents that later occurred, accurate impressions about people, places, and events of which she knew nothing—so, having a sudden, intuitive feeling while at Biddulph Grange was nothing unfamiliar.

"I know it sounds crazy," she said," and I can't

explain why or how I know, but I feel that we're embarking on a..." Jodi searched carefully for the right word. "A quest, if you like, where what we discover along the way may be just as important, maybe *more* important, than the relic itself."

"I don't think it's crazy at all," Graham said. "'Quest' is precisely the word Jenny used."

He and Jodi had worked together on investigations in the past, one involving the search for the biblical Ark of the Covenant. They hadn't found it, but they had made significant discoveries during the investigation and witnessed extraordinary events. So, "questing"—a term sometimes applied to hands-on research into historical mysteries during which extraordinary events and seemingly meaningful coincidences occurred—was familiar territory.

Jodi put down her phone. "So, what's next?"

Graham took a swig from his drink before summarizing his thoughts. "I think we can say with certainty that the Order of Meonia was a serious occult group and that the Heaths and Batemans were heavily into the mystical and supernatural. Likewise, they regarded little Mary as a young psychic who'd led them to find something they regarded as an ultra-powerful relic, which was eventually hidden by Laura Heath or perhaps someone on her behalf." He shrugged. "But what next? If we *have* found the actual B Stone Jenny referred to, then new clues might present themselves."

Jodi agreed. "Although the Heart of... You know, I'll call it the Heart; it's easier. Although the Heart might not be hidden at the Bridestones, there might be indications there concerning its location."

Graham sighed. "The place has been dug up and virtually ransacked since Laura Heath's time."

"It must have some relevance, or why Jenny's message?" Jodi remained optimistic. "Let's look at the footage we took of the area."

Jodi fetched her laptop so they could view their photos and film in detail. The pair examined the images of the site taken earlier in the day, finding nothing unusual—until they watched the video recorded by Graham during the brief storm. The film began with panning shots of the sunlit tomb before a clear, bright day abruptly darkened and the rain fell in torrents. A flash of lightning, an immediate crash of thunder, the trees bent violently by the wind. The camera wobbled as Graham ran for cover, he and Jodi shouting to be heard above the racket of the storm. After about three minutes, the rain ceased, and the wind dropped. Graham continued to film as he headed toward the car. Just as he reached the gate, some 20 feet from the monument, a bright circle of white light slid onscreen from the direction of the Bridestones, grew smaller, appeared to move over the gate, and continued to diminish in size until it seemed to disappear over the wall on the far side of the lane.

"It must be lens flare," Graham replayed the footage for the umpteenth time.

"I don't think so," Jodi took over the keyboard and played the movie, frame by frame. "It's large when it comes into view, seemingly close to the camera, and then grows proportionally smaller until it flies over the wall and disappears into the bushes. For all the world, it looks like a white glowing orb about the size of a tennis ball. There's no way that's lens flare. Besides, the sun wasn't even out at that point."

Graham had to agree. "But I didn't see anything at the time. Did you?"

"No. But weren't we both looking at the sky?"

"Right, we were. Even though I kept filming, we were both gazing up at the single dark cloud responsible for the downpour." They carefully examined the other images captured that day, finding no further anomalies. "We need it examined by an expert."

Graham called his friend Mike, an IT consultant, shared a copy of the film, and asked for his opinion. The man showed it to colleagues, who agreed that the light was probably some temporary fault with the phone, not due to lens flare. It was suggested that the digital camera might have been affected by the ionization of the atmosphere caused by the electrical storm.

With a possible explanation for the light, Jodi and Graham turned their attention to browsing the celeste, after which the Bridestones was named.

"Look at this!" Jodi pointed to her laptop screen. "According to this site, in Celtic mythology, Bride would sometimes manifest as a sphere of light during a violent storm." She turned to stare at Graham. "Like the white ball in our footage? Regardless of what caused the effect, you must admit it's a strange coincidence, appearing during a freak storm that occurred when we just so happened to be there."

"The storm was certainly strange," Graham

agreed. After checking a weather site that revealed only sunshine over the North Staffordshire hills during their time at the Bridestones, Graham called Biddulph Grange to ask if there had been a flash storm earlier in the day. The receptionist said there had been nothing, not a drop of rain, although she recalled hearing a few claps of thunder in the distance.

"An extraordinary storm," Jodi emphasized when Graham finished the call. "Localized to the area around the Bridestones. And only when we were there. The film's light distortion may be due to electrical interference—but it resembles a shining orb, something associated with Bride!" Jodi stared Graham in the eyes. "Something's trying to tell us something."

Jodi and Graham had enough experience with synchronicities over the years to not ignore when fate seemed to be guiding them. Remarkably, it often proved helpful, sometimes providing new leads when an investigation had reached a dead end.

"Perhaps you should try one of your remotes," Graham suggested. "Concentrate on the Bridestones and see what you pick up."

Jodi had spent many years training in diverse martial arts and mind-focusing techniques, combining both Eastern and Western disciplines to formulate her unique style of meditation. She could sometimes concentrate her "remotes" (short for remote viewing), as she called the altered state of consciousness she achieved, onto specific locations, themes, or ideas. But like for Jenny all those years before, the results were often fragmentary: images, coupled with sounds or words forming in her mind, which were usually obscure—like lucid, vivid dreams. And, like dreams, the meaning was often jumbled into a cryptic, though sometimes meaningful, mental scenario. Interpreting Jodi's remotes could take some doing, but although not consistently successful, they *had* led to some remarkable breakthroughs during historical investigations they had conducted together. The problem was that Jodi could only occasionally achieve such states of mind.

Jodi was hesitant. "It's all very hit and miss. I might lead us on a wild goose chase."

"Nothing to lose," Graham said.

That night, in the seclusion of her hotel room, Jodi relaxed and focused her mind on the stillness where images would form.

The English countryside. A bright summer day with a little girl and boy playing around a stone circle beside a grass-covered mound. The mound has fallen away at one end, revealing a small opening resembling a giant rabbit hole, the entrance to the tomb inside. The girl clambers in, calling for the boy to follow.

Jodi told Graham of her vision the following morning over breakfast in her hotel. "The girl resembled the typical depictions of Alice in Wonderland. I assume that's my mind's way of forming an image associated with a little Victorian girl."

"You think it was Victorian times?" Graham asked.

"Yes. The boy was dressed from that period too." Jodi had a strong impression of what was occurring. "I think the girl was Mary Heath as a child. Are there any pictures of her from that time?"

"Sadly not. No photos or paintings. None of her at any age that I've been able to find."

Jodi sighed. "Pity. I'm certain that I saw the Bridestones when Bateman had the stone circle moved. And the mound was the tomb as it was at the time."

"James Bateman moved the stones in the spring of 1851," Graham said. "Mary was born in 1844, so she *was* around seven. The boy may have been a young Robert Bateman, two years older than Mary. She had lived at nearby Clough Hall at the time, and the pair were childhood friends. They could well have played around the Bridestones." Pouring himself a cup of tea, Graham added, "So what do you think it means?"

Jodi recalled the feeling she had during the vision. "I've no idea what, but I think something important happened when the girl entered the tomb."

"Perhaps if we return to the Bridestones, you might get more," Graham suggested. "I'd certainly like to film it again. With luck, something weird will happen. Another freak storm or images on film?"

When they returned to the Bridestones later that day, no unusual weather occurred, nor did camera footage capture anything unusual. Neither did Jodi receive any new inspiration. It seemed like a non-event. However, when they clambered into the open tomb, they found that someone had placed a playing card on top of the collection of objects left in the metal offering bowl since the previous day.

"The Queen of Hearts," Jodi said, picking it up. She turned it over. Just an ordinary playing card. "Does the Queen of Hearts hold any particular significance to Wiccans or New Agers?"

"Not that I know of." Graham took the card to examine it himself.

"So why leave it here?"

"I guess it held significance to someone. People sometimes refer to Princess Diana as their 'Queen of Hearts.' Maybe it was in memory of *her*."

Something suddenly occurred to Jodi. "During my remote, the little girl looked like Alice in Wonderland—the blue dress, white pinafore, headband, and long blond hair. I thought it was just my mind's way of depicting a Victorian girl. But there might be more to it. Alice met the Queen of Hearts in Wonderland, didn't she?"

"Yes, but how would that tie up with anything?"

"Another synchronicity! Whatever reason someone had for leaving the card, it has me thinking of the Alice story. She went down a rabbit hole to reach Wonderland. The tomb entrance, which the little girl in my vision entered, looked like a large rabbit hole."

Graham laughed. "You think little Mary entered Wonderland?"

"No. But seriously, my remote could indicate that she found something important inside the tomb. Something connected with a queen and a heart."

"Like what?"

"The *Heart* of the Rose! You say it might have been a mystical stone fashioned by an ancient Meonian *queen*."

Graham thought carefully. "I'm the last to dismiss synchronicities, and it's a fascinating idea, but it's likely Mary found the relic in Greece."

"Does the memorial pamphlet specifically mention a Greek tomb?"

"No," Graham had to admit. "It only refers to a sepulcher. No location is given."

"Your theory that Mary found it in a Greek tomb is based on its possible origins in ancient Meonia. It might have been made there, but surely it could have ended up somewhere else—like the Bridestones tomb."

Graham agreed that it was possible. He explained how numerous items of Mediterranean origin had been found in Celtic tombs. "Before the Bridestones tomb was built around the year 500, Britain had seen centuries of Roman occupation. Travel and trade between here and other parts of the Roman Empire, which included the ancient Greek world, were commonplace."

As they explored the area around the Bridestones, Graham mulled over the possibility that the young Mary Heath had entered the tomb. She and Robert likely played here as children and might even have been around when James Bateman was moving the stone circle megaliths in 1851. However, he was doubtful that this was the location of the sepulcher where Mary found the Heart of the Rose.

Graham voiced his thoughts. "If the young Mary did go inside the Bridestones tomb, as in your vision, then she can't have been the first to do so," he said. "Anyone had access to the site. Anything of value would have been discovered well before her time." He stopped talking and rethought. "Then again, it's quite possible that if the Heart of the Rose was a *small* stone, it could have been overlooked or remained hidden in the soil."

Jodi was examining the bushes on top of the wall on the other side of the lane, where the light in the film had seemed to vanish. "We have no descriptions of the Heart, so it could well have been small," she said, finding nothing of interest where she was searching. Only undergrowth, creepers, insects, and one very annoyed bird that flew noisily right over her head. She jumped back in shock.

"What size were Omphale stones?" Jodi said when Graham had stopped laughing.

"Anything from small enough to fit in a ring to a few feet high. The larger ones were usually made of marble or other sculptured rock carved into rounded cone shapes, sometimes decorated with patterns. The smaller ones were usually precious or semi-precious gems, cut and polished into various shapes."

"So, the Heart of the Rose could have been a stone carved into the shape of a heart or rose," Jodi offered. "And it may have been small enough to have gone undiscovered until little Mary came along. She was considered psychic; maybe she was inspired to dig where others hadn't."

"Okay, it's possible Mary found the Heart here. But that doesn't tell us where it is now," Graham said as they walked down the lane back toward the main road.

Jodi stopped at the boundary stone. "If Jenny was right, there must be some reason that us finding this would initiate the quest." She listed the recent events: the strange storm, the photographic anomaly, the Queen of Hearts, and her vision of Mary looking like Alice. "They indicate that the game's afoot, as you said."

Hoverflies hung above the boundary stone, and a solitary bee buzzed around Graham's head as he gently waved it away. "According to the memorial pamphlet, the Heart of the Rose was the Order of Meonia's prize possession," he said. "The Meonia group seems to have been established when the Celtic glen —the first shrine—was created in the spring of 1851. If Mary did indeed find the relic here at that time, then it might have been the event that started the whole thing. Perhaps the stone *did* something." Graham shrugged. "No idea what, but if its discovery did initiate the founding of an occult society and the building of four elaborate shrines, it must have been something extraordinary."

Jodi frowned. "How would finding this boundary stone instigate our quest."

"Well, if this is where it all began for the Order of Meonia, with them finding the Heart of the Rose, perhaps this is where it should start for us."

Jodi was only partly on board. "It seems to be the Bridestones that are important. So why would Jenny not refer to them directly? Why the B Stone?"

"Maybe to indicate that this area is important," Graham suggested, looking back towards the tomb some 30 yards away.

"I agree, but I think there must be more to this particular stone." Jodi was searching on her phone when her eyes widened. "Now that *is* interesting." She had been looking for anything concerning that specific boundary stone in greater detail than they had discovered the day before. "This stone was erected in May 1851."

"*Very* interesting," Graham said as he stepped backward to narrowly avoid being hit by a passing tractor. The driver glanced angrily in their direction. Graham held up his hands in a gesture of apology. "Exactly the time Bateman moved the stones," he continued. "And perhaps the very time little Mary found the Heart of the Rose."

Jodi was still examining her phone. "More happened than just the stones being moved," she said. "An archaeologist erected the boundary stone while excavating the Bridestones tomb." Her voice rose as she related what came next. "And guess what, the archaeologist was one Thomas Bateman—none other than James Bateman's cousin!"

Graham was dumbfounded. "That must be significant. Does it say if he found anything?"

Jodi shook her head. "He only uncovered a few fragments of broken pottery. But if pottery fragments survived, so could a gemstone. If that's what the Heart really is."

Graham opened the same website Jodi was viewing on his own phone. "Evidentially, Thomas Bateman's notes on the dig still survive at a museum in the town of Leek, just seven miles from here. We should check them out. The dig *must* be relevant."

"And we would not have found out about it if we hadn't browsed for the boundary stone," Jodi said as they returned to the car. "So, the B Stone *was* important."

Graham froze. "Forty years ago, Jenny—or whatever spoke through her—not only appears to have foretold what's happening now but also seems to have predicted the internet."

* * *

As Graham drove across the rolling uplands of the Staffordshire Peak District, every so often passing one of the towering rocky outcrops for which the area is famous, he explained his cryptic "internet" remark. "Jenny said that the search for the Heart of the Rose could only begin when the stone carved with the letter B was found. While at just such a stone, we discover what may be an invaluable new lead—Thomas Bateman's dig. That wouldn't have been possible without the World Wide Web—years in the future in Jenny's time."

Jodi had been gazing out the passenger window, intrigued by the ancient drystone walls that traversed the windy moorlands, dividing the grazing land of the area's scattered sheep farms in the valleys below. She turned to Graham. "I see what you mean. Back in the 1980s, the only way to learn of Bateman's excavation would entail examining hundreds of books and documents in dozens of locations. We'd probably never have done it without the internet." The car slowed as a flock of sheep ran across the road to scamper effortlessly up the hillside. "But does that mean that Jenny predicted the internet? It's difficult to get your head around how these synchronicities, visions, and psychic impressions even work."

"You're not kidding."

Jodi and Graham were traveling between the Bridestones and the small town of Leek, where Thomas Bateman's journals were preserved at the Nicholson Museum and Art Gallery. Graham explained that the area they were in, a roughly triangular region delineated by the modern towns of Biddulph, Congleton, and Leek, which contained the Grange estate and the Bridestones, was known as Wolfside, named after depictions of a wolf on the district's heraldic crest.

"Is there a reason the Irish decided to settle here, specifically?" Jodi asked.

"Very likely. The hill rising above the Bridestones —called the Cloud, from the old word *clud*, meaning 'peak'—is known locally as the hill of the double-setting sun. It is so-called after an unusual spectacle. Each year, on the midsummer solstice, the sun sets behind the hill, only to rise again further down its slopes and set for a second time. The day marked an important festival for the ancient Celts, so the hill that made such an annual display possible was revered. The locations from which the event could be observed, to the southeast of the hill—all in the Wolfside district—meant that the region was considered special."

They were reaching the brow of a hill, as Graham explained they could see the Cloud on the horizon behind them.

"Can we stop and get a photo?" Jodi said.

Graham looked along the road, then glanced in his mirror. "There's no place to pull over and too much traffic. I'll drop you off, turn around further on, and come back and pick you up."

The moment she was left alone on the side of the road, watching Graham's car disappear over the crest of the hill, Jodi regretted it. The skies opened, and the downpour began. She was without a coat or a sweater as the wind-driven rain soaked her skin. To make matters worse, there were no trees or cover, and a heavy, damp mist had blanketed the hilltop. The minutes passed, Graham had still not returned, and Jodi grew worried.

"Are you okay, dear?" A car had pulled over beside her; the sole occupant, an elderly lady, had opened the front passenger window and was leaning across with a concerned expression.

Jodi bent down to peer in. "Yes, my friend just dropped me here to take photos. He'll be back any minute."

The lady was clearly finding it hard to believe anyone would happily leave a lone woman in the middle of nowhere, on a barren, misty, windswept moor, during a storm. To take photographs! As she looked around her, Jodi realized it sounded insane. She couldn't see more than a few yards before her face. Photographs of what? The woman drove off, seemingly with some reluctance, as cars were beginning to line up behind her, angrily sounding their horns. Embarrassingly, another driver, a less than congenial-looking middle-aged man, stopped his car. Jodi held out a hand. "I'm fine," she said as he opened his window. He drove off, disturbingly slowly at first, only for another vehicle to begin to pull over, this time containing a carful of grinning teenagers. With one hand half covering her face, she waved them on.

"Graham!" Jodi cursed as, at last, his car appeared out of the mist on the other side of the road. "What the hell! Where have you been?" she demanded, flopping angrily into the passenger seat, drenched through, and freezing cold.

"I couldn't find anywhere to turn, then got stuck at road works." Graham tried to make light of the matter. "By the way, Bride also had power over storms. Consider it a privilege to be caught in a Bridal shower."

Jodi was in no mood for stupid jokes. "Drive!" she commanded.

- 4 -

The Stone Heart

After stopping at a pub where Jodi could dry off and change, they arrived at the Leek Museum just after lunch. Inside, Graham scrolled through faded film on an antique microfiche reader in its study room, examining copies of Thomas Bateman's papers.

"The Bridestones dig certainly took place during May 1851," Graham said. "The first *two* weeks of May, to be precise. The report is mainly dry academic stuff about what was found, which wasn't much, just pottery shards confirming the site's dating to the post-Roman, late fifth or early sixth centuries. Nothing spectacular like a lost relic or anything that might be the Heart of the Rose." He read on. "James Bateman is referenced moving the megaliths with the help of several workmen while Thomas and his assistant Samuel Carrington were excavating the tomb. Also present during the dig was local councilor Robert Heath. That would be Mary's father." Graham paused. "Interestingly, there's mention of children being there. Thomas doesn't name or reveal how many, but he says they had to rope off the area to prevent them from hampering the dig. Notably, he refers to *the* children, not just children. That implies they were related to people in some way involved with the excavation. James Bateman was Robert Bateman's father, and Robert Heath was Mary's dad."

Jodi was stunned. "Then little Mary and Robert could indeed have been playing in the area at the time of the dig, and Mary might well have crawled into the tomb just as I saw in my remote." Jodi was always astonished when her visions proved accurate—but witnessing an event that may have occurred well over a century and a half ago was mind-blowing. "As the tomb in my vision was pretty much intact, what I saw may have occurred just before the excavation."

Graham continued to scroll through the microfiche records while Jodi was at one of the adjacent computer terminals, quietly looking up references to Thomas Bateman's other work. Suddenly her voice echoed through the room. "Amazing!" An employee staffing the nearby information desk glared in her direction and held a proverbial finger to his lips. "Sorry." Jodi continued quietly, pointing to the screen as Graham moved across to join her. "This old book refers to a site excavated by Thomas Bateman where they found—guess what—a small stone heart."

Intrigued, they examined the relevant chapter in the book, *Memorials of Old Staffordshire,* published in 1909. The author, a local priest called William Beresford, described an ancient tomb mound excavated on the edge of Leek by Bateman and Carrington in January 1852. Known locally as Cock Low ("low" is a regional term for an ancient mound), it was similar in design to the Bridestones tomb, seven miles to the west. Nothing of great interest was found then, but when the site was leveled in 1907 to make way for re-development, Beresford and local historians tried to prevent it. They failed but were allowed to carry out hasty excavations before the work commenced. It was during this dig that they found an old pottery urn. In-side was a small stone around two inches high, two inches wide, and an inch thick, carved in the shape of a heart. Jodi and Graham stared at the page that in-cluded photographs of the two items taken at the time. The type of stone from which the heart was made was impossible to determine from the old monochrome picture, unaccompanied by a detailed description.

"Could this be the Heart of the Rose?" Jodi looked animatedly at Graham, who appeared deep in thought. "We even speculated that it might have been a small stone heart," she prompted. "The Heart was hidden around 1897, and the Cock Low dig was ten years later. The Meonia group could have hidden it in this second tomb to be inadvertently uncovered by Beresford's team."

Graham frowned. "Somehow, I can't see the Or-der of Meonia hiding their prize possession some-where treasure hunters might ransack at any time." He took over the mouse and keyboard and read through the account as Jodi waited patiently. "Bateman and Carrington could well have missed it," he said at last. "The second dig was much deeper. I'd say the chances are that the item had remained buried there since the mound was built, but the Bateman excavation had been too limited to uncover it."

"But the stone heart must be relevant. Surely! It's too much of a coincidence." Jodi stared at Graham, waiting for a reply.

He remained silent, intently searching online, comparing the urn picture with examples of ancient British ceramics. "The style of the flat-bottomed pot suggests a post-Roman funerary vessel," he said eventually.

Jodi recalled something in the Beresford account. "We are told that, along with the stone heart, fragments of burnt bone were found inside the urn, so it was certainly a cremation vessel. Was it usual for the Celts to cremate their dead and bury their ashes with stone hearts?"

"Cremations, where the ashes were deposited in funerary urns, were common in late Celtic times," Graham said while browsing. "Although, as far as I know, no stone hearts have been found. However, precious, or semi-precious stones, believed by the Celts to channel mystical power, have been discovered in the tombs of Druids. The Cock Low artifact may represent a local variant of the same tradition. Although, from what I can tell, no similar finds are recorded elsewhere in the Wolfside district. Most burial mounds in the area were robbed, vandalized, or leveled by builders and farmers long ago, so it's unknown what they contained. All we can go by are the Bridestones and Cock Low excavations."

Graham swiveled his chair, rolling it back to the microfiche reader, as Jodi made hard copies of the old urn and stone heart photographs. "That's interesting," he said as Jodi rejoined him. "These detailed illustrations of the pottery shards found during Bateman's dig at the Bridestones are fragments of an almost identical vessel to the intact urn found by the Beresford team at Cock Low." He pointed to the images, comparing them with Jodi's printouts. "See here, on the pottery fragments, are the same ring and crisscross engravings seen around the top of the urn. It seems Thomas Bateman unearthed the remains of an identical funerary vessel to the one found in Leek. Unlike the one at Cock Low, however, it had been broken open sometime in the past, maybe by vandals or perhaps through natural decay."

Jodi was none the wiser. "What does that tell us?"

"That the Cock Low tomb was likely built by the same people who erected the Bridestones tomb around AD 500. As the person buried here had been buried with a stone heart—"

Jodi immediately caught on. "So might the person buried at the Bridestones."

Graham smiled. "Exactly."

Jodi's eyes widened. "So little Mary may have found a small stone heart, just as we thought."

"Indeed, except the vessel that contained it was no longer intact but broken into the fragments discovered by Thomas Bateman. Like the one found in Leek, a stone heart could easily have fallen out in the past and, if compacted in the earth and covered with centuries of caked mud, would have been indistinguishable from an innocent small rock or pebble."

"Explaining why it wasn't found before," Jodi recalled her vision. "I saw the little girl clamber into the tomb alone. There were no adults around at the time, only the boy. Mary may have found a stone heart before the archeologists began their work." An intriguing idea occurred to her. "If it did have mystical properties, maybe the one found at Cock Low did too."

"There's nothing about anything strange happening in Beresford's account." Graham was back at the computer terminal and scrolling through the *Memorials of Old Staffordshire*.

Jodi leaned in to read over Graham's shoulder. "What happened to the stone heart found at Cock Low?"

Graham continued to search various databases and websites. "There are no further references to it." He leaned resignedly back in his chair.

Jodi wandered over to the man who had shushed her earlier, showed him the picture of the artifact, explained how it was found, and asked if he knew anything about it.

"Well, it's not in *this* museum," Jodi said on returning to the terminal. "He's going to speak to one of the curators and see if she can help."

As they waited, Jodi voiced something that had been on her mind. "Why would these stone talismans be shaped like hearts?"

Graham offered a possible explanation. "The heart shape that now represents love and affection originally had nothing to do with a human heart, which bears little resemblance. It represented the leaf of the common mulberry tree. First cultivated in China and later by the Greeks and Romans to nourish silkworms, the plant's leaf signified wealth and luxury. It symbolized the epitome of good fortune. An Omphale stone shaped like the mulberry leaf would suggest it was specifically associated with the power to change fate and fortune, just like everything else we're discovering about the Meonia group."

That mention of the fabled Meonian queen had Jodi thinking. "The Heart of the Rose was found in a Celtic tomb; why would the Order of Meonia have considered it one of the legendary Omphale stones?"

"Who knows? Maybe someone had a psychic message like Jenny did at Biddulph Grange. Or little Mary revealed it through clairvoyance."

Graham's suggestion only raised a new question from Jodi. "You explained how an Omphale stone could have got from ancient Greece to the British Isles, but would the Celts have revered such items?"

"Over the centuries, the Celts were greatly influenced by the mythology of Mediterranean cultures. They knew of and sometimes claimed to possess legendary artifacts from ancient Greece and Rome. Celtic mythology incorporated various quests to discover such fabled relics as the Golden Fleece, the helmet of Hermes, and Pandora's Box. So yes, it's quite possible the Druids came to venerate stones they believed to have been fashioned by Omphale."

"Then why not call it The Heart of Omphale or

The Heart of Meonia? Why the Heart of the Rose? What's a rose got to do with anything?"

Graham held up his palms in acquiescence. "Beats me. The only reference I ever discovered to anything called the Heart of the Rose was the name of an early twentieth-century tapestry."

Graham explained how a wall hanging titled *The Heart of the Rose* was made by the British textile company Morris & Co in 1901. "That was the business run by William and Jane Morris, the same Jane associated with the Meonia group. It intrigued me at first—I was sure there must have been a connection—but my research led nowhere.

"Maybe we're now better placed to find a link," Jodi suggested.

They found an image of the tapestry online. It depicted the robed figure of a young man stretching out his hand over a wooden fence, about to touch a giant red rose, surrounded by a tangle of vines and leaves, with the reclining profile of a woman's head, as if asleep, at its center.

"From what I remember," Graham said, "it was inspired by a thirteenth-century French poem called *Le Roman de la Rose*—The Romance of the Rose. The narrative concerns a character called the pilgrim who, by using a magic mirror, experiences visions of a huge, enchanted rose with the power to find him an ideal lover, and he embarks on a quest to find it. I don't remember much more."

While Graham was talking, Jodi had been browsing further. "The picture on the tapestry wasn't just associated with *one* likely member of the Meonia group, but *two*. Not only Jane Morris but Edward Burne-Jones." She summarized the website revealing that the tapestry was copied from an original Burne-Jones monochrome drawing dating from 1872. It even had the same title, *The Heart of the Rose*. "Interestingly, he created a second picture called *The Heart of the Rose*." She opened the relevant image. Dating from 1889, it was an oil painting depicting the same figure of the pilgrim, this time accompanied by a winged figure with a bow, both standing before a beautiful, young, red-haired woman seated in a tangle of rose briars. "Both pictures represent a particular verse in the poem."

They located an online English translation of *The Romance of the Rose*, elucidated by accompanying commentary. It concerned the pilgrim discovering the giant, enchanted rose, its influence symbolized by the girl who sleeps at its center—its heart. The secret enclave where the rose grows is guarded by the goddess Venus who shoots a magic arrow into the rose to awaken the girl who, it transpires, is blessed with miraculous powers to grant the pilgrim his wish. This verse contained the only mention of the Heart of the Rose in the entire poem when referring to the sleeping girl by this name.

"This was what Burne-Jones's two pictures depict, the pilgrim discovering the rose and the sleeping girl having been awakened," Jodi said.

Graham shook his head. "I still don't see any link with the Order of Meonia."

"I do," Jodi said excitedly. "The guardian of the site where the rose is hidden is Venus. Bride was associated with the planet Venus."

"Bride was also associated with the sun, moon, and the dawn, but they're not mentioned."

"But Bride was represented with feathered wings —as is Venus in Burne-Jones's painting. Yet there is no mention of her having wings in the poem. Was it usual to depict Venus with wings?"

Graham typed the words "winged Venus" and other variations on the same theme into the browser with no results. "Seems not."

"And does Venus have a bow?"

Graham did a further search online. "No."

"Just as I thought. Maybe not in the poem, but in Burne-Jones's mind, the woman who shoots the arrow to awaken the girl is a hybrid supernatural being —a winged celeste—just like Bride."

Graham agreed. "So, why do you think Burne-Jones made the drawings?"

"The poem, a typical medieval love allegory, was written by a French poet around 1230, so it had no connection to the pagan Celts, a magic stone, or Omphale of Meonia. And it had nothing to do with a stone heart found at the Bridestones centuries later. Yet Burne-Jones's pictures strongly suggest someone in the Meonia group saw similarities in the poem's symbolism to Mary Heath finding the stone heart. It gave her mystical powers conferred by a celeste. I think they knew of the poem and regarded it as an apt analogy. Accordingly, they decided to name the relic, which happened to be shaped like a heart, after the young woman in the poem who personified magical power—the Heart of the Rose."

Graham was impressed. "Which would imply they didn't know its original name. If it had one, or they knew it but kept it secret, not even revealing it in the memorial pamphlet."

"So, this is the possible scenario," Jodi leaned back and folded her arms. "The Meonia group's prized possession, the Heart of the Rose, was a stone heart thought to have magical powers which they believed had been fashioned by Omphale of Meonia over three thousand years ago. By the fifth century, it ended up in England with the Celts of this area, where it was ultimately buried with the remains of a high priestess or oracle of Bride entombed at the Bridestones." Jodi remained silent for a while. "But why *bury* such an important relic?"

Graham mulled it over. "Because she may have been the last such priestess. A British monk called Gildas, who wrote around 545, implies that this area had been Christianized shortly after AD 500. I guess no one remained who had the gift to use it."

"Until little Mary came along." Something suddenly occurred to Jodi. "I think I know why Edward Burne-Jones drew his original *Heart of the Rose* picture in 1872. It was in memory of Mary Heath. That was the year she died."

"You're asking about the stone heart?" Jodi and Graham turned to face a woman who had appeared silently behind them. Perhaps around thirty, with flowing red hair and a long green dress, she reminded Jodi of a Pre-Raphaelite model. It seemed the curator had at last arrived.

"Yes," they replied in unison and introduced themselves.

"It's not in any collection I know of. Probably lost or stolen long ago." The lady spoke in a pleasant, melodic voice that seemed to be a Welsh accent. "Same as the one found at the Bridestones. It used to be in the hands of the Heath family of Biddulph Grange. Who knows where it is now? Good luck finding it." With that, she abruptly turned and left.

Graham was shocked by her brusque departure. "Sorry. Excuse me. How do you know a stone heart was found at the Bridestones?"

"Or that the Heath family owned it?" Jodi called out as the woman reached the exit and left the room.

Jodi and Graham stared at each other in stunned silence for a second or two before leaping to their feet and bolting in pursuit into the adjacent gallery. Oddly, no one was in sight except a young couple examining an exhibit. They hadn't seen anyone; they said when questioned.

Jodi and Graham returned to the information desk. "Can we have another quick word with the curator?" Jodi asked the man.

"Sorry," he said with a confused expression. "I was about to tell you. I've just been told she won't be in today."

"But we just spoke to her. Red-haired lady in green," Graham said, looking around.

"Don't know whom you spoke to, but it wasn't her." He told them that the curator looked nothing like the person they described. He hadn't noticed any-one even vaguely matching that description in the gallery. Mystified, Graham and Jodi searched every public space in the building and questioned visitors and staff alike. No one recalled seeing anyone re-motely resembling the woman who had spoken to them in plain sight.

"How *did* she know about a heart stone being found at the Bridestones?" Jodi said as they stood outside the museum, looking up and down the empty, rainy street. "There's nothing about it in Thomas Bateman's journals or anything else we examined. And how did she know the Heaths had it? Or, for that matter, that we were looking for it?"

"Maybe she overheard us talking."

"If she were close enough to overhear us, we would have seen her. And so would others. She wasn't exactly hard to miss."

Graham shook his head. "Who the hell was she?"

* * *

Driving back to Birmingham, Jodi and Graham puzzled over the mysterious woman who seemed to have known precisely what they were doing. Particu-larly strange was her appearance. It wasn't that she had reminded Jodi of just *any* Pre-Raphaelite model, but the one in the painting they were examining when the woman appeared—Burne-Jones's second *Heart of the Rose* picture. Although the woman was older than the girl in the painting, her hair was the same shade of red and cut in a similar style, with short bangs (or a fringe, as they say in England), while her dress was almost an ankle-length version of the long, dark-green gown worn by the figure in the picture. The mysterious woman was a flesh-and-blood human being, no ghost or spirit. Nevertheless, it was uncanny that the enigmatic stranger, with her equally enigmatic message, should bear any resemblance to the model in the painting at all. Jodi voiced her thoughts, and Graham agreed.

"How come no one else saw her?" Graham said as they hit the evening rush hour and came to a stop.

"I suppose visitors were particularly engrossed with exhibits," Jodi suggested, "while the man on the information desk was preoccupied with work."

"I suppose," Graham echoed. "Well, whoever she was, and however she knew what we were investigating, we should take her as another synchronicity confirming we're on the right track. Apart from anything else, she confirmed that a stone heart was discovered at the Bridestones." He glanced over at Jodi. "I wonder if there are clues in the Burne-Jones painting to reveal where it was hidden."

"I doubt it. The Heart seems to have been hidden around 1897; the oil painting dates from 1889—eight years earlier."

An idea struck Graham. "In the poem, the Heart of the Rose girl personified the supernatural power the pilgrim sought. We reasoned that Burne-Jones's painting represented the power of the stone heart discovered by Mary Heath. What if the woman in the picture *was* Mary Heath when she had grown up?"

Jodi's expression turned doubtful. "Then again, the little girl in my remote was blond."

"The Pre-Raphaelites often gave their models red hair, regardless of their true color. For some reason, it was considered medieval." Graham sighed. "Anyway, I've failed to locate a single painting or photograph of Mary. I assume they all went up in smoke during the Biddulph Grange fire."

"I'm sure I'd recognize the little girl in my vision," Jodi said, as at last, the traffic began to move. "It's a pity we don't know what Mary looked like as a child."

This was soon to change in the most unexpected way.

-5-
Alice

During the remaining days of Jodi's visit to England, nothing unusual happened, and no further insights were gained. Even her remotes failed to provide anything new. They contacted the museum hoping to view surveillance footage of the red-haired stranger but were informed it had been copied over. Consequently, with nothing else to go on, and as they were both going to be busy with other projects, they agreed to put the Meonia mystery on hold until Jodi returned to England later in the year. However, things took a surprising turn.

Graham's sister visited him and, along with a friend, they went to the Bridestones. Nothing strange transpired while they were there but later, when he viewed this new footage, something odd again occurred on film. The camera panned around the stones when the sound briefly became crackly and distorted. Graham once more shared the footage with IT expert Mike, who suggested that the anomaly might again have something to do with electrical interference. However, there had been no thunderstorm this time, and there was nothing around the site, such as a transformer or power lines, that might have caused it. Hoping to discover the reason for the sound distortion, Mike adjusted the audio and isolated what seemed to be a voice in the background. It was barely discernible over the crackling, but everyone who heard it agreed that they could hear what seemed to be a little girl saying—*Follow me*.

It was indeed possible that the voice belonged to a child playing somewhere out of sight, beyond the trees, although none of them recalled hearing anything at the time. Strangely, the voice was only recorded during the brief period of sound distortion and not at any other time during the more than ten minutes of video. The moment Jodi listened to the shared footage during a video chat with Graham, an image of the playing children from her vision came vividly to mind.

"The little girl in my remote was beckoning for the boy to follow," she said. "'Follow me!' That's what the voice is saying. I'm sure our attention is being drawn to my vision." An idea struck her. "Alice in Wonderland!" she said excitedly. "Little Mary being dressed like Alice wasn't just my subconscious way of depicting a Victorian child. There's more to it. The Alice story and the Meonia mystery are somehow connected."

"How?" Graham couldn't see a link.

Jodi shook her head. "I've no idea—but I'm sure of it."

She decided to return to England immediately.

Strange Fate

After Graham collected her from Manchester Airport, they decided to visit the Bridestones and Biddulph Grange en route to her hotel in Birmingham. But after the trip revealed nothing new, they focused on the potential Alice in Wonderland link Jodi felt existed.

Alice's Adventures in Wonderland is a novel first published in 1865 by the English author and mathematician Charles Dodgson under the pseudonym Lewis Carroll. It concerns a girl named Alice who enters a rabbit hole to find herself in a fantasy world populated by various bizarre creatures, including playing cards brought to life in distorted human form, the chief of whom is Alice's adversary, the Queen of Hearts. The book's title character is generally thought to have been inspired by Alice Liddell, the daughter of Henry Liddell, dean of Oxford's Christ Church College where Carroll lectured on mathematics. However, although he dedicated the book to Alice Liddell and probably named his character after her, Carroll always denied that she had been his inspiration. Photographs of Alice Liddell taken at the time the book was published show her with dark hair cut in a bob with bangs, whereas in the book illustrations, taken from Carroll's original drawings, Alice has long blond hair without bangs. Besides, Alice is seven years old in the story, while the Liddell girl wasn't even born when he first conceived the idea in the early 1850s and thirteen when the book was published. Nonetheless, Lewis Carroll often implied that he *had* based his character on a real little girl, although he kept her identity a secret he took to his grave.

That night, as Jodi lay on the bed in her hotel room, looking at a picture of Carroll's Alice on her laptop, she was overcome with déjà vu. Until now, she had only thought there might be a *link* between Mary Heath and the Alice story; now, Jodi was struck with the overwhelming feeling that the young Mary Heath had been the mysterious person who inspired it.

Over the next couple of days, they discovered that there was indeed a direct connection between Mary Heath and Lewis Carroll. In 1851, Carroll, a student at Oxford University, completed the first part of his degree in mathematics and took a sabbatical, working as an in-house tutor to the children of the wealthy landowner Sir Charles Wood at their home of Hickleton Hall in Yorkshire. In August of that year, Mary's father, Robert Heath, was Sir Charles's guest, there to discuss mining rights in the area. According to the scant records that still survived concerning the activities of the Heath family, during the visit, Robert had been accompanied by his wife Anne and their seven-year-old daughter Mary. So, astonishingly, as a child, Mary Heath must have met Lewis Carroll while at Hickleton Hall. Could the young Mary Heath have inspired the story of Alice, ultimately published some years later as Jodi now believed?

Although Jodi had previously experienced visual images and mental impressions concerning things she knew nothing of that later proved correct, she was always amazed when her feelings and visions were accurate. And this appeared to be another such occasion. She had known nothing about the life of Lewis Carroll or any links he had with Mary Heath. So, when they discovered that Carroll's first notes for what would eventually morph into Alice's adventures, plus some of his early drawings for the story, were made during that same summer of 1851, Jodi was blown away. But there was more. The fictional Alice was seven years old—exactly Mary Heath's age. None of Sir Charles's three daughters were Alice's age in August 1851. One was eleven, one was a toddler, and the other hadn't even been born. Remarkably, it was indeed possible that little Mary Heath had inspired Lewis Carroll's character.

As they had found a definitive link between Mary Heath and Lewis Carroll, Graham suggested that Jodi try another remote. Her visions became unclear, chaotic, and indecipherable if she attempted them too often. Nevertheless, she agreed.

A hazy image, clearing to become the exterior of a large country mansion. The vision switches to what Jodi is sure is the interior: what seems to be a library, a room surrounded on all walls by bookshelves. The same little girl from her remote of the Bridestones, again dressed as Alice in Wonderland, peers out from a gold-framed mirror above the fireplace. Bizarrely, she exists only as a floating reflection; the room is empty. The vision fades.

"No, that's not the house in my vision," Jodi said the following day when she met Graham for breakfast at her hotel. He was showing her an old photograph of Hickleton Hall on his phone.

Confusion showed on Graham's face. "Are you sure? That's where Mary Heath and Lewis Carroll stayed in 1851."

"The architecture was completely different, built from red brick, not pale stone like that place."

"And it wasn't Biddulph Grange?"

"Nothing like it. I don't think it's anywhere we've been."

After breakfast, they spent the morning looking at pictures of English stately homes on Jodi's laptop that might be the one in her vision. From Jodi's description, it seemed to be a Victorian mansion, which helped concentrate their search, but it was still lunchtime before they found it.

Graham examined the photograph. "Hoar Cross Hall, central Staffordshire. You're sure that's it?"

"Positive."

"Well, there's certainly a link with what we're investigating." Graham was scanning a relevant webpage. "In the late 1800s, it belonged to a politician named Hugo Francis Meynell-Ingram—that's a mouthful—who married Lady Emily, the daughter of Sir Charles Wood of Hickleton Hall, the very place where Lewis Carroll and Mary Heath stayed in 1851. Emily came to live at Hoar Cross Hall after her marriage in 1864."

"How old was she?" Jodi asked.

Graham clicked on a link to Emily Charlotte Wood. "She was born in 1840, so around 24."

"I mean in 1851 when Lewis Carroll tutored the Wood children."

Graham screwed up his face to make what should have been a simple calculation. "Eleven."

"So, she must have been one of Carroll's pupils."

"Could she have been the little girl in your remote?"

"No." Jodi was adamant. "Too old. The girl I saw in the mirror was the child from my vision of the Bridestones—same age, same appearance—and I'm certain *she* had been a young Mary Heath."

Graham thought for a moment. "Your vision was certainly surreal. A little girl stuck in a mirror. But it might be symbolic. All the same, I think you've added a new perspective."

"What?"

"Alice Through the Looking Glass!"

Alice Through the Looking Glass, originally titled *Through the Looking Glass and What Alice Found There*, was the sequel to *Alice in Wonderland*. It was published in 1871 and set shortly after the first tale. In the story, Alice sees yet another strange world, reflected in a large mirror hanging above a fireplace. She clambers onto the mantelpiece to peer in, finding she can enter this fantastic domain by passing through the mirror. Like Wonderland, the world she enters is inhabited by strange beings. Still, this time the chief protagonists are not anthropomorphized playing cards but personified chess pieces, her main rival on this occasion being the Red Queen. (During the nineteenth century, chess pieces were often red and white rather than the black and white of today).

"That never occurred to me," Jodi said. "I guess it could have been my subconscious connecting the two stories."

"If you're sure it was Hoar Cross Hall, we should visit the place; see if it ever had a library matching your description."

Hoar Cross Hall is now a luxury health resort and hotel, but many of its decorative features remain from the nineteenth century. Although the west wing is new, much of the east wing is original. Here, the long gallery, just off the reception, is today a bar and rest area, with wood-paneled walls, old portraits, tapestries, and a ceiling of intricate plasterwork. It is lit by large windows on one side, while the other has oak doors leading to the dining room and a lounge called the library.

When they entered the library, Jodi gasped in recognition. It was the room in her remote. The bookshelves still lined the walls, filled with old volumes, many dating from the 1800s. The owners, they later discovered, had endeavored to keep much of this wing of the building as authentic as possible, even going to the trouble of tracking down original furnishings that had been sold off over the years to repair and return them to the once stately home of Hoar Cross Hall. Apart from the tables, couches, and chairs where patrons could eat and drink, the lounge was just as it had been when the room was a library in the nineteenth century. The fireplace and mirror matched precisely what Jodi had seen. From the receptionist who offered to show them around, they learned that the mirror had been restored to its original condition in the 1990s and, as far as she knew, rehung where it had been during the 1800s.

To their surprise, Jodi and Graham found a secret door disguised as a bookshelf in one corner of the room that opened onto a corridor; the receptionist showed them another, in the opposite corner, leading to the dining room. "There are many mysteries at Hoar Cross Hall," she said with a smile. "For instance, this old library is supposed to be haunted by the ghost of a little girl." They stopped in their tracks.

"A little girl!" Jodi said as she and Graham exchanged glances.

The receptionist seemed taken aback by Jodi's surprise. "Err, yes. I've never seen anything myself, but guests and staff have claimed to see a little Victorian girl."

"Why Victorian?" Graham asked.

"People say she's dressed like Alice in Wonderland. That's Victorian, isn't it?" Jodi and Graham could not believe what they were hearing. Not wanting to prompt the woman, Graham asked her to elaborate. "She's not only been seen *here* but also on the grand staircase, in an upstairs corridor, and in one of the bedrooms," she said.

"How old is she?" Jodi asked as the receptionist led the way from the library and up the grand staircase.

"The ghost? Around seven, from what I've heard."

Jodi turned to Graham. "Same age as the girl in my remote," she said quietly.

"And Alice in Wonderland," Graham whispered back.

The house, they learned, had a long reputation as being haunted. The family who lived there during the 1970s and their visitors reported hearing unaccountable sounds and voices. On many occasions, they claimed to witness the apparition of a little girl—not dressed in day clothes, but in what seemed to be a long nightdress, standing outside the lounge, on the grand staircase, and floating down an upstairs corridor. The most frightening encounter was when the lady of the house awoke one night to see the phantom child hovering over her bed. The alleged haunting dates back to the Victorian period when Emily lived here; during the mid-1860s, her brother Charles Lindley Wood, later to become Lord Halifax, stayed at Hoar Cross Hall and was so astonished by the phenomena he witnessed that he acquired a life-long interest in the paranormal, traveling the country collecting accounts of hauntings that he published in two books: *The Ghost Book of Charles Lindley, Viscount Halifax,* and *Lord Halifax's Complete Ghost Book.*

"Halifax wrote of his experiences here," the receptionist explained. "Strange noises, footsteps, and the specter of a little girl dressed in what he described as contemporary clothes. Contemporary for *his* time, that is."

Leading Jodi and Graham upstairs, the receptionist took them along the supposedly haunted corridor, telling them that various guests had heard footsteps here, like a child running, although nothing was seen. She stopped at room number 432. "Other than the library, this is allegedly the most haunted room," she said, opening the door and ushering them inside. Everything seemed quite normal for a hotel room. A double bed, en suite bathroom, with an old stone-frame window overlooking the gardens. "People claim to have heard strange noises here, plus a knocking at the door to find no one there, and it's said that the Victorian girl's been seen." She pointed to the window. "There."

"In day or night clothes?" Jodi asked.

"Both, I think."

"Why do creepy ghost girls always appear in night dresses?" Graham quipped.

The receptionist stayed close to the door, seemingly reluctant to enter. "I must admit this room creeps me out," she said. "We often get calls from here, down in reception. When we answer, no one's on the line. Some of the girls say they hear a strange crackling sound."

"Probably a bad line," Graham suggested.

"When the room's unoccupied!" the receptionist added with a visible shiver.

Suddenly Jodi grabbed Graham's arm. "Look!" she said, pointing to the plate with the room number on it.

They had already noted that all the rooms were numbered and named after aristocrats: Lady, Countess, Princess, something or other, such as Maria,

Natasha, and Elizabeth. Room 432, the one they were in, was "Lady Alice."

"What is it?" the receptionist asked.

"You said the ghost looked like Alice in Wonderland," Jodi said. "Was this room named after her?"

The girl took a step backwards. "How odd. I never considered that."

When they returned to the lobby, the receptionist made inquiries. Although some of the rooms were named after people who had lived or stayed there in the past, such as the Halifax Conference Suite, after Lord Halifax the ghost hunter, as far as anyone knew, most of the rooms were randomly named by the current owners after various titled figures with no connection to Hoar Cross Hall to give the place an aristocratic feel. The identity of the Alice the room was named after was a mystery.

"Who's the ghost meant to be?" Jodi asked.

"People have suggested a serving girl," the receptionist said.

Graham considered the possibility. "I don't think little children were employed as housemaids during Victorian times. Besides, her clothing—her daytime attire, that is—suggests someone from money. So why a servant?"

"Probably for lack of another candidate." The receptionist explained how the owners in the late nineteenth century—Hugo and Emily—were childless and how, after Emily died in 1904, the house remained empty for years. "There doesn't seem to have been any children living in the house during the Victorian era. A servant, or possibly the daughter of a servant, seems to be the only possibility," she concluded.

Taking tea in the library, Jodi and Graham searched independently online to see what else they could discover about Hoar Cross Hall during the Victorian period. "The place was already haunted by the child's ghost when Lord Halifax stayed here in the 1860s," Graham mused. "Who lived here before that?"

"No one," Jodi said. "Emily's husband built the present hall, so that's as far back as it goes."

Graham frowned. "So, who's the little girl?"

"You're the ones who've been asking about the ghost?" said a waitress who had come to clear away one of the tables.

They both smiled and nodded.

"She's supposed to haunt this room. People say they've seen her in the mirror," she said, pointing to the one above the fireplace.

Jodi was astonished. The mirror in her vision! "What do they see?" she asked.

"The little girl," the waitress repeated.

"They see her floating there?" Graham asked, recalling Jodi's vision.

"I think they just see her reflection like she's standing in the room. But when they turn around, she's gone."

Jodi was astonished by the similarity to what she had seen in her vision the night before. "Do you know anyone, personally, who's seen her?"

"Only this one guy who worked behind the bar."

The girl told them of the young man's strange encounter. One night, as his shift ended, the bartender entered the library to clear away glasses. When he looked in the mirror, he saw the reflection of a little girl with long blond hair standing in the corner, at the other end of the room where the secret door led to the dining area. He assumed she was in fancy dress, wearing what he described as an old-fashioned blue dress and white apron. She was staring at him with a blank expression. Wondering why she was up so late and on her own when the bars and dining room had closed, he turned to ask if she was okay. But she was gone. Thinking she had left quickly through the secret door, he walked over and followed, only to find the dining room empty. Assuming she had run out into the long gallery, he went back into the recess that led to the library and again saw her in the mirror—now standing in the doorway where *he* had been when he first saw *her*. She was staring at him again, this time with a mischievous smile. By the time he rounded the corner to re-enter the library, she had disappeared. Thinking she was playing games, he trotted through the room and out into the long gallery, but she was nowhere to be seen.

"He couldn't work out how she moved so fast," the waitress said. "It was only the next day when he learned that no children had been staying here that he realized he may have seen the ghost."

"Well, what do you make of it?" Graham asked Jodi when they were alone.

"The ghost must be connected to the little girl in my vision. They certainly have the same appearance: the right age, blond, and dressed like Alice in Wonderland. And I only saw her reflected in the mirror. Just like the bartender. He never got to look at her directly."

Graham walked over to the fireplace. "True, but other people do claim to have seen her face to face, so to speak."

"I know, but I think the mirror is important."

"How?" Graham asked expectantly.

Jodi just shook her head.

- 6 -
Wonderland

The next morning, over breakfast in Jodi's hotel, they assessed what they had inferred concerning the Order of Meonia at the time of its formation.

"It seems the Meonia group was founded when the first shrine was constructed," Graham said. "That being the Celtic glen. As Thomas Bateman refers to his cousin James moving the Bridestones megaliths, presumably for that purpose, during his excavation, which occurred during the first two weeks of May 1851, this was when the whole thing began. If Mary found the Heart of the Rose around the time the dig commenced, as your vision implies, it means that within a short time something had persuaded the Heaths and Batemans not only that the little girl had developed some kind of extraordinary supernatural gift but that they should establish a secret society."

Jodi concurred. "Whatever their objective, it was obviously considered important. Building the four shrines was a considerable undertaking."

"If they were hoping to utilize the power of Bride, as we've reasoned, perhaps they originally intended to construct only the Celtic glen," Graham suggested. "We speculated that there were gaps in their knowledge concerning ancient Celtic belief, necessitating them to employ other, similar forms of mysticism from various ancient cultures."

"Leading to the later building of the Egyptian, Chinese, and Roman shrines." Jodi shook her head. "I wonder what kind of revelation could have inspired them to do all that."

"Well, as all their activities seemed to relate to supernatural entities associated with opening portals to other worlds, I'd guess it involved someone, presumably Mary, accessing an alternate reality. Or as far as they believed."

"That's it!" Jodi said, suddenly losing interest in her breakfast. "I think you're onto something. Last night I read up on Celtic mythology; it's full of tales concerning children gaining strange powers after venturing inside burial mounds, some of which were believed to conceal tunnels leading to fantastic underground lands inhabited by fairy folk. We've been assuming that it was the Heart of the Rose that enhanced Mary's paranormal abilities. Maybe it did have mystical properties—whatever they happened to be— but her clairvoyance might have been amplified by the tomb itself.

"You think there's some truth in these Celtic legends?"

"Yes, maybe something in the tomb changed little Mary."

Graham seemed doubtful. "Why just Mary? Why

not others who entered the tomb?"

"In Celtic mythology, it only happened to *special* children. Those who already had fairy blood."

"Mary Heath had fairy blood!" Graham said incredulously.

Jodi waved a dismissive hand. "Someone like her might have been *thought* to have, in the past. Today we might say she had the right DNA. She was already different."

Graham considered the scenario. "You thought I was onto something when I said Mary might have accessed an alternate reality. What did you mean?"

"Wonderland."

"Lewis Carroll's Wonderland?"

"I think what happened to her might have inspired his story. Think about it. Mary crawled inside a small opening in a hillock to experience something remarkable, just like Alice discovered a magical world down a rabbit hole. I doubt Mary entered another reality, but the upgrade to her mind—or whatever you'd call it—might have involved an extraordinary experience, perhaps something like my remotes, which the child was unable to comprehend. All she remembered was a meaningful, but jumbled, lucid dream. When Mary met Carroll at Hickleton Hall just a few months later, the episode was still fresh in her mind. She was probably full of the story, and Carroll was intrigued by it. I don't suppose that living playing cards, white rabbits, and Mad Hatter's tea parties were part of Mary's experience, but they may have been surreal enough to provide the author with a backdrop to be elaborated by his imagination."

"So, what *do* you think did happen to little Mary in the mound?" Graham asked, intrigued.

"Perhaps something she couldn't explain, her young mind embellishing her experience into time spent in a world of magical creatures. Like Celtic children envisaging fairies. Maybe not precisely those that Carroll ultimately imagined, but weird enough to give him the idea."

Graham nodded thoughtfully. "It does hang together, no matter how weird it sounds. There certainly seems to be something strange about the Bridestones. That bizarre storm, the weird light, and the seemingly disembodied girl's voice. Not to mention the fact that someone *coincidentally* left a playing card that got us thinking about the Alice stories." Graham paused. "So, what's causing it all?"

"Who knows? Maybe some kind of essence, energy, or intelligence the ancients called Bride. Whatever we're dealing with, it wants our attention."

For Graham, a big question remained unanswered. "I know you think the girl in your visions was Mary Heath, but she can't be the child ghost of Hoar Cross Hall?" he said. "Mary didn't die until she was in her late twenties."

"I suppose," Jodi shrugged, adding, "But as Mary met Lewis Carroll at Hickleton Hall perhaps we should go *there*."

"Unfortunately, the place is a boarded-up ruin," Graham explained what he had discovered when researching Lewis Carroll, the previous night. The

Wood family sold the Hall in 1947 and it was turned into a girls' school; in 1961 it was sold again, and for over forty years it remained a care home run by the charitable Sue Ryder Foundation. "There's very little about the place online. Maybe we can learn something from the last occupants."

Having spoken to the Sue Ryder Foundation, Jodi and Graham arranged to meet with the person they were told would be the most helpful: Grace Perry, a lawyer working for the charity in the 1990s who had carried out some historical research on Hickleton Hall. She now lived in Telford, not too far from Birmingham. Driving around the town, looking for the woman's house, the GPS kept going haywire, leading them back, again and again, to the same traffic roundabout. Giving up on technology, Jodi and Graham tried to navigate by road signs alone but still ended up back where they started. On about their sixth return to the roundabout, Jodi shouted in surprise.

"Look at that!"

"What?" Graham almost swerved the car as he tried to see what Jodi was pointing at. On the next orbit of the roundabout, he saw it: a large public information sign pointing to *Wonderlana*.

"I swear that wasn't there before," Jodi said. She quickly began browsing on her phone for "Wonderland, Telford."

Graham agreed. "I've looked at all the signs at this roundabout, over and over, and never noticed that. How could we miss it?"

Jodi stared incredulously at her phone. "You

won't believe this, but it's an Alice in Wonderland theme park. The only one in England, according to their website."

"I've never heard of it. But we should check it out." Graham turned off at the appropriate exit.

They arrived to find a kids' adventure playground with rides and mockup villages featuring the different places and characters Alice encounters during her trips to Wonderland and the mirror world.

"What are the chances of us bumping into this place?" Jodi said as they paid to get in.

"Well, as there's only one in the entire country, pretty remote I'd say."

Graham followed Jodi through the turnstile and to the various attractions. They could imagine the place bustling with children on a sunny day, but it was cold, raining, and almost deserted. From a drenched, shivering, student, dressed as Alice and working part-time as one of the park guides, they learned that Wonderland had been there for years and was open all year round. But following their early euphoria, hoping that the place might hold some serendipitous clues to help them discover something relevant concerning the Alice mystery, the place was disappointing. None of the features revealed anything, while the staff knew next to nothing about Lewis Carroll or the historical background of the Alice tales. However, on visiting the gift store on the way out, they did acquire something that was to prove invaluable: a rare edition of both Alice stories, complete with a historical introduction and original artwork.

By the time they returned to the car, they were late for their meeting with Grace Perry. Graham called her to apologize, only to discover that she was soon to go out and would be unavailable to meet again for several days. She had, however, located a file concerning Hickleton Hall and was able to answer their questions over the phone. Although the file contained little more than they already knew concerning the history of the building, it did provide a detailed description of the interior. Graham put the phone on speaker so that Jodi, sitting in the passenger seat and flipping through the Alice book they had just bought, could hear.

By the time the Sue Ryder Foundation had taken over Hickleton Hall, Grace explained, it contained none of the original furnishings. Nevertheless, many of its nineteenth-century fixtures and fittings still survived. She went on to describe the Hall, which had clearly been a grand place to live, but Graham didn't think it was of much help in their research. He was about to thank the woman for her time when Jodi interrupted. "Does it describe a drawing room?" she asked.

They could hear Grace flipping through papers before answering. "Yes, it was where the family received guests."

"And did it have a fireplace?" Jodi said.

More rustling of paper. "Yes. There are no photographs, I'm afraid, but there's a detailed description of all the original fixtures for insurance purposes."

Graham looked quizzically at Jodi as she asked if

the lawyer could email them a copy of the inventory. "What is it?" he asked after he had hung up and they waited for the document to arrive.

"In the Looking Glass story, the magic mirror is in the drawing room. It hung over a fireplace." Jodi held up the open book. "Here's Lewis Carroll's illustration of Alice having clambered up onto the mantelpiece before she steps through the mirror. The fireplace is quite distinctive. If it matches the one from the drawing room at Hickleton Hall—"

Graham interrupted before Jodi could finish. "I thought we reckoned that *Alice in Wonderland*, not *Alice Through the Looking Glass*, was inspired while Carroll was at Hickleton Hall."

"According to the introduction to this book, he initially began working on both stories in tandem during his time at Hickleton Hall in 1851."

Graham caught on. "So, Hickleton Hall's drawing room may have been his setting for the Looking Glass story?"

"And if the fireplace illustration matches the one in Hickleton Hall's drawing room—"

"It pretty much confirms it."

"Exactly."

By the afternoon they had still not received the email from Grace Perry so decided to visit Staffordshire's central library in the county town of Stafford to check out further details concerning Hoar Cross Hall. As they examined various papers in the local collection, Jodi found something of considerable interest.

"When Emily Wood came to live at Hoar Cross Hall after she married in 1864, she brought certain furnishings with her, including a collection of ornate, gilded-framed mirrors which had previously hung in Hickleton Hall. What if they included the one from the drawing room? We know that the Hoar Cross library mirror was there in the 1800s. Perhaps that's it."

"The haunted mirror in the Hoar Cross library might have been the very one that inspired the Looking Glass story?" Graham said enthusiastically.

"It makes sense."

Graham began flicking through the Alice book. "Can I see a photo of the Hoar Cross library mirror?" he said.

Jodi opened the relevant image on her phone. The mirror was about 4 feet high and 3 feet wide, surrounded by a gold-colored frame. The top was lavishly decorated, but the sides were adorned with simple corded designs, resembling straight pieces of golden rope.

"They're pretty similar," Graham said, pointing to the book's illustration of Alice about to enter the looking glass. The picture only showed the bottom left corner of the mirror, but the golden corded design matched the one in the photograph. "Lewis Carroll insisted that his original illustrations were copied by the artist John Tenniel for both books when they were published," he continued. "It doesn't *prove* it's the mirror from the drawing room—the corded design was probably fairly common—but the Hoar Cross library mirror is a much better contender than the one generally thought to have inspired Carroll's looking glass."

Graham explained how, in popular tradition, the mirror that inspired the story belonged to Alice Liddell's grandparents, as the Liddell girl, who often stayed with them, is said to have been fascinated by it. It still survives in the same building, now a private house at Charlton Kings in the county of Gloucestershire. He searched online for a picture and showed it to Jodi. The mirror was 6 feet high and 5 feet wide, its frame elaborately decorated on all sides with carvings of interwoven branches, foliage, and various animals.

"It's nothing like the one in the book illustrations, "Jodi observed. "Why has no one figured that before?"

"They have. Literary historians don't think it has anything to do with the story. More of an urban legend. It seems few actual scholars believe the mirror in the book illustrations is the one at Charlton Kings."

"But it could be the one at Hoar Cross Hall."

Graham again compared the photograph with the Alice mirror. "It's not exactly the same, but it's not far off."

"Well, it *certainly* came from Hickleton Hall!" Jodi said excitedly." She held open a local history book concerning the village of Hoar Cross that included a contents inventory of the Hall from the late Victorian era and pointed to the relevant paragraph. "Here, the library mirror is included in a list of the furnishings added by Emily Wood in 1864."

"It all comes down to Hickleton's drawing-room

fireplace," Graham concluded, taking the book from Jodi to read it for himself. "If it matches Lewis Carroll's illustration, then the mirror that hung over it *must* be the one that inspired his story. And, as the Hoar Cross library mirror *dia* come from Hickleton Hall, and it is remarkably like the Alice mirror, I think we could safely say we've located the original Looking Glass."

It was late that afternoon before they finally received the email from Grace Perry. But not before yet another extraordinary happenstance. They were walking through Stafford town center, looking for somewhere to eat, talking about the peculiar coincidences that had already occurred.

"It's so weird how that Wonderland theme park happened to be just where we were," Graham said, as they entered a back street.

"I swear, I looked at every road sign at that roundabout at least half a dozen times," Jodi said. "I would have noticed if there had been a sign to 'Wonderland.' It just seemed to have appeared out of nowhere."

"Another of the strange synchronicities that seem to be guiding us. Like the Queen of Hearts someone left at the Bridestones, the storm, strange camera effects, the little girl's voice, and the haunted room coincidentally being named the Lady Alice suite. If we hadn't gone to Wonderland, which we only found because we inexplicably kept returning to that same roundabout, we wouldn't have the book with its informative introduction, original text, and illustrations. It could all be coincidence, but if we get another synchronicity..." Graham clicked his fingers as if he could make one happen.

Jodi stopped dead in her tracks, grabbing Graham's arm. "I think we just have." Right in front of them was a small café called the Mad Hatter's Tea Emporium, its window festooned with images from the Alice stories.

Graham stood there open-mouthed for some seconds before speaking. "I've been around here many times and never saw that."

"Well, you just asked for another synchronicity," Jodi said, staring in through the window.

"And got one. Almost as if—"

"It's confirmation that fate *is* helping us."

"You think?"

Jodi shrugged. "It's certainly weird." She ushered Graham towards the café. "Be careful when you click your fingers," she said.

As they walked on, Graham did try clicking his fingers again, asking for things to appear, but without success.

A few minutes later they were sitting in the Mad Hatter's Tea Emporium waiting for their order. All around them, the place was decorated with Alice memorabilia: dolls, paintings, surreal ornaments depicting characters and scenes from Wonderland and the mirror world; even posters for the Johnny Depp movies. Before long, their pot of tea arrived—and so did the email from Grace Perry. They had already identified the precise type of Victorian fireplace depicted in the *Alice Through the Looking Glass* illustrations, and the inventory from the Sue Ryder Foundation concerning the fireplace in the Hickleton Hall drawing room matched precisely: A wooden Corbel mantlepiece, a relatively simple design of two flat pilasters to either side, with ornately grooved brackets to support the shelf. The fireplace was of the Lytton design, a rounded rather than rectangular, cast-iron inlay around and above the grate. All identical to Lewis Carroll's original artwork.

"The likelihood of those exact, combined features occurring by chance must be astronomical," Graham concluded. "There's now no doubt in my mind that the Looking Glass story was first conceived in the drawing room at Hickleton Hall. And its mirror —highly likely to be the one now in the Hoar Cross Hall library—was the very item Lewis Carroll had in mind. Which all suggests that Mary Heath—the only girl of the right age at Hickleton Hall at the time both stories were conceived—really *was* the inspiration for the fictional Alice."

"But if Mary Heath inspired Carroll's character, why call her Alice?" Jodi queried.

"After Alice Liddell," Graham said. "And for the same reason he dedicated both his Alice books to her. It's generally thought that he hoped to curry favor with her father, his boss the dean of Christ Church College where he lectured by the time the books were published. He also included some cryptic allusions to the Liddell girl in his works. For instance, he used the first letters of each line of a poem at the end of

Through the Looking Glass to spell out her name, and he set the *Wonderland* story on May fourth, Alice Liddell's birthday,"

"The Wonderland story is set on May fourth?" said Jodi, surprised. "Once again—my birthday!"

It was Graham's turn to sound surprised. "I've just realized something! Thomas Bateman's Bride-stones dig occurred during the first two weeks of May 1851. If little Mary entered the tomb just before the excavation commenced, it might well have occurred on May fourth, the same day Alice entered Wonderland."

"Wow! More evidence Carroll based his story on her. So, Alice Liddell's birthday is just a coincidence."

Graham let out a long breath. "I don't even know what 'coincidence' means anymore."

"May fourth is also the date of the Mary Heath memorial event in 1897," Jodi said. "Maybe that's what the occasion was commemorating."

Graham widened his eyes. "Not her death, which we know was on October thirteenth, but when she entered the tomb, gained her power, and the whole Meonia thing began. You could be right."

Jodi shook her head in disbelief and began scanning through the Alice book. "You said Lewis Carroll made coded allusions to Alice Liddell in his works. Surely, if he did base his story on Mary Heath, there must be some implied reference to her too." She spent a few moments flipping through the book before pointing animatedly. "And it looks like there is. When the white rabbit, which she followed into Wonderland, first speaks to Alice, he calls her 'Mary Ann'—four times. Alice assumes that he is mistaking her for his servant." Jodi continued reading for some minutes while Graham patiently sipped his tea. "Yet no character of that name appears in the story, and it goes unexplained why the rabbit addressed Alice as Mary Ann. Wasn't that Mary Heath's full name?"

"You're right. That's how the epitaph writers refer to her in the memorial pamphlet. Wow!" Graham stared up at a poster on the café wall depicting Alice climbing into the looking glass. "Everything considered, I guess we can safely say that your intuition was right. Alice *was* based on Mary Heath."

* * *

It was some time before the investigation continued, upon Jodi's next visit to the UK. Graham had been researching and developing a working hypothesis concerning the ghost girl at Hoar Cross Hall. It seemed far-fetched, but no less so than some other aspects of their investigation.

"I originally thought your vision of the girl in the mirror was simply your mind's way of revealing that Mary Heath inspired the Alice stories," Graham said after he picked Jodi up from the airport and headed for Hoar Cross Hall on that dull, rainy afternoon. "But I reckon there's more to it. The Hoar Cross ghost would appear to be the child you saw in the mirror during your remote. They seem to be the same age, are dressed alike, and both have long blond hair. You're sure the girl you saw in the mirror was the same little girl you saw in your Bridestones vision?"

"Yes," Jodi replied from the passenger seat.

"And you're certain *that* was Mary Heath?"

"*Yes.*" Jodi was growing impatient. Graham had not yet explained what he had figured out. He was doing one of his dramatic, reveal-it-at-the-last-moment things "Come on, tell me what we're doing."

"Okay," Graham relented. "All considered, your visions imply the ghost is Mary Heath, right?"

"I agree. But it can't be. She died as an adult."

Graham turned and smiled knowingly. "But it might be her tulpa."

Jodi frowned. "Her what?"

"Tulpa. It's a concept originally from ancient Tibet, still prevalent in Japanese Shinto. A phantom manifested by the power of human thought or intense emotion. Gifted children are sometimes believed to unwittingly create them to act out their fantasies as mischievous spirits."

"Like poltergeists?"

"More like the girl from *The Ring*."

Jodi shivered slightly as they passed through a dark stretch of woodland. She had always found that film disturbing. "You mean it's malevolent?"

Graham laughed. "In the movie, yes. But not usually in Japanese tradition."

"But what I saw *was* Mary, at least an ordinary-looking girl, not some weird-looking, creepy entity created by her mind," Jodi said confused.

"Children's tulpas are often a spirit copy of themselves. A kind of psychic clone, stuck at the age of the child when it was formed."

"And they create them deliberately?"

"Adult mystics supposedly can. But with children, it's evidentially a subconscious thing. Something like how kids are meant to be unconsciously responsible for poltergeist activity."

Jodi was not sure how to react to the idea of a bizarre, look-alike thoughtform that had survived for over one and a half centuries. "You believe this?"

"Well, we have had some very weird experiences. I wouldn't rule it out," Graham said with a shrug.

Jodi wasn't convinced. "From what we've discovered, Mary Heath may have been an exceptionally psychic child, but surely she wouldn't have the power to create one of these things."

"Maybe she did."

Jodi was perplexed, interrupting Graham before he could elaborate. "But if the ghost is a thoughtform created by Mary Heath as a child, what's it doing at Hoar Cross Hall?"

"It came with the mirror," Graham proposed. "In Japanese tradition, mirrors are revered. They are thought to have the power to capture one's essence. Japanese mythology is filled with tales of sorcerers using magic mirrors to create supernatural copies of themselves. Allegedly, such tulpas are tied to the mirror but can appear elsewhere in the building in which it hangs. They are said to act as site guardians, to protect tombs or temples, or sometimes they're a way to preserve knowledge or secrets."

Their car passed an old country church, its graveyard reaching the roadside. The mold-covered statue of a mournful angel over one of the graves seemed to watch them as they passed.

"These things can think?" Jodi said incredulously.

"I gather these phantom clones are regarded more like we'd consider a computer program rather than a conscious entity," Graham explained how a Shinto shrine, or *jinja*, is believed to house *kami*—elemental and ancestral spirits—venerated by devotees. The most hallowed part of the shrine is the *honden*, a separate sanctuary containing a *shinkyō*, a sacred mirror in which the kami are said to reside. In Shinto belief, a kami from one shrine can be copied in the form of a *bunrei*, meaning "divided spirit." "Priests perform a special ritual known as *kanjō*, where they duplicate the spirit from one shrine by cloning its essence into a second shinkyō mirror so that a copy is made to be housed in a further shrine where the mirror is taken," Graham concluded.

"Wow! Spirits are copied like you'd copy a file. That's an amazing concept. I've visited Shinto shrines, and knew about the mirrors, but had no idea what they were for."

"They're central to Shinto belief," Graham said. "It means that the spirits of revered ancestors can be venerated and communed with in more than one location."

Jodi widened her eyes in surprise. "So, you think Mary Heath somehow copied herself into the mirror when she was just seven years old? How?"

"It might have something to do with whatever happened to her in the Bridestones tomb; some ancient mystical knowledge may have been transferred into her mind?"

Jodi stared dubiously at Graham. "You're serious?"

Graham shrugged. "In your remote, you felt that Mary had been changed when she entered the tomb. You reckon that's how she became whatever she became. Perhaps she also emerged with some ancient wisdom somehow preserved there." Jodi remained silent. "Like it was downloaded into her mind," he added, assuming she hadn't grasped the idea.

"I know what you mean," she said. "If it was a Japanese tomb—then maybe. But the Bridestones tomb is Celtic."

Graham had already considered that. "The ancient Celts may have had a similar tradition. They *also* believed that mirrors, in their case made from polished bronze, could capture the human essence. From what I can tell, pre-Christian Celtic belief shared much in common with Japanese Shinto."

Jodi wasn't convinced. "But there's no way such a mirror would still have been lying around in the tomb in Mary's time. People would have taken it."

"True, but maybe the stones themselves held the knowledge. The ancient Celts believed that standing stones could preserve the wisdom of gods or the dead. And Mary had the right kind of, I don't know, psychological makeup to receive it." Graham smiled. "To be honest, I've no idea. I'm just considering possibilities for the impossible,"

Jodi decided to suspend disbelief for the time being. "Even if your right, surely a seven-year-old wouldn't understand any of it?"

"True. Perhaps she did when she was older. But she might have *inadvertently* created it as a child when staring into the mirror at Hickleton Hall."

Jodi clasped her hands together in concentration. "Let's see if I have this crazy notion right. I assume that somehow the person is copied to appear how they were dressed at the time the procedure occurred. Mary was presumably dressed in the clothes Lewis Carroll depicted her in for his Alice illustrations at the time she duplicated herself in the mirror. So, what about her also appearing in a nightgown?"

"I've wondered about that. Maybe she created two of herself, one during the day and one at night."

Jodi groaned. "That would complicate things."

"Or the nightgown girl might be someone else entirely. Perhaps a regular ghost. As far as we know, only the Alice lookalike has appeared in the mirror. We've no idea how it works, so for now let's just assume the Alice lookalike *is* Mary Heath. We've already reasoned that little Mary's account of what happened to her at the Bridestones inspired the *Alice in Wonderland* story. Maybe Lewis Carroll saw the phantom doppelganger in the mirror, or something equally weird, which set his imagination alight to further conceive the idea for the Looking Glass story. And he depicted her in the clothing she wore when the mirror tulpa was created."

Jodi considered the idea for a while, before agreeing that Graham's theory at least held a kind of internal logic. "So, how's it done? How do you copy yourself into a mirror?"

"As far as I know, today Shinto priests are the only people who claim to know how to do it, and you must be initiated to learn the secret. But I think we could *communicate* with Mary's tulpa—if indeed that's what it is."

"Really?"

"Possibly."

Jodi pondered the idea. "It would be an astonishing experience. But even if we could communicate with her, would it help our investigation?"

"Maybe. By August 1851, when Mary stayed at Hickleton Hall where the mirror was, the Order of Meonia had been founded, they possessed the Heart of the Rose and the building of the Biddulph Grange shrines was underway. There might be a wealth of relevant information contained in the…" Graham paused for the right words, "copy of Mary's mind made at the time."

It was growing darker, and Jodi noticed how the clouds were now a deep, threatening grey. "Okay, so how do we call her up?"

"Maybe in the same way that Shinto priests commune with a bunrei. Three times, they clap their hands, bow, and repeat the spirit's name."

Jodi recalled seeing something similar in Japan. "It's a long shot. Even so, surely, you'd have to be trained, initiated, or whatever, to be successful."

"Or the bunrei, tulpa—call it what you will— wants to speak to *us*. Little Mary seems to have come to you in your visions, and we recorded what may be her voice on film."

As they turned into a narrow country lane, flanked by thick hedgerows, Jodi saw the first signpost to Hoar Cross Hall. "So, we're coming here to try to contact Mary's copy in the mirror," she said. "Like Superman communicating with his dad's hologram in a Kryptonian crystal."

"You'd better hope it's that easy."

"*I'd* better hope! Why me?" Jodi said with surprise.

"Because *you're* doing it."

- 7 -
The Looking Glass

The rain was falling heavily by the time they arrived at Hoar Cross Hall. The red brick façade, tall chimney stacks, steep gables, and high, decorated towers stood out darkly against the ominous, overcast sky as they pulled into the parking lot. It looked less like the welcoming spa resort they had visited previously and more like the cinematic portrayal of a haunted Gothic mansion. The old east wing was virtually deserted, with just a couple drinking at the long-gallery bar. Jodi and Graham ordered drinks and made their way to the library. They were alone. All was quiet. Even the calming background music had been switched off.

Jodi stared at the mirror, recalling what they had learned. Its gilded wooden frame had been repainted since Victorian times, and although it had been re-silvered, it still held the original glass. It once hung above the fireplace at Hickleton Hall, where it inspired the story of *Alice Through the Looking Glass*; did it also contain the bizarre spirit copy of a young Mary Heath?

Graham broke Jodi's reverie. "Mary came to you

in your remote. You're the one who's seen her. That's why I think it should be you who tries to communicate."

"Thanks," Jodi said sarcastically as Graham took pictures of the room and mirror with his phone.

It was murky outside, and although the lights were on in the library, the dark paneling and shelves of old, musty books gave the room an ominous atmosphere rather than the regal, relaxing ambiance intended by the owners. After a few minutes, Jodi felt ready to begin. As Graham watched, she stood before the mirror, took a deep breath, clapped, bowed, and repeated Mary's name three times. Then she erupted into laughter.

"Sorry," she said. "I can't help thinking of that game we played as kids. We'd scare each other, looking into a mirror and repeating the name 'Bloody Mary' three times. She was supposed to appear but never did."

Graham knew of the American folktale. "It may not be so different." He explained how the creepy tradition originated in the nineteenth century, after the practices of the Theosophical Society. "Theosophy was an esoteric doctrine founded in 1870s New York by the Russian occultist Helena Blavatsky. Her beliefs were an amalgamation of various Eastern traditions. Just the other day, I read how she spent time in Japan and incorporated Shinto ideas into her teachings. She believed spirits could be summoned into mirrors by calling their names three times."

"Japan must be full of similar folktales."

"It is. The most famous concerns the spirit of one Hanako-san, a young girl said to appear in a mirror in the locker room at a girls' school in the city of Yamagata. Like the little girl here, she's been seen both as a reflection in the mirror and roaming the building."

"What does she look like?" Jodi said hesitantly. The image of a corpse-like face, half covered by long black hair, had formed in her mind.

Graham guessed what she was thinking. "Not like Sadako."

"Who?"

"The girl in *The Ring*. Hanako-san appears just like an ordinary schoolgirl but in clothing from the 1950s."

"Are these things always young girls?"

"Quite often, which is why creepy ghost girls regularly appear in Japanese horror movies."

"And they're always associated with mirrors?"

"Much of the time."

"So, who was Bloody Mary?" Jodi asked.

"Mary Tudor, a sixteenth-century English queen famous for executing heretics. But how she ended up in an American folktale, I've no idea."

Graham noticed that Jodi had grown more concerned. "Are you okay?"

"I was just thinking; it's strange that we're calling on a Mary."

"I think that must be a *genuine* coincidence. At least, I hope so."

Jodi forced a weak smile. "Thanks for the reassurance." Steeling herself, she again repeated the summoning. This time any impulse to laugh was quickly dispelled. An unexpected sensation flooded her mind. "*You* have to do it." She said after a while.

Graham laughed. "You worried about Bloody Mary?"

Jodi was serious. "No, it's not that. I can feel something trying to communicate. It's like in my remotes, but I get the impression that you need to call her."

"Okay, but why me?"

"No idea. Perhaps she wants to relate something concerning the occult. A subject you're more familiar with. Maybe she thinks you'll understand better. I don't know." Jodi realized just how strange her idea was. The notion that a thoughtform might have the power to reason was beyond weird.

"Fair enough." Graham gazed into the mirror, clapped, bowed, and said "Mary Heath" three times. Suddenly he noticed the reflection of movement behind him. A bartender had entered the room. "Err, that's how Mary Heath used to clean her teeth," Graham said to Jodi as an explanation for his odd behavior. The man smiled uncomfortably and left.

"Cleaned her teeth!"

Graham shrugged and was about to continue when Jodi offered a suggestion. "Call her Mary Ann," she said. "That's what her friends and relatives called her."

While Jodi filmed him, Graham completed the summoning, expecting nothing to happen, at least for a while. But, almost at once, he felt dizzy as the background in the mirror seemed to shift, although his own reflection remained still, an odd experience that nearly threw him off balance. Then a vivid image formed in his mind's eye.

Daytime. A jumble of grey-tiled roofs surrounding a square tower, complete with balustrades and ornamental stone urns, atop a three-story mansion dominating the skyline a couple hundred yards away. A little blond girl, dressed in a coat and bonnet, seems to be leading a group of around a dozen adults, both men and women, all dressed in Victorian attire, up a long, straight path running through a neatly-cut lawn, bordered to either side by thick, tall trees. A little boy wearing a short jacket, knee-high socks, breeches, and a peaked cap, strides enthusiastically beside her. The girl seems in a hurry, impatiently trying to drag along a man sporting a black frock coat and top hat. The impression fades.

"Well?" Jodi asked as Graham turned to face her in stunned silence.

"That was weird," he said as he sat on one of the library's sofas.

Graham had experienced vivid, mind's-eye impressions like this in the past, at so-called haunted houses, when he concentrated hard enough. Most proved meaningless images, but some contained relevant information he could not have known. But this was different—he hadn't needed to concentrate at all.

Moreover, the images were seemingly overlaid with mental impressions. And he felt dizzy. That was new, too.

Still dazed, Graham described what he had seen. "I assume the girl was Mary Heath; maybe the boy was Robert Bateman. She was leading those people somewhere." He interlocked his hands behind his head to help focus his mind. "I had the feeling— that's all I can call it—that I was witnessing a pivotal event."

"What event?"

"I've no idea."

"Any idea where she was taking them?"

Graham leaned forward to clear his head. "I think wherever they were heading was at the end of the path."

"Do you know where the path was?"

"Somewhere in the grounds of Biddulph Grange. I recognized the house."

They returned to the table to finish their drinks. Jodi watched the video footage she had taken with her phone while Graham looked into the mirror. "Nothing unusual," she said. "Pity, I was hoping we'd capture something strange."

Feeling better, Graham scrolled through the photos he had taken earlier. "Nothing here either," he said, handing Jodi his phone. "If we're to believe it, others have seen her in the mirror. I wonder what makes her appear sometimes and not others. Shame *we* didn't get to see her."

"But you did," Jodi said with a frown.

"Only in my mind's eye. Not like a ghostly figure or solid-looking—"

"There seems to be an unusual shaft of light in this image," Jodi interjected, showing Graham one of the photographs he had taken of the fireplace from the window side of the room. In the lower left-hand corner of the mirror, a thin strip of white ran diagonally across the bookshelves reflected in the background. "Wow! Look at this!" she exclaimed, zooming in on the relevant section of the picture.

"What? The light? It could just be—"

"No, below it."

It was in the bottom left-hand corner of the mirror. Although it seemed to be made up from variations in the wood grain on the reflected doorframe leading to the long gallery, it looked to all the world like a faint, transparent image of a little girl with long blond hair in the mirror. She seemed close to the glass, looking down towards the mantlepiece.

"It looks like a little girl." Graham was unable to suppress his amazement.

Jodi pointed in turn to what seemed to be facial features. "You can distinguish the eyebrows, lashes, nose, and mouth. She even seems to be wearing a hairband," she added, her excitement growing.

And look," Graham indicated below what appeared to be the chin. "The blue part here might be a garment."

"Like the bodice of Alice's blue dress."

Graham walked briskly over to examine the mirror and discounted the possibility that the image resulted from dirt, staining, or irregularities in the glass. "It must be a 'simulacrum,'" he suggested. "An image resembling a face, formed by the chance juxtaposition of features in wood or brickwork, that sort of thing."

They both examined the doorway reflected in the mirror to see what might have been responsible but found nothing that matched.

"Take another photo from the same position. See if it happens again," Jodi urged.

Comparing the layout in the photograph, Graham took a new series of pictures from precisely the same spot, but nothing remotely similar was captured again. "The lighting conditions might have changed," he said. "Altered by shadows or the lights in the bar."

They persuaded the bar staff to help by trying to remember what lights had been on or off in the long gallery over the last half hour. Graham then took photo after photo under various lighting conditions but could still not obtain the same or even a vaguely similar image.

The photograph fascinated staff members, but one of them, an IT student working part-time, was skeptical. He insisted on copying the picture onto one of the PCs in the hotel's reception and blew it up to reveal its pixels. He messed around with the image for some time before finally shaking his head. "It's not a double exposure or edited image," he said.

"I know, we just took it," Jodi said irately.

The student continued. "Well, if it isn't just coincidental features in the woodwork—"

"Which we've checked," interrupted one of the

receptionists, exasperated at the guy's cynicism and smiling at Jodi.

"Then it's a problem with the camera," the student said, indignation in his voice.

"That just so happened to have produced the semblance of a little girl in a mirror that's said to be haunted by a little girl," Jodi said firmly.

Some staff members gathered enthusiastically around the computer and began to laugh, while others made mock scary sounds. But the receptionist remained deadly serious.

"I'd say you've just photographed our ghost," she said.

Jodi and Graham returned to the library and spent the afternoon trying to get something else to happen. They repeated the mirror summoning, took more photographs and footage, and Jodi even tried one of her remotes. But nothing unusual occurred. They then showed the picture to other members of staff and some customers to judge their reaction. Interestingly, only half the people who saw it could see anything unusual, even when the image of what appeared to be the little girl was pointed out.

"I suppose it could be just a simulacrum," Graham said. "Although it's certainly another synchronicity. And a dramatic one."

"But your vision was important."

"Without a doubt. We should go back to Biddulph."

The next day Jodi and Graham returned to Biddulph Grange. In the tearoom, adjoining the gift shop, there was a free-standing information board with historical material and old photographs relating to the house and its gardens' nineteenth-century past. There were pictures of those involved in the history of the estate, such as James Bateman and Robert Heath, but none of Maria Bateman, Mary Heath, Laura Heath, or other women associated with the place.

"Typical Victorians," Jodi observed. "The women didn't count. Their stories went untold."

"At least we know something about Maria. She was responsible for much of the gardens' layout and the construction of the shrines. And something about Laura and her occult interests. As for Mary, we know next to nothing. She probably kept a diary and other records, but any such documents seem to have been destroyed in the fire." Graham pointed to an old photograph taken of the Grange right after the event, its center reduced to a smoldering shell, showing the staff and firefighters who had extinguished the blaze standing proudly in front of the building.

Jodi read aloud the plaque beneath it. "'Biddulph Grange after the fire of 1897.'"

"Serious damage," Graham observed. "Although, according to a newspaper article of the time, there were no casualties."

"How did the fire start?" Jodi asked.

"No one seems to have known. At least, it wasn't reported. When I came here in 1980, one of the nurses from the hospital, as it was then, mentioned a rumor that it broke out during a séance in the house."

Jodi motioned to the photographs of James Bateman and Robert Heath. "Were they in your mirror vision at Hoar Cross Hall?"

"I didn't get a good look at their faces, not even the little girl. My vision seemed to pan from the house to the path they were on; from then, my perspective was from slightly behind them. But I'd guess it was Mary Heath leading her parents, the Batemans, and others somewhere."

"Would you recognize the location you saw?"

"If it hasn't changed too much."

Graham found the setting in his vision by orienting his position in relation to the Grange. They ended up on a path, some 200 yards southeast of the mansion, which led in a straight line, starting at the tea terrace, passing directly in front of the Grange facing the gardens, passing the Egyptian temple, and on through the woods. As in Graham's vision, the path was flanked by a wide strip of lawn to either side, separating it from the trees. The only differences were that the muddy trail was now graveled, and a row of well-tended fir trees had been planted to the left and right. Graham had never visited this area of the gardens before and was staggered by the similarity with what he had seen in his mind's eye at Hoar Cross Hall.

"Apart from the fir trees, it's almost the same," he said.

Jodi felt the first drop of rain on her face. "In your vision, you're sure the little girl was leading those people somewhere?"

"Positive. She was virtually dragging the one guy. In this direction." Graham pointed along the path, away from the Grange.

From the map, they learned it was called the Wellingtonia Avenue, which they followed until it reached a dead end about half a mile from the house. Here, they found themselves staring up at a massive stone urn at the edge of the property, behind which was an iron gate set into a high, thick hedge. It was like an enormous drinking goblet, consisting of a pedestal, stem, and bowl; it was some 8 feet tall, its rim around 5 feet wide.

"Well, she wasn't leading them to this," Jodi said, examining the guidebook. "The urn was a relatively late feature, from the 1860s when Mary would have been in her late teens. Your vision has Mary as a child."

After they thoroughly checked the area, finding nothing relevant to their investigation, Graham had a question. "If our tulpa theory is right, and I was picking up Mary's memories, why did I see the episode from an external perspective, not through her eyes?"

"I suppose it was your mind's way of interpreting what happened. Others might have seen things differently." An idea occurred to Jodi. "If you did experience Mary's memories as they were when she stayed at Hickleton Hall in proximity to the mirror, then what you saw must have occurred sometime before August 1851. The question is, how long before?"

"If it relates to the Order of Meonia, then after she entered the Bridestones tomb."

Jodi agreed. "We speculated that Mary entered the tomb on May fourth. So, your vision relates to an event between May fourth and August 1851."

Graham nodded. "Makes sense. So, what event *dia* I witness?"

"The memorial pamphlet says that Mary inspired the Batemans and Heaths to begin the Order of Meonia shortly after she found the Heart. She must have done something extraordinary to convince all these adults to trust her. You said your mirror vision concerned a pivotal event?"

"That's what I felt."

"Then what you saw could relate to whatever Mary did to persuade the adults to begin the Meonia group."

"I reckon you're right. I just remembered something. When I gazed into the mirror, the question at the forefront of my mind was: 'How did the Order of Meonia begin?'"

Jodi smiled. "And I think the pivotal event occurred *very* soon after she found the Heart?"

"What makes you say that?"

Because James Bateman moved the stones to build the Celtic glen—the first of the Meonia shrines —even while his cousin's dig was still in progress. The excavation lasted two weeks, so by the middle of May, Mary must have convinced the adults of her newfound powers at the latest."

"So, Bateman moved the stones on Mary's instructions." Graham frowned. "But why do what she said?"

"Precisely! Because she had already revealed something astonishing. Something that proved her abilities and impelled them to establish the Order of Meonia and all it involved."

"Like what?"

"Whatever it was, it must have been during the first two weeks of May—and it must have been something astounding." Jodi's face suddenly flushed; she became unsteady on her feet and leaned against the urn as if about to faint.

Graham rushed over to steady her. "What's wrong?"

"I don't know… I feel dizzy."

Graham led her to sit down on a nearby garden bench, where she closed her eyes and immediately passed out. There was a sudden crash of thunder.

A heavily wooded hillside where overhanging branches, creepers, and thorn bushes partially obscure the entrance to what appears to be a cave, cut deep into the darkness of a sheer, rocky outcrop. Judging by the surrounding vegetation, it is around 8 feet high and 8 feet wide. The same little girl and boy from her vision of the Bridestones are standing at the entrance, beckoning to be followed inside.

Jodi awoke to find the rain falling and Graham holding one of her hands, slapping it on the back. Now fully alert, as if she had enjoyed a good night's sleep, Jodi described her vision.

"That's never happened to me before, experiencing a vision without practicing a remote. But it was just as vivid."

"What does it mean?" Graham asked, relieved that Jodi had recovered.

"I think I saw what Mary was leading the people in your vision to: a cave."

"A cave?" Graham said. "I don't know of anything around here like what you described."

"I'm certain it exists. We should ask at the house."

"Sure you're okay?" Graham said, helping Jodi to her feet.

Jodi was quite capable of standing on her own. "I'm fine," she said, then started laughing.

"What's funny?"

"You. Patting the back of my hand when I woke up."

"That's what you're supposed to do when someone faints."

"Only in old black-and-white movies."

As they returned along the Wellingtonia Avenue, Jodi struggled to open an umbrella that abruptly turned inside out in the rising wind. "In both our visions, the young Mary is accompanied by a little boy, presumably Robert Bateman," she said. "Remind me what we know concerning his occult connections."

"His mentor Edward Burne-Jones was an authority on the subject and a member of a Druid order, as was his father. He was close friends with the actress Florence Farr, the author A. E. Waite, and the poet W. B. Yeats, all members of the Golden Dawn and prolific writers on mystical matters. Apart from his contribution to Mary's memorial pamphlet, he left no writings, at least that we know of. He died in 1922 at the age of eighty."

Graham stopped walking to stand dead still in the pouring rain.

"Graham?" Jodi thought he had fallen into a trance.

"Talking about Robert Bateman's associates has me thinking. I can't help wondering if the whole Occult Revival of the late nineteenth century might have begun here at Biddulph Grange. Individuals and small groups had been students of the occult for centuries. Still, the founding of societies practicing it openly started with the Theosophical Society in 1875, then the Hermetic Order of the Golden Dawn in 1888. These groups inspired a variety of other occult societies, such as the Order of the Temple of the Orient, the Kabbalistic Order of the Rose Cross, the Ancient Mystical Order of the Rose Cross, the Sphere Group, and the Stella Matutina. If the Order of Meonia was up and running in the 1850s, it preceded them all."

"And it may all have started with whatever young Mary was about to show them in your vision."

Graham whistled. "It must have to be something spectacular."

Arriving at the main house, they took tea in the tearoom, the one room in the building still open to the public to remain unchanged from when Biddulph Grange was a stately home. Its elaborate, cream-colored walls were paneled with bright gold trimmings, punctuated here and there by delicate plasterwork depicting shells, flowers, foliage, and carved angelic heads. Above them, the ceiling was decorated with a circular fresco surrounding a chandelier, where intricate paintings of cherubs were interspersed with cameo figures from classical mythology. Jodi and Graham dried themselves before a roaring fire, its marble mantelpiece supported by the busts of ancient goddesses with garlands in their hair, like pure white figureheads of old sailing ships from a Greek odyssey.

One of the guides joined them at their table to helpfully answer their questions about the Wellingtonia Avenue, which, they were told, was named after the botanical term for the young redwood trees that flanked the pathway.

"Has anything unusual been found along or around the path, possibly at the end of it?" Graham asked.

"Nothing I know of." The lady explained how it was originally a dirt track where the owners would exercise their horses. "It *is* curious, though, being dead straight and precisely aligning with sunset on midsummer's day."

"It aligns with the midsummer sunset," Jodi said, her attention seized. "Any idea why?"

"I suppose it was the symmetry of keeping it parallel with the passage in the Egyptian building."

Jodi and Graham both had the same thought. Midsummer was an important date in many esoteric traditions, particularly in the Wolfside area, where the double-setting sun could be observed on that day.

"The midsummer sunset shines directly down the corridor of the Egyptian temple?" Graham asked enthusiastically.

"Not anymore, sadly, because the gardeners have planted a big hedge in the way," the guide said. "But until recently, on the midsummer solstice, around June twenty-first, the last rays of the sun would penetrate the chamber and light up the Ape of Thoth. It's the only time of the year it happens." The woman knew little more about it and had no idea why that specific date might be significant.

Graham looked around at the magnificently decorated walls of the tearoom. "So, this is unchanged since the 1800s?" he asked the guide.

The lady shook her head. "No, it was completely redecorated after the fire of 1896."

"You mean 1897," Jodi said.

The guide frowned. "The fire was in 1896."

"It *was* 1897," Graham added, as politely as possible, not wanting to embarrass the woman by drawing attention to her mistake.

Jodi stood and walked over to the information board they had been examining earlier. "It says here that…" She stopped mid-sentence.

"What?" Graham got up to join her.

Jodi screwed up her eyes. "This is crazy. This *does* say that the fire occurred in 1896."

"No way. We both read that caption just an hour ago. It said 1897. I've been researching Biddulph Grange for years; I've seen the original newspaper article, everything; it's always been 1897."

Jodi pointed to the plaque beneath the old photograph of the firefighters outside the building. "Has this just been changed?" she asked the guide.

The woman looked confused. "No one's altered it since I've worked here."

To the guide's bewilderment, Jodi and Graham abruptly left her. They entered the gift shop, where they began frantically browsing through the literature concerning the Grange, its gardens, and its history.

"That's impossible," Graham said after they had examined over a dozen different books and leaflets. "They all give 1896 as the year of the fire. "This is completely insane. It makes no sense."

Jodi laughed, but there was little humor in it. "Unless, like Alice through her looking glass, we're in another reality."

-8-
The Cave

Following a meticulous inspection of the Stafford-shire public records and a painstaking online search, Jodi and Graham were confounded to discover that everything confirmed how the Biddulph fire occurred in 1896—and not 1897 as they believed—same date, January 16, but one year before. Furthermore, every-one they knew who was familiar with Biddulph Grange also thought it happened in 1896. Yet, as far as they could determine, everything else in the world was exactly as they remembered. They checked out other events concerning Biddulph Grange, such as the date of the memorial event, the Bridestones exca-vation, the building of the mansion and its shrines, the lives of those involved with the Order of Meonia, and much more besides, but apart from the date of the fire nothing had changed. The Meonia group even disbanded at the time they remembered, in early 1897.

"Well, we're not in another universe," Graham concluded as they sat in the living room of his Birm-ingham home. "I've read through all my notes con-cerning Biddulph Grange, and they still relate how the fire occurred in 1897. If we *were* in a parallel world, I assume the date would also have changed in my writings. So, somehow, I must have made a mistake."

"No, you didn't." Jodi was adamant. "After we first visited Biddulph together, I found numerous on-line references to the fire occurring in 1897. I swear they've all changed."

"You probably saw what you expected to see after I told you the year the event happened. The *wrong* date, as it turns out."

Jodi was frantically browsing on her laptop. "I know I saw the year 1897 because one site mentioned the fire occurring in the same year Bram Stoker's novel *Dracula* was published. I just confirmed that was indeed the year that book came out." She shook her head in bewilderment. "Strangely, I can no longer find the relevant article on Biddulph Grange."

"The author probably realized the mistake and took it down."

"We both saw the date 1897 on that information board in the Biddulph tearoom, and an hour later, it had changed to 1896," Jodi said doggedly. "Did you take a picture of it?"

"No, not the first time. You?"

"No. There was no reason to. Dammit!"

Graham held out his upturned hands in a gesture of surrender. "Besides us, everyone thinks the fire was in 1886. So, *we're* the ones who've got it wrong."

Jodi still didn't buy it. "The Meonia group seems to have been involved in something concerning portals to other realities. Now *this*. It means something."

"If we *have* entered some alternative reality, then my notes, which include the fire date as 1897, would have to have been plucked from our original world to cross over with us! How would that even work?"

"Regardless of how impossible it all seems; do you still remember repeatedly seeing the date of the fire as 1897?"

Graham combed his memory. "Yes, I do."

"As do I. I think that, for the time being, we should suspend disbelief and accept that something crazy has occurred."

Graham reluctantly agreed.

For the remainder of Jodi's time in England, they revisited Biddulph Grange, Hoar Cross Hall, and other locations hoping to throw more light on the perplexing situation. Still, nothing unusual occurred, and no new information was gained. Jodi attempted a remote repeatedly but drew a complete blank. At the same time, Graham spent an entire evening staring into the library mirror at Hoar Cross Hall, hoping to receive another vision but got zilch. They even returned to the Bridestones, getting soaking wet as Jodi meditated inside the ancient tomb, to leave with nothing more than a common cold.

"So, what *is* going on?" Graham asked when he dropped Jodi off at the airport.

"I don't know," she said. "But it has to mean *something*."

As he drove away from Manchester Airport, Graham recalled hearing of something dubbed the "Mandela effect," a psychological phenomenon of conflicting memory shared by multiple people. The term was coined due to false memories concerning the death of South African leader Nelson Mandela in the 1990s. Thousands of people worldwide were stunned to hear that he had been elected president, swearing to remember the news that he had died in prison.

"That has to be it," Graham said to himself. "If it can happen to a multitude, then it can certainly happen to two. Somehow, we've both got confused." But even as he said those words, he didn't fully believe them. Like Jodi, deep down, he too felt something beyond strange had occurred.

* * *

They had already searched for a cave in the Biddulph area matching the one from Jodi's impromptu remote —where she thought little Mary had been leading the people in Graham's mirror vision—but found nothing. When Jodi returned home to California, she attempted unsuccessfully to solve the dilemma with a remote. She was about to consider her vision of the cave purely symbolic when her attention was snatched by something she found online: a link to a book titled *Mr. Bateman's Garden* by British novelist Priscilla Masters. It was a children's fantasy set in the gardens of Biddulph Grange, but the book's cover immediately had Jodi transfixed. It was a painting depicting a young girl and boy at the entrance to a cave partially overhung by vegetation, around and above which were trees. Apart from a giant frog in the foreground and bats flying out of the cave, the picture

146

was extraordinarily like her vision.

How come she hadn't found this book before? All she had to do was enter "Biddulph Grange" into the browser, and the relevant link appeared on the first page. But the book wasn't new. It had been in print for some years. How could she have missed it? Although Jodi was reluctant to consider this as further evidence that reality had somehow bizarrely changed, she could not help but wonder if it was fate's way of telling her not to abandon the search for the cave in her vision.

Having downloaded a copy of the book, Jodi read through the tale to find that no such cave appeared in the narrative. She then video-called Graham to discuss what she'd seen.

"Nothing in the book specifically ties up with what we're investigating," Jodi explained. "All the same, suddenly finding this book cover with a cave similar to the one in my vision with a young girl and boy in front of it must mean something."

Graham examined the book cover online, accepting that it was a strange coincidence. "Fascinating. Strange, we never noticed it before."

"Should we contact the author to ask what inspired the painting?" Jodi asked.

"What would we say? I'm sure she gets loads of crazy fan mail. I do, and if I were contacted by someone wanting to know about the sort of stuff we're investigating, I'd—"

"—think they were mad," Jodi concurred. "One way or another, I'm sure that finding the picture just when I did is fate's confirmation that the cave exists. It's too much of a coincidence. The cave must be where little Mary led those people in your mirror vision."

* * *

After all the strange new events surrounding Biddulph Grange, Graham decided to try an experiment. He invited a few friends to join him in what psychical researchers call a "sitting" to see if anyone could pick up any impressions concerning the Order of Meonia. It wasn't a séance, exactly—there was no ouija board or trances—those present sat around a table hoping that any thoughts or mental images might prove meaningful. Graham decided to increase the chances of success by streaming the event live to see if anyone, anywhere, could be of assistance. He revealed nothing about their search for a cave.

When nothing out of the ordinary happened, one of those present, a historian, opened a map of the Biddulph district and spread it out on the table. Graham had told him about the Bridestones, Cock Low, and the Cloud, and the man asked if there were any other sites associated with the Druids nearby.

Graham leaned over the map. "There is *one* that I know of." He pointed to a forested area just south of Biddulph called Knypersley Park. "Gawton's Well. It's a natural spring feeding into a rectangular stone basin enclosed by ancient brickwork. It's thought to have been constructed by the Celts. Interestingly, it's still referred to as a Druid shrine."

As Graham explained how the well was named

after a legendary hermit who supposedly once lived nearby, the man returned to the map, asking for a pencil and ruler. On it, he drew a straight line between the Bridestones and Gawton's Well.

"What are you doing?" Graham asked.

"Druidic sites were often constructed along straight lines, not necessarily ley lines, but local alignments for ceremonial purposes," The historian elucidated. "I'm wondering if there's anything else between them." The man suddenly raised his voice. "That's interesting," he said, pointing to the line where it passed directly through the end of a straight footpath running from Biddulph Grange into the middle of a forested area marked "Spring Wood." "After running in a dead straight line for around a mile, the path stops. It must lead to something. Whatever it is, it's not only *on* the line between the Bridestones and Gawton's Well but *halfway* along it." The historian returned his attention to his laptop and opened a satellite image of the area on the map. "The path ends close to the far edge of the wood, but you can't make out anything at the location because of the trees. I wonder what's there."

In another part of England, one of Graham's friends, Clark, who had been watching the live stream with interest, decided to shuffle a tarot pack to see if it might help answer the question about what lay at the end of the path. He cut the pack and turned over the top card. It depicted the inside of a craggy, rock-cut tunnel, leading away towards what appeared to be a blocked, arched exit formed from fashioned stones

—an artificial cave. Clark immediately photographed the card and sent a copy to Graham, explaining why he had used the pack. Graham was astonished. No one other than him and Jodi knew anything about their search for a cave.

"What is it?" The historian asked, wondering what had seized Graham's attention.

Graham turned his phone so that the man could see. "I think *this*—or something like it—might be what's at the end of the path." For the first time, he revealed details of Jodi's vision. On examining the map, Graham realized with astonishment that the woodland path was, in fact, a continuation of the Wellingtonia Avenue. He and Jodi had followed it for around half a mile to the edge of the Biddulph gardens, where it appeared to terminate at the giant urn. But, because of the bushes and undergrowth on the other side of the iron gate, they hadn't realized the path continued for a further half mile. Browsing the history of Biddulph Grange, Graham discovered something he had overlooked. When the Heath family sold the place to become a hospital in 1923, the property was divided, and the area of the woodland track beyond the gate had become part of a separate estate called Biddulph Park. Today, Biddulph Park is owned by the local council and open to the public, and the pathway is still a muddy track, unaltered since the nineteenth century. During the Batemans and Heaths' time, the path would have continued, unobstructed, across the eastern side of the Grange's land to end close to the far side of what is now Spring Wood, the very place the historian had located halfway along his line on the map.

Graham considered the collective events as he tried unsuccessfully to find anything on the internet to reveal what lay at the end of the track. After his experience with the mirror, he felt that the Order of Meonia began with whatever little Mary had found at the end of the Wellingtonia Avenue. He had wrongly assumed that the path ended at the urn. Because of the historian's fortuitous idea to draw a line between the Bridestones and Gawton's Well, Graham now knew that the path ran for another half mile through Spring Wood during Mary Heath's time. So, what was at the end of the original path? Jodi's remote, not to mention the coincidentally-discovered book cover, seemed to imply a cave. And, quite by "chance," Clark had sent them a card depicting what appeared to be an artificial tunnel, a card he picked when specifically asking what was at the end of the woodland track. Understandably, Graham decided to drive over to Biddulph as soon as possible to see what lay beneath the tree cover where the path ended.

Graham made his way along the narrow trackway leading up the hillside to the east of Biddulph Grange. It had recently been raining, and water droplets continually fell on him from the overhanging trees, soaking his clothes. The path and surrounding ground had been reduced to a muddy quagmire, making the ascent an arduous climb. After repeatedly slipping, sliding, and falling on the treacherous, ever-steepening slope, he finally reached the end of the path. A 15-foot sheer rock face stood before him, with fern-covered ground rising to either side; bushes, and more trees grew on top. And there it was. Halfway along the outcrop was a cave, around 8 feet high and 8 feet wide—precisely what Jodi had described from her vision—the pathway leading directly into its dark interior.

Graham entered the cave. "This is no natural formation," he thought, examining the walls with the light on his phone. He could see where the rock had been hacked and chiseled. Making his way deeper inside, what seemed like a cave, narrowed to a dank, dark tunnel, around 6 feet high and 4 feet wide. It ran for some 50 feet, to broaden again to form a cave-like exit, blocked with a wall of large, fashioned stones. Light from the outside world filtered inside in bright shafts created by gaps in the stonework. Peering through the cracks, he could see out onto the opposite side of the hill, but the leaves of thick trees blocked his view of the landscape beyond. Something important surely lay on the other side of the exit. But try as he might, Graham could not get to it. The hillside was too steep, slippery, and dangerous. Eventually, he gave up, deciding he would need to return during dry weather.

That night, Graham video-called Jodi to update her on the latest developments. She was delighted to hear that, taken together, her and Graham's visions had proved astonishingly accurate.

"That's what I saw," she said, examining the photos Graham had taken of the cave. "It *must* be where little Mary led the people in your vision. So, what is it?"

Graham explained that although Spring Wood was part of a public park, the cave went unmentioned online. Even members of staff at Biddulph Grange he had spoken to that morning had never heard of it. "Which is no surprise, I suppose, as it's no longer on their land."

"What about the local council who now owns Biddulph Park? Have you spoken to them?" Jodi asked.

"Yes. Same thing."

"You mean no one knows it's there?"

"People do. There was rubbish like beer cans inside, but it's not a well-known landmark. It's not even marked on any map I've found."

"You said the tunnel is artificial. We need to know *who* made it. When. And why."

Graham turned the conversation to the sitting he'd held in his home the previous evening, describing what happened and sharing the footage he'd shot of the tunnel. "It's incredible," he said. "Although from outside it looks like a cave, inside it becomes a passage, just like the one depicted on the tarot card Clark sent. And the other end is blocked, exactly as shown on the card."

Jodi shook her head. "How's that possible. We're not talking about clairvoyance here, which, although unproven scientifically, is at least a rational concept—we've experienced it ourselves—but someone randomly cutting to a card that depicts an image of what was at a location you had just pinpointed on a map. How is that even possible?"

Graham mulled it over. "When last night's session began, no one, besides you and me, had any idea that we were looking for a cave, tunnel, or anything like one. We were hoping to get a new lead on the Biddulph Grange mystery. Without any prompting from me, our historian friend pinpointed the location of that cave right at the end of the same path from my mirror vision, which precisely matched what you had seen during your remote. I told no one of our visions or even mentioned the Wellingtonia Avenue before the sitting began. I think someone randomly cutting a card that closely resembles the place I visited today is no less weird. Although, to answer your original question—how's it possible—I have absolutely no idea."

When Graham next visited Biddulph during dry weather, he was accompanied by his American friend Tara who had more than a passing interest in the Grange. She had visited the place on a previous trip to England with her colleague Jack and had a strange experience while in the Egyptian temple. Although she saw nothing unusual, while standing in the central chamber, she had the feeling that someone or something was next to her in the direction of the bench alcove.

Along with Staffordshire journalist Wayne and his friend Gary, who were interested in the history of Biddulph Grange, Tara and Graham made their way up the now dusty track leading to the cave. On the way, they met a man walking his dog, who had lived in the district his whole life. Stopping to talk with them, he related the local tradition that the tunnel had been cut through the hill by James Bateman so that estate staff who lived in the village of Biddulph Moor, on the other side of the hill, could more easily get to work. However, he explained, this wasn't the case. Estate workers may have used the tunnel, but it was already there years before the Batemans' time. He told them he even possessed a copy of an Elizabethan map showing it had existed as early as 1600, and the parish archives recorded it as being old even then.

Arriving at the cave, the four of them thoroughly examined the interior, agreeing with Graham's initial evaluation that it was an artificial tunnel, presumably cut through the hill to reach the other side. From the map, it seemed that there was only a short continuation of the pathway, leading to an outbuilding belonging to a local farm. The whole notion of the tunnel being cut—at whatever period of history—so that people could travel more easily from Biddulph Moor made no sense; the direct route from the village to Biddulph Grange missed the hill entirely. Yet, the tunnel, which would have required considerable time, labor, and expense to construct, must have been made to lead to something just beyond the now-blocked exit.

As the others examined the area around the cave, Graham climbed the hill to gain an unobstructed view of the land beyond. Between him and some modern farm buildings, an outbuilding with a corrugated plastic roof immediately caught his attention. Although its roof was modern, and some of its walls were re-cent, the building had clearly been constructed using the shell of a much older structure. The hefty, weath-ered stones of one gable end still survived, and part of what had once been a window could be discerned. From what remained, there was little doubt in Gra-ham's mind that this had once been an ecclesiastical building, such as a church, chapel, or abbey, its ruins later incorporated into a barn. Moreover, from the ar-chitectural style, it was medieval. As there was nothing else but modern buildings in the area, and the ruin lay precisely below the cave, it was obvious that the tun-nel had been constructed to link the original building by a straight path to what is now Biddulph Grange.

When Graham rejoined the others and described what he had found, Wayne had a good idea of what the building might be and why the tunnel was dug. Graham listened with interest as he explained what he had researched concerning the early history of what would ultimately become the Biddulph Grange estate. Over the years, there had been various buildings on the site of the Grange, but archaeology had yet to be conducted to determine what these buildings were. Records, however, did go back almost a thousand years. Shortly after the Norman Conquest of 1066 (when the northern French invaded Anglo-Saxon England), the new king, William I, gave the land to his standard bearer, a man known as Richard Forester, who became the first Lord of Biddulph. Around 1100, Richard's son Ormus le Guidon inher-ited the property. According to local tradition, Ormus had been a crusader knight. In the 1120s, he returned from the Holy Land with a contingent of Arab stone-masons needed to construct a monastery somewhere in this area.

"The building you describe could be the monastery's chapel," Wayne concluded.

"Where did Ormus live?" Graham asked.

"It's not known for certain, but very possibly in a manor house that stood where the Grange is now."

"So, the tunnel might have been created by Ormus le Guidon as a direct route between his home and the chapel, if that's what it was."

"It makes sense," Wayne agreed.

On his return home, Graham again called Jodi to discuss the turn of events. The site where the barn stood, they discovered, was called Rockfields Farm. But, despite an in-depth online search, they could find nothing relating to any ancient buildings there. Just as they were about to hang up, Jodi was struck by an intriguing thought. She had been examining the area of Biddulph Grange and Biddulph Park on a detailed map.

"As we were told, the path runs parallel with the Egyptian temple passage," she said. "And we know that aligns with the midsummer sunset. Therefore, so does the path and presumably the tunnel at the end of it."

Graham considered the implications. "You're right. If there were fewer trees around, the summer solstice sunset would shine directly into it. That can't be a coincidence."

"It suggests the tunnel was more than just functional. More likely created for some ceremonial purpose."

Graham clapped his hands in conclusion. "I reckon it was at the chapel that little Mary revealed whatever it was that convinced everyone that she had an extraordinary gift."

"And persuaded them to start the Order of Meonia and build the shrines," Jodi added. "As I said before, it must have been something astounding."

- 9 -

Spring Wood Priory

When Jodi returned to England, she and Graham immediately visited Rockfields Farm to examine the mysterious building beyond the cave. They soon discovered that the farm was now a construction company, and the barn was on the edge of a builders' yard. Surrounded by pallet loads of tiles, stacks of bricks, piles of lumber, and bags of cement, the pair looked up at the skeletal remains of an old building. Large, mottled, rough-cut stones comprised a section of its wall and a complete gable end, where the remnants of what was once an old window stood out above the level of the modern roof. Here, the structure backed onto the forested hillside of Spring Wood, where the overgrown, sealed-off tunnel exit could be seen at the end of a short pathway running upwards through the trees. Graham explained how the irregular stonework, the construction of the window surround, and the steep pitch of the gable suggested that the building had been a small church or chapel dating from the Middle Ages, making it over 500 years old.

The ramshackle setting was nothing like Jodi had been expecting. She stared at the years of rubble that had accumulated against the outside wall of the partially-collapsed gable end facing the hillside: a nettle-covered rubbish dump reaching as high as what had once been an upper window. All around lay piles of discarded bricks and sections of broken fencing.

"In the States, buildings only a century old would be tourist attractions," she said. "Something like this would be a national monument. It's sad to see something so treasured from the past now lay in discard."

"This is certainly where the path led," Graham observed. "It comes down from the tunnel exit to disappear beneath that rubble against the gable end. There must be the remains of a doorway under there."

At that moment, a pickup truck stopped beside them, its wheels throwing up a cloud of dust. "Can I help?" the driver said curtly.

The man's tone softened when Graham told him of their interest in the building's history. He confirmed that it had been used as a barn when it was a farm. However, he knew very little concerning the history of the area and doubted his fellow employees were any wiser. The old building, he told them, was now a workshop. Jodi and Graham peered inside to see that it was filled with heavy machinery bolted to a solid concrete floor. Graham was at least pleased to see that a bricked-up doorway was still visible at the far end. It consisted of a pointed arch, supported by simple columns to either side, exactly what would be expected around the entrance to a small medieval church.

Calling crows echoed over the Spring Wood hillside as Jodi and Graham left the site. If the workshop was once a chapel, its records might be preserved at the nearby parish church—their next stop.

* * *

The church of St. Lawrence, with its castellated tower, vibrant stained-glass windows, and sandy, beige-stone walls, stands just a few hundred yards to the southwest of Biddulph Grange. Although it existed during the Middle Ages, much of the current structure dates from the nineteenth century, having been rebuilt by James Bateman's father, John, in the 1830s when the family still lived at nearby Knypersley Hall. Unfortunately, the church was locked, so Graham and Jodi wandered through the surrounding cemetery.

"I assume the Heaths and Batemans are buried here," Jodi said, gazing across the graveyard. Deep green yew trees grew everywhere as if standing sentinel over the final resting places of generations past. Tombstones of every shape and size—some new, of polished marble, still tended by loved ones, others moss-covered and aged, their inscriptions faded long ago—numbered in the hundreds. Yet, throughout this somber scene, colorful wildflowers were alive, with bees and butterflies busying themselves in the hazy midday sun. "Can we see Mary's grave?" she asked.

Graham shook his head. "I've searched the church, the cemetery, and the parish burial records but can't discover where she was laid to rest. Perhaps she was cremated. She died in London, so maybe she was buried there. Nevertheless, bearing in mind the memorial pamphlet and the esteem it implies her family and friends held her, it's odd that there is not so much a commemorative plaque or inscription in memory of her anywhere in the church."

"Perhaps, as the leader of an occult group, she didn't want to be buried on holy ground or be remembered in place of Christian worship," Jodi suggested.

"It didn't bother the others. Maria, Robert, Laura, they're all buried here. And inside the church, plaques are dedicated to other Heaths and Batemans buried elsewhere." Graham stopped and pointed. "This is Laura's grave." A tall, white-stone cross was mounted on a pedestal inscribed with her name, date of birth and death, along with that of her husband, Robert Heath Jr. Although more significant than most of the gravestones in the churchyard, it was relatively plain for such a wealthy family.

'I wish Laura's spirit could tell us where she hid the Heart of the Rose." A thought struck Jodi. "We seem to be communicating with Mary. Why not Laura? She ran the Meonia group for twenty-five years."

Graham looked down at the grave. "We seemingly contacted Mary's tulpa in the Hoar Cross Hall mirror. Maybe Laura couldn't create such a thing."

"It's not just the mirror," Jodi said. "I seem to have picked up on Mary three times in my remotes. Twice before we even discovered the mirror. It was a vision of Mary that led us to find the mirror in the first place."

Graham gazed skywards in contemplation. "Maybe it's not so much Mary's spirit communicating with us but part of a learning process."

"Learning process? You've lost me."

"We've noticed that *fate* seems to be guiding us. It's just a wild thought, but perhaps something—don't ask me what—is revealing the story of the Meonia group chronologically, one step at a time, starting at the beginning. First, Mary found the Heart at the

Bridestones, then she led her family and the Batemans to the chapel where she convinced them to start the Order of Meonia and build the shrines."

Jodi was intrigued. "With all the weird synchronicities, it makes sense. But why *now*?"

"Because we found the B Stone?" Graham proposed.

Jodi considered the scenario. "It was forty years ago that Jenny said you would find it. Presumably you weren't meant to find it until now."

Graham exhaled. "Once again. Why now?"

"Perhaps because the Heart of the Rose is needed again." Jodi offered.

"We don't even know what it was used for in Mary's time."

They returned to the church, where a series of horizontal weathered stones were held up with blocks to be used as benches along one of the exterior walls. Each around 6 feet long, 2 feet wide, and 6 inches deep, they were carved with a simple design of two parallel lines along most of their length that joined a double circle around 18 inches in diameter at one end. Inside the circle was a cross, its arms narrow at the center and broader at the tips, which indented in the shape of a letter V.

"These look like very old gravestones. Why are they being used as seats?" Jodi said with a frown.

"No idea," Graham frowned too. "But they look like Templar gravestones to me."

Jodi and Graham reflected on what was known about the enigmatic Knights Templar. In 1119, twenty years after a combined European army had captured Jerusalem from the Arabs during the First Crusade, a French knight, Hugues de Payens, established a militia to protect Christians on pilgrimages to the Holy Land. They made their headquarters in Jerusalem on the site of the ancient Israelite Temple, where they adopted the name *The Poor Knights of Christ and the Temple of Solomon*—Knights Templar or Templars for short. In 1129, the pope made the Templars an official military sect of the Church, affiliating them with the Cistercian order of monks. Although rank-and-file Templars were required to swear monastic vows of chastity, poverty, and obedience—making them Christianity's first warrior monks—their leaders were often wealthy aristocrats who were married, rich, and a law unto themselves. By the end of the twelfth century, the Templars had become a full-time crusader army. Outside the Holy Land, in countries like France and England, they established preceptories. A cross between a military barracks and a monastery, a preceptory was a training center for Templars who, between crusades, often fought as mercenaries in battles between opposing Christian kings.

Because such preceptories were heavily defended by some of the only full-time, professional soldiers in Europe, the rich and powerful would increasingly pay these institutions to safeguard their wealth. When their effects, such as gold, silver, and jewels, were entrusted to the Templars, the owners would be issued a paper note that promised to pay the bearer whatever had been deposited. (One half of a signed document that could be uniquely matched with the other half the Templars retained.) Increasingly, when transactions occurred, rather than carry around bags of cash or cart-loads of valuables, the buyer would hand over the Templars' guarantee, which the vendor could now use to collect what was owed or pass it on in a future deal. In this way, the Templars not only became Europe's first bankers but also introduced Christendom to the concept of paper money. They also made loans, with interest, to some of the most important figures of the time, ultimately leading to their downfall.

By the fourteenth century, with Jerusalem lost to the Arabs, the Templar high council was situated in Paris. Both the French king, Philip IV, and the pope, Clement V, were heavily in debt to the order, and together they orchestrated a plan to bring about its demise. From occult texts acquired during their time in the Middle East, the Templars had become steeped in various forms of mysticism, and it was this that was used against them. With papal backing, on October 13, 1307, the Paris Templars were arrested on blasphemy charges, quickly tried, and burned at the stake. As other kings were indebted to the Templars, they too followed suit. However, the Templar order did not disappear overnight. They were heavily armed and well-trained, but the sheer numbers against them led to their extinction within a few years. One country in which the Templars persisted longest was England, where its king, Edward II, had not only fallen out with the pope but, fearing invasion by France, needed their backing. The Templars survived here in dwindling numbers until the mid-1300s when the Black Death finally finished them.

"How do you know these are Templar gravestones?" Jodi asked as she dusted confetti off one of them that had presumably been used for seating during a recent wedding.

"The cross for a start," Graham said, indicating the designs carved in the circles at one end of the slabs. "It's called a formée, the Templar emblem. That, coupled with the modest style of the carving, without names or inscriptions, is typical of the first Poor Knights of Christ. Their tombs became more elaborate the richer they grew, so these stones probably date from their early period—the 1100s."

Jodi shook her head. "And they're now being used as seats. Weird. Presumably, they weren't always bench tops, so they must have been moved here from somewhere else."

"Indeed, they were." Jodi and Graham turned to see that the voice behind them belonged to a middle-aged, bearded man leaning on a garden fork. It turned out that he was one of the churchwardens tending to the graveyard. "I couldn't help but overhear. You're right; they are Templar stones. Though not grave markers but coffin lids placed over stone sarcophagi in medieval churches. Probably not this one; detailed records of the rebuilding of St. Lawrence's in 1836 include no reference to any such tombs, so they most likely came from another church."

"Any idea where?" Graham asked.

The man was keen to share his knowledge of the church's history. "Well, James Bateman, the owner of Biddulph Grange, had them placed around the church in 1851. It wasn't until the 1940s that the vicar decided unceremoniously to use them as seats. Sadly, where they came from is not recorded."

The same thought simultaneously occurred to Jodi and Graham: 1851, the year little Mary led the Heaths and Batemans to the ruined chapel. The gravestones could have come from there. They told the warden of their interest in the barn beyond the

cave at the far end of Spring Wood and how they believed it may have been a small church.

The warden knew nothing about the building itself, but he did know about the property. "During the
Middle Ages, all the land around there belonged to
Cistercian monks, with whom the Knights Templar
were affiliated, so I guess that Bateman moved the
coffins from somewhere in that area when creating
his gardens. If you're right about the barn being a
chapel, they could have come from there."

"So, Bateman owned the land beyond the tunnel?" Graham said.

"Yes. When the Batemans' successors, the Heath
family, sold up in the 1920s, it became a farm. Before
then, it was an extension of Spring Wood."

"Why would Bateman move the Templar
graves?" Jodi asked. "And why here?"

The man thought for a while. "If the barn was a
chapel, perhaps a ruin in the mid-nineteenth century,
James Bateman might have been renovating the place
as a setting for one of his scenic gardens, like the
Egyptian temple and the Chinese sanctuary closer to
the Grange. It's possible he arranged to have any human remains reinterred on what was still consecrated
ground—this church—having their old sarcophagus
lids placed in the graveyard here." The warden took a
pen and notepad from his pocket and jotted some-

thing down. "If you want to know about Spring Wood, you should speak with the local expert." He handed them her name and number.

* * *

Just to the southeast of Rockfields Farm lies the village of Biddulph Moor. Until the growing industrial region of Stoke-on-Trent encroached upon it in the late 1800s, it was a remote, hillside farming community, a reclusive settlement of just a few hundred people who seem to have lived in virtual isolation for centuries. Curiously, old records indicate that the village consisted of two separate communities: one of red-headed people, thought to be descended from the Celts who built the Bridestones, and a dark-haired people who were said to be descended from the Arab stonemasons whom Ormus le Guidon employed to build his monastery in the Spring Wood area during the early 1100s. Biddulph Moor is now a commuter neighborhood; most of the indigenous population has left or long ago assimilated with newcomers. A few, however, remain, and the person the warden suggested they contact was one of them. Edith Murrow, an elderly lady whose family claimed descent from the Arab stonemasons, was regarded as a leading authority on the history of Biddulph.

As Jodi and Graham sat in Edith's living room, they were reminded of the character of Miss Marple from the films and TV shows of the Agatha Christie novels. Not only was she around the right age, dressed in a dark tweed suit, and exhibiting a sharp intelligence, but her cottage seemed to have been stuck in the 1950s, the period of the Miss Marple stories. Net curtains filled the windows to keep out prying eyes, heavy red drapes were held neatly back by cords, and the wallpaper was a loud arrangement of multicolored flowers, as was the thick shag carpet on the floor. Photographs of family members spanning generations filled almost every space on sideboards, tables, the mantelpiece above the fire, and the top of an upright piano against one wall. Everything appeared to have its place. All was immaculately clean and smelled of furniture polish. Edith was seated in a large crimson armchair while Jodi and Graham sat on an adjacent matching sofa.

"You want to know about the old chapel up by the tunnel?" Edith said as she poured tea into china cups that she had set out on the low coffee table before them, just about the only piece of furniture to remain uncluttered. She spoke with a North Staffordshire accent, the one thing about her that was not like Miss Marple. Agatha Christie's character is always portrayed with a posh, upper-class voice.

Graham nodded. "A friend thought it might have been built by the lord of Biddulph, a man called Ormus le Guidon, who employed Arab stonemasons he brought back from Jerusalem in the 1120s."

"It's possible," Edith said. "He certainly built a monastery in that area."

"We gather your family is descended from the stonemasons," Jodi said.

"On my mother's side, yes. But it may be just a legend."

"So, you don't think the Arabs *did* build it?" Graham asked.

"I don't know if they're my *ancestors*," Edith replied, staring at Graham as if disapproving of his inaccurate presumption. "I think it's possible that stonemasons from the Middle East were involved in its construction. The Arab world was architecturally far more advanced than Western Europe at the time, and Arab captives were employed to build ecclesiastical buildings in various parts of England during the Middle Ages."

"So, it *was* a chapel? The ruined walls that are now incorporated into a barn—well, a workshop now?" Jodi asked. "It looks like *an old chapel or church,* but we can't find anything to prove it."

Edith smiled. "It took me much digging to piece together its history, but it helped that I already knew for certain that it was a chapel."

Jodi glanced at Graham. "How?"

"I have an old drawing of it. My mother got it from the Grange when it was a hospital." Edith opened a manila folder and took out an old sepia print showing a ruined ecclesiastical building. The drawing was of the gable end, all overgrown by ivy with trees on either side. It was built from large stone blocks surrounding an arched doorway with a single, similarly arched window directly above. "You can see that it's the end of the building that still survives—the side facing the tunnel—except now the doorway has been bricked up, and the upper part, including the top of the window, has collapsed." Edith pointed to the bottom left corner of the picture. "It's dated September 1851. It's not signed but was probably made by James Bateman's wife, Maria. **She** was an artist from whom her son Robert inherited his talent to become a Pre-Raphaelite painter. She also had a passion for historic buildings, and was something of an architect, designing the ornamental structures like the mock Egyptian tomb in the Grange gardens."

Jodi and Graham were captivated. That date again —1851. "What do you know about the chapel?" Jodi asked.

"For a start, it was called Spring Wood Priory."

"Spring Wood Priory?" Graham repeated.

"That's what it was called before it became a barn," Edith explained.

"Is a priory the same as a church?" Jodi asked.

"A priory was a small monastery," Edith said, offering them biscuits. "What remains was probably its chapel. There are a few passing references to the building as Spring Wood Priory over the years, but the strange thing is that it does not appear in any Church records. I've not even discovered to what saint it was dedicated."

Graham examined the picture of the ruin as it was in 1851. "It certainly looks like an ecclesiastical building. But might it have been a folly?" He was referring to buildings constructed purely for decoration, such as mock medieval ruins often erected on the grounds of stately homes.

Edith shook her head. "No, it's far too old. Follies date from the eighteenth century onwards. The medieval archives are scant, but there is record of Spring Wood Priory already being there in the 1500s."

"Do you think it might be all that remains of the monastery built by Ormus le Guidon?" Jodi asked.

"I'd say so." As the warden had told them, it was evident by the authoritative way Edith spoke that she was a retired university lecturer in medieval history. "The door and window are lancet type—pointed—a feature of medieval Gothic architecture. However, the rudimentary design would place it before Gothic architecture generally flourished in England. Early to mid-twelfth century, is my guess. That's Ormus le Guidon's time, and his monastery is the only ecclesiastical building known to have existed in that area during that period." Edith sipped her tea before continuing. "Unfortunately, no archaeology has been conducted there to establish a date. James Bateman's cousin, Thomas, was an archaeologist and wanted to excavate it in the 1850s, but the family put the place strictly out of bounds. They erected a fence around it and even bricked up the tunnel exit to prevent people from gaining access. The place became a farm when the Batemans' successors, the Heaths, sold up in the 1920s, and the farmer turned it into a barn. There wasn't much left to excavate after that."

"When exactly did the Batemans fence it off?" Graham asked.

Edith sorted through her folder, removed a printed sheet of paper, adjusted her reading glasses, and read it through. "In 1851," she said after a moment.

Jodi cast a glance at Graham. Once again, the year little Mary may have led the Heaths and Batemans to that exact location. One of Edith's many cats brushed itself against Jodi's leg, and she bent down to stroke it. "Why *did* the Batemans close it off?" she asked.

Edith furrowed her brow." No one knows. The

Batemans were very secretive about the place. In my great-grandmother's day, there were rumors they'd found treasure there."

"Treasure?" Graham said enthusiastically.

Edith shook her head and held up a curtailing hand. "Don't get too excited—just local gossip. I've found nothing to prove it. Although the place must have held *some* special significance to James and Maria, otherwise why fence it off?"

"Was there any mention of Templar graves?" Graham asked, explaining how they wondered if the sarcophagi lids James Bateman moved to St. Lawrence church came from Spring Wood Priory.

Edith shook her head. "No specific mention. But if the stones are Templar, which I'd say is highly likely, they probably did come from Spring Wood Priory. That is if Ormus le Guidon built it. He was a Knights Templar.

That was news to Graham. "I knew he was a crusader but didn't realize he was a Templar."

"Yes, one of the first," Edith replied. "Although he inherited the Biddulph estate in 1100, he returned to the Holy Land for some years and was in Jerusalem in 1119 when the order was founded. In 1129, when the Templars became affiliated with the Cistercian monks, he gave a strip of his land, eight miles south of here, to that order, where they built the monastery of Hulton Abbey."

"Was that the same monastery built by Ormus le Guidon?" Graham asked.

"No, completely different."

"So, Spring Wood Priory seems to have been part of Ormus's monastery, not Hulton Abbey," Jodi said for clarification.

A cat jumped onto Edith's lap as she nodded in confirmation. "Correct. The abbey only later obtained it. In 1219, Ormus's descendants—by this time having adopted the family name, Biddulph, after their estate —gave the land where the priory is situated to the abbey. Before then, though, it still belonged to the Biddulphs, many of whom were Templars. As such, I would guess that the monastery was originally a Templar preceptory, and what was later called Spring Wood Priory was its chapel. Preceptories were usually separate from Cistercian monasteries, run directly by Templar lords."

"So, the ecclesiastical building Ormus had the Arab stonemasons build was not just a monastery, but originally a Templar preceptory?" Graham said.

"That's right. It may have been one of the first, if not *the* first, preceptory built outside Jerusalem," Edith said.

"So, the barn, or workshop, that now survives was likely the preceptory chapel," Graham mused.

"How big would it have been?"

"Probably around the size of a small parish church."

"And when was it abandoned?" Jodi asked.

Two cats were now on Edith's lap. She stroked one with each hand as she spoke. "In 1538, when Henry VIII broke away from the Roman Catholic Church to establish The Church of England, Hulton Abbey was stripped of its assets, and the Crown confiscated its lands. By this time, Spring Wood Priory belonged to the abbey, and the scant surviving record of the building refers to it as being on land confiscated by the king being sold to Ormus's descendant Richard Biddulph in 1542. He still lived at Biddulph Manor where the Grange now stands."

"So, the family got it back." Graham was puzzled. "How come they still lived at Biddulph? As Templars, wouldn't they have lost their lands after the order was dissolved?"

Edith shook her head. "That didn't happen so much in England. Often, so long as he publicly renounced the order, a Templar lord could retain his status and estates. The Biddulphs continued to live here for a further century. By the late 1500s, Richard's son Francis had inherited the estate and built a new home at nearby Biddulph Old Hall, but he left his daughter Mary to run the manor, which included the land on which the priory stood. Most unusual for the time, letting a woman run an estate. It was the Puritans who eventually left the place a ruin. The last of the Biddulphs were killed during the English Civil War. In 1642 the manor was destroyed, and the Puritan army used Spring Wood Priory for canon practice."

Jodi was unfamiliar with the English Civil War, so Edith explained how the conflict—between 1642 and 1651—saw the defeat of King Charles I after a revolt led by Parliament. The man who emerged as the country's new leader was the head of the rebel army, Oliver Cromwell. He and his soldiers were zealous puritans, hostile to any elaborate worship. They destroyed and defaced many old churches before Cromwell died, the regime collapsed, and the monarchy was restored in 1660.

Edith had told them all she knew concerning Spring Wood Priory, so Graham changed the subject. "Do you know if the Heaths and Batemans were involved in anything…" he tried to think of the right word to use, "strange or unusual?"

Edith cocked her head to one side as if to aid her memory. "From my grandmother, I learned a bit about the Grange during the time of the Heath family. Few outsiders were allowed anywhere near the place once the Heaths took over. Mary Heath ran the estate with the help of James Bateman's son Robert who lived nearby. My grandmother's mother, my great-grandmother, had been convinced they were having an affair. The pair also had an unconventional circle of friends: Pre-Raphaelite painters, romantic poets, bohemian actors, militant academics, and wealthy socialites, that sort of thing. Mary Heath's sister-in-law, Laura, ran the place after Mary's death in 1872 until she died in 1897. Staff at the Grange spoke about odd, nocturnal gatherings on the grounds when both women ran the estate, and many of their visitors were so-called occultists. Although I can't recall any names. My grandmother said the Heaths referred to these meetings as 'fetes.'" Edith turned to Jodi. "In America, you probably don't have such things. A fete is a traditional English fair."

Jodi smiled. "We have them. They're called Renaissance fairs. Although they are more medieval."

"What Mary and Laura organized were nothing like the usual kind of pageants country folk call fetes," Edith continued. "My grandmother said they were held after dark, for one thing. And the public was excluded. Even the staff were given the night off."

"Was your grandmother around during Mary and Laura's time?" Graham asked.

"She was born in 1890 and was just a child when

Laura died. No, she heard it all from *her* mother, who knew servants at the Grange."

"What were Mary, Laura, and their friends doing, do you think?" Jodi asked.

"My grandmother didn't know. The rumors were all rather vague. All she'd heard was that they'd put on fancy dress and got up to various shenanigans."

"So, it was all about drink, drugs, and..." Graham stopped himself from completing the sentence.

Edith laughed. "Orgies? Possibly. But I'd say they were into the craze of magic, spiritualism, and other such nonsense that was popular at the time. You know, it was said that the fire of 1897 began during a séance when a candle was mysteriously knocked over?"

"We heard that," Jodi said.

Edith waved her hand dismissively. "Just rumor. The cause of the fire was never established, and as no one was hurt, there was no official inquiry. But my grandmother always maintained that it was caused by lightning. There was a storm that night, and a maid who lived in one of the Grange's outbuildings said she witnessed the strike."

"Laura Heath died shortly after the fire, didn't she?" Graham said.

"Yes. She was very ill with tuberculosis, or consumption as they called it back then. Her daughter-in-law Lady Phyllis then took over the running of the estate." Edith poured them another cup of tea. "She wasn't strictly a 'lady'—the wife of a lord or knight of the realm—but that's how the head women of stately homes were usually addressed: Lady Maria, Lady Mary, Lady Laura, Lady Phyllis. Phyllis oversaw rebuilding the house after the fire as her husband was occupied with business affairs. She remained the lady of the estate until the Heath family went broke—their mining and ironworking endeavors collapsed after the First World War—and the Grange was sold to become a hospital in 1922. As far as I know, rumors of the strange goings at Biddulph had ceased by Phyllis's time."

"Sorry!" Jodi was staring intently at Edith. Something had just occurred to her. "Earlier, what year did you say the fire happened?"

Edith seemed rather shocked by the intensity of Jodi's question. "The fire at Biddulph Grange? 1897."

"You're sure?" Jodi said, still staring. "The literature at Biddulph Grange says 1896."

Edith fumbled through her folder and produced an old photograph of people standing in front of the burned-out center of the building. It was the same picture they had seen at Biddulph Grange. "These were the firefighters and other local people who'd helped put out the fire posing in front of the house the following day. I wrote the date on the back." Edith turned it over to show them. "January 16, 1897."

Jodi explained how they also thought the fire occurred in 1897. But every piece of information online, in books, in literature at Biddulph Grange, all said it happened a year earlier, in the early hours of January 16, 1896.

"No, that's not right," Edith said firmly, lifting the cats from her lap, standing up, and walking over to a bookcase. When she removed one of the books and flicked to a page, her eyes opened wide with surprise. She took out a second book, a third, and a fourth, thumbing through each, progressively more urgently, before speaking. When she did, her voice was quavering. "That's not possible!"

"What is it?" Jodi asked, knowing what she must have found.

"They all say the fire occurred in 1896, but I know these very same books recorded the event exactly a year later, in 1897." Edith returned to the coffee table and picked up her folder. One after another, she produced her notes, all confirming that the fire occurred in the year she believed it had happened. She sat back in her armchair, looking decidedly unwell. "That's impossible. I know I'm right." She dropped her notes on the table, and Jodi picked them up. According to everything Edith had written herself, the fire occurred in 1897.

Edith was now staring into space in shocked confusion. Graham was about to tell her of their experiences. Like hers, his notes still contained the 1897 date, while other material had seemingly changed, as had everyone's memories. But Jodi shook her head and put a restraining hand on his arm.

"I don't think she's up to it," she whispered. Edith just sat there in silence, seemingly oblivious to their presence.

-10-
The Secret Vault

"Well, we're not the only ones who think the date's changed," Jodi said as she and Graham sat in her hotel room. They had checked and rechecked everything online to establish that the day of the Biddulph fire was still a year earlier than they—and now Edith—remembered. Yet bizarrely, all their own notes and writing still recorded the event as having taken place in 1897.

Graham shook his head, bewildered. "I'd decided that I must have mixed up the date and that you'd inadvertently gone along. But now Edith! She's an academic. That she made the exact mistake we did! I don't buy it."

"So, what *is* going on?"

Graham held out his upturned palms. "I've no idea."

For the first time in a while, Graham opened his text messages. He was about to contact Tara's friend Jack, an authority on occult history and the Knights Templar, and ask him about the coffin slabs at St. Lawrence Church. Surprisingly, Jack had already sent *him* a message. Tara had told him of her latest trip to

Biddulph and had shared photographs of the tunnel. Jack was immediately reminded of something: an illustration from an old book depicting an artificial cave very similar to the one in Biddulph Park. Enigmatically, Jack only sent Graham a copy of the picture with no accompanying note. He obviously thought that Graham would get the connection. And he did.

"What does it mean?" Jodi asked when she saw the image.

Graham remained silent for a moment, staring at his phone. "I think I know what little Mary may have found at Spring Wood Priory. It's all to do with the original Order of Meonia."

"The *original* order? Remind me."

"Remember, an Elizabethan group also called the Order of Meonia existed in the late 1500s and early 1600s. I doubted the two groups had any connection with one another. For a start, they existed two and a half centuries apart. I thought they had coincidentally used the same name for their groups merely because the land of Meonia was considered the birthplace of Western mysticism. Other than that, I assumed there was no link. Now, I'm not so sure."

"How would the Elizabethan Order of Meonia have any relevance to what little Mary found in Spring Wood years later?"

"I'll give you my take on it soon. First, there's a place you should see."

* * *

"You're doing your usual thing by keeping me in suspense," Jodi complained from the passenger seat as Graham drove them across the Midlands of England the following morning.

"Yes ... and no."

"What's that supposed to mean?"

"You need to understand the background to my thinking."

"Can you at least tell me *where* we're going?" Jodi said with a sigh.

"Canons Ashby House. About seventy miles north of London."

Canons Ashby House, near Daventry in the East Midlands, is a Tudor manor dating back to the late 1500s, the period of Queen Elizabeth I and William Shakespeare. The rear of the house is faced with honey-colored blocks of local Cotswold stone from a later era, but most of the building has remained unchanged since it was first built. An archway, through which carriages would once have passed, leads to a central courtyard: a cobbled enclosure surrounded by red-brick walls, diamond-leaded windows, high chimney stacks, and steep, grey-tiled roofs, all the fashion during Elizabethan times. And overlooking the scene, a whitewashed tower topped by a domed cupola with a wrought-iron weathervane.

After they paid to enter the now publicly-owned building, Graham led Jodi inside, through the entrance hall adorned with portraits of those for whom this was once home, and up a winding staircase that creaked and groaned with time. Navigating a series of narrow, plastered corridors, they arrived at a second-floor chamber, redolent with fresh polish, pleasantly overlaying the musty smell of age. Glass-fronted cabinets displaying a collection of china and silver ornaments were set against the walls. At the center of the room was a large mahogany table, a reminder of when the head of the household used the place as an office. Graham indicated to a mural covering one wall. Much of it had worn away, but enough remained to make out the general composition. The once-colorful painting had faded to resemble a monochrome charcoal drawing depicting an Elizabethan family posing together in a stately hall. He pointed to the top center of the mural, where a series of barely discernible letters were surrounded by an array of lines depicting a shining manifestation, something like the sun.

"This represents a new star that appeared in 1572," he said.

Jodi frowned. "Stars can just appear?"

"They thought so at the time. It was what today we'd call a supernova: an exploding star. The flareup of these stellar explosions, visible from Earth for many weeks, outshines all the other stars in the Milky Way, making it seem like a new star has just appeared. So rare are such celestial events that none have been observable with the naked eye for the last four hundred years."

"And the letters?"

"The four Hebrew characters spelling the word for God. In English, it's normally rendered as *Yahweh*. Many people thought the supernova was a sign from God, heralding a new age, something like how the

Star of Bethlehem proclaimed the birth of Christ."

"Presumably, the people who lived here believed that. Who were they?"

"In the late 1500s, the owner was Erasmus Dryden, a man fascinated by the occult."

"Wouldn't that have been considered witchcraft back then?" Jodi noticed the look of concern on the face of a nearby visitor at overhearing the mention of witchcraft.

"Interestingly, no. Elizabeth's reign was relatively tolerant regarding such matters. Subjects like astrology, magic, and alchemy weren't considered witchcraft. The queen even employed an astrologer, Dr. John Dee, and it's with him that our story begins."

Jodi listened carefully as Graham explained. Born in 1527, John Dee was one of the most learned men of his age. After studying at Cambridge University, he briefly entered the priesthood. But the appearance of the new star in 1572 changed everything. Dee had always been interested in esoteric matters, but from age 45, he became consumed with astrology, mysticism, and the occult. The 1572 supernova was known as Tycho's Star, after the Danish astronomer Tycho Brahe, the first to write about it. Brahe was an astronomer who observed the night skies with pragmatic interest; conversely, John Dee was an astrologer who regarded the positions of the heavenly bodies as portents to future events. Dee also wrote about the new star, considering it a sign that profound worldly changes would soon occur in religious, scientific, and mystical affairs.

"Dee's reasoning regarding the new star fascinated the wealthy statesman and explorer Sir Walter Raleigh, and together they established a society to prepare for this imagined new age of enlightenment," Graham concluded. "With its membership boasting several leading academics—such as the philosopher George Chapman, the mathematician Thomas Harriot, the physician Heinrich Khunrath, and the polymath Robert Fludd—it was called the Order of Meonia."

"The Elizabethan Order of Meonia?"

"That's right."

"So, what did they get up to?" Jodi asked, noticing how visitors were beginning to gather around, assuming Graham to be an official guide.

"Publicly, they merely discussed philosophy and new discoveries. But they were primarily fascinated by magic: the summoning of angels to answer questions, the conjuration of spirits to do their bidding, the scribing of enchanted symbols called 'sigils' to open doorways to hidden realms, and the quest to comprehend nature's secrets through the practice of alchemy."

"Alchemy! Turning lead into gold?"

"That was largely allegorical. The crucial idea was to transmute the soul. To gain enlightenment through meditation and elaborate rituals."

"How did they supposedly know all this stuff?" Jodi asked.

"They took it from an esoteric belief called Kabbalah or Kabbalism. It was found in various *grimoires*

—books filled with incantations, occult symbols, and instructions for magical rites—compiled during the Middle Ages. They were copied from sacred texts discovered in the Middle East during the crusades."

Jodi felt rather conspicuous now that a small crowd had assembled around them. "So, the group could openly admit to practicing all this without fear of recrimination?" she asked.

"At first, yes. But in 1591, the queen adopted a more fundamentalist approach to religion. The society officially disbanded, and John Dee formally renounced his ideas. On the other hand, Raleigh continued to lead the group in secret until he was arrested in 1603 and spent the next thirteen years in prison. It's unknown where the society continued to meet, but I think it was here."

Graham had been so engrossed with his discourse that he'd been unaware of the interest he was attracting. The small audience waited for him to continue, but when he remained silent, they began to disperse.

"What makes you think that?" Jodi asked when they were alone.

Graham ushered Jodi into the corridor and up a narrow, twisting flight of steps, which led to a smaller room with wood-paneled walls painted with colorful heraldic crests. "These shield designs are the coats-of-arms of those who met here: supposedly, influential landowners who gathered to discuss financial matters. But look what people that included." Graham pointed in turn to various crests as he identified their owners.

"Beside Erasmus Dryden, who owned the place, we have Walter Raleigh, George Chapman, Thomas Harriot, and Robert Fludd—all members of the Order of Meonia. As these shields date from the 1590s, after the society was supposedly disbanded, this was almost certainly where the first Order of Meonia continued to meet."

A bright shaft of sunlight shone through the large bay window to one end of the room as Jodi looked around her at the shield representations depicting animals, mythical beasts, and various symbols. "What suggests these meetings had anything to do with the occult?" she asked.

As if to order, an officious-looking guide entered with a party of tourists. "This chamber was used for gatherings involving those whose crests surround us." She indicated to the heraldic shields. "But, until recently, we had no idea what such meetings might entail."

The guide explained how, in 2013, a secret alcove was discovered beside the entrance, hidden behind lath and plaster for four hundred years. The visitors assembled around her as she showed them the fascinating discovery. The recess, some 6 feet high, 3 feet wide, and 2 feet deep, had a shelf halfway up, flanked on either side by wooden depictions of fluted pilasters joined by an arch. In the top corners of this miniature, stage-like façade were red-painted designs resembling upturned letter Ls. Below the shelf was a similar fascia, but in place of the L-shaped motifs were brown, inverted V-shape figures.

"The pillar designs represent the two columns of the Temple of Solomon, while the L-shapes are squares, and the Vs are compasses, the most identifiable symbols of Freemasonry," the guide explained. "The alcove is thought to have held a ceremonial washing basin, implying the chamber was a meeting room for early Masons. Masonic halls had such basins at their entrance."

As the guide described how discovering the secret alcove made national news, Graham told Jodi the relevance of these Masonic signs. A metal L-shaped tool, rather misleadingly known as a "square," is used in carpentry and stonemasonry to measure right angles accurately. While the "compass," not to be confused with the device for finding magnetic north, is a technical drawing instrument used for inscribing circles and as a divider to measure distances on charts, blueprints, and maps.

"Together with the twin pillars, they were adopted as emblems to represent the knowledge of the stonemasons that constructed the biblical Temple of Jerusalem, whose sacred conventions the Masons contend to uphold," Graham explained. "Early Judaic tradition maintains that those who built the temple at the behest of King Solomon, around three thousand years ago, were occultists—Kabbalists, to be precise."

"It involved the occult?" Jodi said, bemused. "That doesn't sound very God-fearing."

"In Kabbalistic belief, the occult—which means 'hidden wisdom'—wasn't devil worship, but sacred knowledge supposedly embraced by the temple's designers. The Masons claimed to have inherited certain aspects of this ancient wisdom, hence their name."

"Why *Free*masons?"

"Because of their perceived freedom from any earthly master."

"I thought Freemasons were basically a glorified college fraternity," Jodi said. "Men who meet secretly to discuss matters of mutual benefit and raise money for charity. Secret handshakes and all that."

"Today, perhaps, but originally, they professed an interest in Kabbalism. Masons still perform what are basically Kabbalistic ceremonies, although they're just symbolic these days. At least, I assume they are, not being one of them."

"Could you tell me if you were?" Jodi jibed.

"No idea. I suppose I could admit to being one, not what they do." Graham took Jodi to one side, out of earshot of the guide and visitors. "But the people who met here can't have been Freemasons. England's first Masonic lodge wasn't founded until 1717, well over a century after the decorations in this room. However, another organization previously used these same Kabbalistic symbols over a century earlier—the Order of Meonia."

Jodi was fascinated but still confused. "Okay, this place was a secret meeting place for the Elizabethan Order of Meonia. But how does all this tie up with Spring Hill Priory and what little Mary Heath might have found there?"

As Jodi moved to a window seat, away from the visitors crowded at the other end of the room, Graham explained. "In 1604, surviving members of the Order of Meonia, such as Robert Fludd and Heinrich Khunrath, started what they hoped to be an international secret society called the Rosicrucians. Although they claimed to follow the teachings of a medieval mystic called Christian Rosenkreuz, this legendary figure was almost certainly allegorical. His name means literally "Christian Rose Cross," the name of the new group's emblem, a Christian cross with a rose at its center. Incidentally, that's where the word 'Rosicrucian'—Order of the Rose Cross—originates.

"They seem to have been quite religious for occultists," Jodi said.

"Almost everyone in England was Christian back then; it depended on how they interpreted the Bible. Few learned people saw a contradiction between Christianity and Kabbalism, which was supposedly practiced in ancient Israel. In the Elizabethan Order of Meonia, only Walter Raleigh seems to have been a committed atheist."

"So, what was the purpose of this Rosicrucian society?"

The tourists moved on, leaving them alone. "It was intended to be an enlarged version of the Meonia group, with the same aims," Graham explained. "Most of its membership and activities remain shrouded in mystery, but the society seems to have lasted for around fifteen years until it disbanded during a Europe-wide conflict between Protestants and Catholics known as the Thirty Years War. Various anonymous Rosicrucian writers claimed that this larger group was started after its founders discovered a secret underground vault containing manuscripts revealing arcane Kabbalistic knowledge."

"Its founders being the Elizabethan Order of Meonia?" Jodi interjected.

"Yes." Graham nodded. "The vault's location, which was resealed when the Rosicrucians disbanded around 1618, remained a secret. However, one person who seems to have known of its whereabouts was Meonia group member Heinrich Khunrath, and in 1605 he included a stylized drawing of a tunnel said to lead to the vault. It still survives in copies of his work, the *Amphitheater of Eternal Wisdom*." Graham remained silent momentarily to accentuate his next words "That was the picture Jack sent me."

Jodi caught on. "The tunnel in Spring Wood leading to the priory. You think Mary Heath found this vault?"

"Churches have crypts—underground vaults. The crypt beneath Spring Wood Priory might have been the vault the Elizabethan Order of Meonia discovered in 1604. If little Mary found it, it would have proved her abilities. It might also explain why the Heaths and Batemans called their group the Order of Meonia, after the society whose secret vault they'd rediscovered."

"What do you think the vault contained?" Jodi asked.

"By Mary Heath's time, it's unlikely to have still held any Kabbalistic manuscripts. They may originally have survived to be discovered in 1604 because they had been sealed inside airtight containers, such as stone or lead boxes. But if they were returned to the vault in 1618, after years of exposure to the air, they would have completely rotted away well before the mid-nineteenth century. However, there could still have been inscriptions or various items in the crypt to reveal it to have been the vault referenced by the Rosicrucians."

"Maybe it was from such inscriptions that Maria Bateman got the idea for creating the shrines and performing whatever rituals they got up to." Jodi mused.

"Maybe." Graham adopted a stern expression. "Unfortunately, it's impossible to prove any of this— at least for the foreseeable future. We'd never persuade archeologists to excavate the remains of Spring Wood Priory on such speculative evidence. Besides, I doubt the construction company would agree to have their work disrupted, and their property dug up. Even a geophysics scan, using noninvasive, ground-penetrating radar to see what might lie buried, is out of the question. What was once the chapel floor is now a mass of thick concrete."

Jodi stared out of the window. "It can't be a coincidence that the Bridestones and the Rosicrucian vault were both on the Biddulph estate," she said.

Graham joined Jodi at the window. Looking down at a straight row of neatly-trimmed bushes that bordered a freshly-cut lawn, he had an idea. "Remember when we were at the Celtic glen, and I told you how old Celtic shrines were sacred springs, caves, and stone circles? Well, they were often aligned." Graham began to trace a line with his figure on a wood panel to one side of the window recess.

"Excuse me!" The guide's shrill voice filled the room. "No touching," she said sternly, glaring at them from the other end of the chamber.

"Sorry." Graham grimaced while Jodi stifled a laugh. It was like being back in school.

Graham cleared his throat. "Imagine a straight line between a natural spring and a nearby cave. At the same distance further from the cave, in a continuation of the line, the Celts often erected a stone circle, creating an equidistant alignment of the three sacred sites. I think such an alignment existed in the Biddulph area. The priory is right in the middle of the line drawn between the Bridestones stone circle and the Gawton's Well sacred spring. There could have been a cave, sacred to the Celts, over which the chapel was erected. Its crypt may have been fashioned from such a cave."

Jodi needed to clarify. "You're saying that the ancient Celts revered two natural features, the spring and the cave, then created an alignment of three sites by erecting a stone circle the same distance further on, along a straight line from the cave."

"Exactly."

"The sacred cave, at the center of the alignment, became the crypt for Spring Wood Priory, the vault discovered by the Elizabethan Order of Meonia."

"You've got it."

"So, as the priory was built by Ormus le Guidon and his Templars in the 1120s, they created the vault discovered in 1604 from a cave previously sacred to the Celts." Jodi tilted her head slightly. "Would they have revered such a Celtic shrine?"

"Quite possibly. The Templars were into all kinds of ancient beliefs. Local tradition probably told how the Celts once venerated places like the Bridestones, Gawton's Well, and the cave."

"And this is what little Mary's clairvoyance led her to discover?" Jodi turned to Graham with a furrowed brow. "So, how did the *Elizabethan* Meonia group discover it?"

"Maybe they had their own Mary Heath."

* * *

A bright shaft of sunlight shines down through the trees, illuminating the interior walls of a roofless, ivy-covered building: a ruined chapel, its windows long bereft of glass. Fragments of broken statues, dried leaves, fallen branches, and detritus, litter the floor. A group of men in black tunics and calf-length breaches heave up a large stone slab that, judging by the piles of soil surrounding them, they have just exposed in a corner of the church. A woman, perhaps in her mid-forties, wearing a long purple cloak over a brown, front-laced bodice and a long, full skirt, her hair tied up beneath a white bonnet, seems to be directing the men in their work. Jodi's eyes snap open, and she is back in her room.

"I think I saw the opening of the vault at Spring Wood Priory in 1604," Jodi said after describing her vision during a successful remote the previous night.

She and Graham had met at her hotel the following day for brunch. "The building looked very much like the ruined chapel in Edith's picture but less dilapidated," she continued. "I assume the people were the Elizabethan Meonia group. And they were being led by a woman." Jodi shrugged her shoulders. "That can't be right, though, can it? Women wouldn't have been part of such a society back then, let alone in charge, would they?

"I think the leader of the Meonia group *was* a woman." Graham said enthusiastically. "Several anonymous Rosicrucian writers suggested that they were led by a woman who might have taken over the leadership of their founding society after Raleigh was imprisoned in 1603." He explained how the previous afternoon after he left Jodi, he had visited Staffordshire's central archives to examine records concerning Biddulph during the late sixteenth and early seventeenth centuries. "I was looking for evidence that whoever owned the estate at that time had links with the Elizabethan Order of Meonia. And they did."

Graham explained that the family who owned the estate in 1604, when the Rosicrucian tomb was supposedly found, could have been involved with the original Order of Meonia. "Remember Mary Biddulph, the woman Edith told us ran Biddulph Manor where the Grange is now? That was between 1580 and 1620, the same period during which the vault was found. Well, not only was she the niece of Walter Raleigh, the leader of the Order of Meonia, but she had close associations with other members of the group: George Chapman and Thomas Harriot were friends of her brother, Richard, who lived at Biddulph Old Hall, and Robert Fludd wrote about the district of Biddulph while repeatedly staying at the manor when Mary ran the place after the death of her husband. The two were possibly lovers—Fludd remained single, and Mary never remarried."

"So, the woman I saw in my remote could have been Mary Biddulph?"

"Indeed. And, as she was born in 1561, she would have been 43 in 1604, around the age you described."

"Do you think that Mary Biddulph found the vault in the same way as Mary Heath?"

"Psychically, you mean. Perhaps. There are interesting parallels between the two Marys. Both were left in charge of the estate when women had virtually no inheritance rights. Like Mary Heath, Mary Biddulph was held in high esteem. On the other hand, it's possible she discovered clues to the vault's existence in her family records. The Biddulphs were directly descended from Ormus le Guidon, who seems to have had it constructed."

Jodi took a deep breath. "Well, I thought it was confusing enough with three Roberts. Now we have two Marys."

Graham's phone chimed, alerting him to a new email. Viewing the message, he became the epitome of incredulity. "I can't believe it!" he said. "We were just talking about the Elizabethan Order of Meonia, and suddenly I got a message directly concerning it."

Graham reminded Jodi how, 40 years before, he had been part of a team that had located an item that once belonged to the Elizabethan Meonia group—a short sword made from a single casting of steel. It was around twenty inches long, the blade about two-thirds of that length, separated from the hilt by a small, two-inch cross-guard. It was identified as a dirk, a long thrusting dagger. However, as it had a rounded tip, it was considered a decorative item used for ceremonial purposes. Along its blade was inscribed in Elizabethan spelling, *Meonia fore Marye*—Meonia for Mary.

"The Earl of Coventry, the person on whose property it was found, kept the sword, and for many years it was locked away at his ancestral home of Croome Court. Lord Coventry died in 2002, and the National Trust took over the place. However, the sword remained in the possession of one of the late earl's estate managers. Anyway, someone from the National Trust has just emailed me to say that the sword has been given to a nearby museum and is now on public display."

"That's a remarkable synchronicity," Jodi said, her eyes wide. "It has to mean something."

"I think it does. The inscription on the sword implies that the Meonia group had sworn allegiance to someone called Mary. We always assumed it was Mary Queen of Scots, as the cross-guard was embossed with what seemed to have been her coat of arms. Before her death in 1587, she had close links with members of the Meonia group.

"Oh no … not another Mary!"

Graham grinned and held up a figure. "The sword dated from 1605, way after her death. So, she's probably not important. I've never come up with another candidate for the Mary in question. Until now."

"Mary Biddulph!" Jodi said. "Well, if that's not fate's way of confirming that she led the Elizabethan Order of Meonia, I don't know what is."

* * *

The National Trust had told Graham that the sword was now exhibited in a museum in Upton-upon-Severn, not far from Croome Court. Considering the strange synchronicities, he and Jodi decided to see it. Situated some 40 miles south of Birmingham, the small town had narrow streets, where modern stores were interspersed with buildings dating back to the Middle Ages. When the pair arrived, the community's 3000 population was swollen by hundreds of sightseers enjoying the sunny day to visit the local marina, where pleasure boats embarked for tours along a picturesque stretch of the River Severn, after which the town was named. The black-and-white fronted Tudor House Museum in Church Street lived up to its name, remaining virtually unaltered since its construction in 1550. What is now the museum was originally three separate dwellings, the central section being a rectory, once the home for the parish priest whose church stood directly across the road.

After learning from the lady at the reception desk where the sword was displayed, Graham and Jodi made their way to the second floor. A series of adjoining galleries, once the private chambers of the priest who dwelt here in the sixteenth century, were crammed with mementos of the town's history. Farming and carpentry tools, food-preparation utensils, archaic medical equipment, household items, toys, dolls, boxes, chests, military paraphernalia, weapons, wartime gas masks, crockery, and much more besides, spanning the centuries, were displayed in glass cabinets, or laid out on benches and open shelves around the walls. In center place, at the far end of the longest gallery, the sword was wall-mounted in a glass-covered case. Below it was a low sideboard with a blue ring binder containing information concerning the sword's history, plus photographs showing the people involved in its discovery. Jodi picked it up and flicked through the pages.

"Old photos of you!" Jodi couldn't help but laugh at a picture of a youthful Graham with long, tousled hair, looking thoughtfully at the camera and proudly holding the sword.

"I couldn't help overhearing. You were involved in the sword's discovery?" One of the museum staff introduced himself. "You were one of those who found it?" said the man when Graham gave his name.

"That's right. I've just been told about the new display. Couldn't wait to see it." Graham peered at the sword through the glass. "Would it be possible to take it out of the case? I haven't seen it for almost forty years."

The man excused himself to return with three

other staff members keen to meet Graham. One of the team unlocked the cabinet and tried to remove the item, but it was attached by thick clasps, meaning it would require dismantling the entire display to take it down. Instead, Graham touched the cold steel artifact for the first time in decades.

"It's strange that the sword should end up here," said a rather high-pitched, raspy male voice. Everyone turned to the short, elderly, white-haired gentleman in an ill-fitting, black, three-piece suit standing at the back of the group—apparently a visitor who had arrived unnoticed and had been listening to their conversation. "I gather it belonged to an occult society of the Elizabeth era," he said in an almost monotone manner. "This building was once the home of the most famous Elizabethan occultist—Dr. John Dee."

"Really?" Graham said excitedly. He looked at the guides, who remained silent, unaware of any such connection.

The man smiled. "This was the rectory for the church across the street. In the 1550s, Dee was its priest."

"I knew he was a priest in his early life but had no idea he lived here," Graham said.

"Look it up," the stranger replied enigmatically before turning and wandering nonchalantly off into the next gallery.

As the visitor seemed unwilling to engage in further conversation, Graham took out his phone and began scrolling through a webpage concerning John Dee. "He's right; Dee was a priest for the parish of

Upton-upon-Severn between 1553 and 1555."

"So, you didn't know that John Dee had lived here?" Jodi said.

Graham looked sheepish. "No. I must have missed that."

"It's news to me, too," said the man who had opened the glass case. The three other members of staff shrugged or shook their heads in agreement.

"How did the sword come to be here?" Jodi asked them.

"The Earl of Coventry donated it to us as he was one of our trustees," said the man with the cabinet keys.

"So, it's pure coincidence." Jodi turned to Graham. "What are the chances of the Meonia sword ending up where the very person who started the Order of Meonia happened to live?"

Graham seemed oblivious to the question. His brow furrowed as he stared quizzically at the man who had answered Jodi. "Lord Coventry donated the sword to the museum! Didn't he die in 2002? I thought the sword had only recently been exhibited."

"The display you see *now* has only just been assembled, but the sword has been on show here for years," the man said. "Lord Coventry gave it to the museum in the 1980s."

"But that's impossible. When we tried—" Graham was cut off mid-sentence when Jodi gave a short, covert tug on his sleeve. He turned, and she gave him a slight but rapid shake of the head.

"What?" Graham asked when the staff members

returned to their duties and left them alone.

"I know this sounds crazy, but I think reality has shifted again."

"Reality has shifted! Again?"

"Like it did at Biddulph Grange when the year of the fire changed. Three of us—you, me, and Edith—all remember the date being a year earlier than everyone else. All these people think the sword has been here for years."

"They must be mistaken," he said.

"All of them?" Jodi said incredulously. "Besides, one of the ladies just told me she's worked here for years and specifically remembers moving the sword when it used to be on display downstairs after the placed flooded in the 1990s."

Graham immediately got on his phone and called various people involved with the sword's discovery. Bizarrely, two of them remembered the item being in the Tudor House Museum since the 1980s, and two remembered it always having been at Lord Coventry's home of Croome Court and then in possession of the estate manager."

"I was prepared to believe that confusion might account for the conflicting memories concerning the date of the Biddulph fire." Graham reminded Jodi of the so-called Mandela effect. "But this goes way beyond that. It's possible to mix up the recall of a news event or to misremember a date, but something as detailed as the sword being in two places simultaneously. I recently said that nothing sounded crazy anymore. I take it back. It does now."

"And there's a further synchronicity," Jodi said. "That man just happened to be here to tell us about John Dee's connection with this place."

Graham slowly shook his head. "Changing reality, fate, synchronicities! How the hell does any of it work?"

-11-

Fate, Reality and Time

That evening, Jodi and Graham sat in a pub garden overlooking the river that ran through Upton-upon-Severn. As boats and pleasure craft sailed lazily by in the late afternoon sun, they discussed the bizarre series of events confronting them: fantastic turns of fate, astounding synchronicities, and what seemed to be impossible changes to reality. Both they and Edith clearly remembered many times reading how the Biddulph fire had occurred in 1897. But now, written records, published books, online material, and even other people's memories told a different story—the fire was in 1896. If it only concerned this single event, it might be written off a shared misreading of historical material. But other scenarios also appeared to have involved—for want of a better term—reality shifts. There had been the sudden appearance of the Alice in Wonderland theme park and the Mad Hatter's Tea Emporium, which had seemingly not existed before—at least not in Graham and Jodi's world. Now there was the sword. Over a dozen people Graham had called that afternoon vividly recalled, as did he, that the item had been on Lord Coventry's estate ever since it was found in 1979 and then in the care of the estate manager, while many others he had contacted swore it had been in the Tudor House Museum all along.

Some scientific interpretations of modern physics allow for parallel worlds. These 'multiverse' theories, as they are known, propose that other universes might exist alongside our own. After the date of the Biddulph fire astonishingly seemed to change, Jodi and Graham had tentatively discussed the possibility that they had somehow ended up in one of these other worlds. Perhaps, they reasoned, as they had not been confronted with their doubles, only their minds had made the crossing to be transferred into different versions of themselves. However, even this fantastic explanation didn't seem to fit. It was not just a matter of finding themselves in an alternate reality; if they *had* been transported to another world, things from their universe—their writings, photographs, even several other people—had apparently come with them. A parallel universe might be a weird concept, but what confronted Graham and Jodi was even stranger: a situation where *particular* aspects of one or more universes had been dragged into another. If everything was as it seemed, they now existed in some crazy patchwork reality.

"What exactly *are* we dealing with?" Jodi asked as she drank from a much-needed glass of wine.

Graham was sitting on a low stone wall separating

the pub garden from the river, a few feet from their drinks table. "If Mary Heath was led to discover the secret vault after whatever happened to her at the Bridestones," he said, "as we can infer from your remotes and my mirror vision, then something had evidentially *wanted* her to find it. Perhaps the same applied to Mary Biddulph. Maybe even Ormus le Guidon had been *led* to an ancient Celtic cave where he constructed the vault in the first place. It would now seem that this same 'something' is guiding *us*. Whatever it is, it would appear to have the wherewithal to impart mystic powers to a little girl, copy minds into mirrors, mess with cameras, generate preternatural thunderstorms, and create meaningful synchronicities like—"

"Someone leaving the card at the Bridestones," Jodi cut in. "Not to mention the mysterious woman in Leek, the man in the Tudor House Museum, and us learning about the sword being on display at precisely the opportune moment we did."

Graham agreed. "Furthermore, it can alter history and bend the fabric of existence. Clairvoyance and the paranormal, I can get my head around. But this!"

Jodi looked pensive. "Maybe what I've been seeing is not communication from Mary Heath, but guidance from that same 'something.' After all, I doubt what I saw of Elizabethan times came from her." She added a further thought, "When Jenny visited Biddulph in 1981 and spoke about the B Stone, where was *that* coming from?"

Graham sat down at the table. "As a spiritualist, Jenny believed her messages and impressions came from departed spirits. However, whatever spoke through her in the Egyptian temple totally freaked her out. She had no idea what it was."

"What do *you* think it was?"

Graham shrugged. "The same thing behind what's happening now, I guess. It knew I'd find the B Stone one day, which would start our quest."

Jodi raised her eyebrows. "You think, as with little Mary, us entering the tomb kicked things off?"

"Maybe. I'd visited the Bridestones before but never stepped inside."

"Why not?"

"At the time, it was cordoned off."

"So, why us?" Jodi stopped, rolled her eyes, and held up a hand. "Don't tell me. You've no idea."

Graham gave a wry smile.

"Okay, so what exactly *is* this 'something,' this guiding influence or whatever you'd call it?" Jodi asked.

"Who knows *what* could manipulate reality." Graham paused. "Perhaps, though, we shouldn't ask. Chances are we couldn't comprehend it. Maybe labeling or conceiving it in a particular way limits, negates, or even changes its nature."

"You've lost me."

Graham ran a hand through his hair. "We're not the only ones to have experienced such weirdness. Throughout history, cultures, creeds, groups, and individuals of every persuasion, have attributed inexplicable and extraordinary events to the intervention of just about everything: gods, ancestors, karma, you name it. And often, their encounters, visions, experiences, and even the messages they receive, support their preconceptions. The way the phenomenon manifests may be determined by what people already believe. It could be that the reality behind it gets scrambled by prejudice."

A short way along the riverbank from the pub, a crowd had gathered around a troop of traditional performers with green-painted faces and medieval, leaf-covered clothing, dancing wildly to the accompaniment of a flute and drum. Graham indicated toward them. "If our 'something' had interacted with *their* pagan predecessors, then they may have communicated with the Green Man—the spirit of the forest."

At an adjacent table, a couple of late teenage boys were intently gaming on their phones, oblivious to everything around them. One of their T-shirts was emblazoned with a swirling galaxy. Jodi nodded in their direction. "And they'd probably get aliens." She glanced inquiringly at Graham. "So, none of what we're dealing with involves spirits or anything like that?"

"Maybe some of it. My mirror vision might have come from little Mary's tulpa. Your remotes may include communications with spirits, entities, and supernatural beings. But the guiding hand must be something else entirely. It has powers far beyond any regular ghost."

"Are you sure about all this?"

Graham sighed. "Not really."

"Fair enough. But let's say you *are* right. I assume this—whatever it is—has intention. It seems to want us to figure something out. However, as you suggested, if we get sidetracked by preconceptions, its purpose becomes scrambled, nonsensical, and misleading. So, how do we stop ourselves from thinking about it in a limited, preconceived way so as not to alter its programming?" Jodi held out her hands. "See, I'm doing it already. Thinking of it as a computer. I could end up creating an ethereal robot."

Graham smiled at the thought of a transparent metallic android, then scratched his head. "Judging by their shrines, the Victorian Order of Meonia may have tried to avoid labeling it by adopting multiple belief systems simultaneously: Egyptian, Chinese, Celtic, Roman."

"And us? What should *we* do?"

"The Heaths and Batemans were steeped in the strict religious values of their time. We don't have that problem."

"We don't?"

"What do *you* think is behind it all?"

Jodi spread her hands. "No idea."

"Me neither. So, we're probably okay."

Jodi ran a finger around the rim of her glass. "Is it safe to ask *how* it works?"

"Maybe it interacts with certain people, in certain places, at certain times."

"Such as?"

Graham decided to do some informed guess-

214

work. "People like Mary Biddulph, Mary Heath; maybe Laura Heath, Ormus le Guidon, and now us. Perhaps because we share a particular fascination with the unexplained and are open to unconventional ideas. Places like the Bridestones. Little Mary may not have been the only one to have kick-started events by entering the tomb; Ormus le Guidon and Mary Biddulph might have too. Times such as significant nexus points in history. Ormus lived at the start of the High Middle Ages when European civilization emerged from centuries of Dark Age turmoil. Mary Biddulph lived during the birth of science when people like Galileo began employing experimentation to understand the natural world, laying the foundations for the Industrial Revolution. And Mary and Laura Heath lived precisely when workable theories of electromagnetism were being established, leading to Einstein's relativity and quantum physics, and the age of electricity, radio transmissions, and modern technology."

"So why is it interested in *us*?" Jodi asked.

"Well, not to start a mystical order, perform rituals, or build shrines. If that's what it wants, it's chosen the wrong people."

"Absolutely." Like Graham, Jodi was no fan of organized *anything*."

"I think it wants us to know what happened to the Victorian Order of Meonia. At least to start with. So far, we've been led to learn about their Bridestones excavation, Mary Heath's childhood powers, and their discovery of the Spring Wood Priory vault."

"And we've been guided to those discoveries by

opportunely appearing strangers, convenient syn-chronicities, and…" Jodi realized the next item on her mental list didn't quite fit. "What's with the apparent reality shifts?" she said. "How would changing the date of the Biddulph fire or where the sword was kept help us along?"

Graham took a deep breath. "I think we'll have to come back to that."

Absently watching the traditional dancers, Jodi played back the day in her mind. "When, exactly, do you think reality shifted today?" she asked.

"No idea. Maybe when we were in the museum."

"And what about when the date of the fire changed?"

"Must have been when we were in the Biddulph Grange gardens, between the two times we looked at that information board in the tearoom."

"And did you feel anything? Either time?"

Graham thought back. "No. Nothing at all,"

"Me neither." Jodi finished the last of her wine. "I've just had a weird thought. These reality shifts might be happening all the time;.we just don't notice."

"That's a bizarre idea."

"And that's not all. What happened to the people who used to know that the fire occurred in 1897 or that the sword was not in the museum? Are they in another universe? And what about the two of us with different memories?"

Graham held up a hand. "You could go mad thinking about it."

Jodi decided not to. "Okay, so how to proceed?"

"Perhaps you should try another remote," Graham suggested.

"I had the vision of Spring Wood Priory only last night," Jodi recalled how her visions, at least those relevant to what they were doing now, were sporadic. "It may be some time before I get anything new."

Graham emptied his glass. "I think you get the necessary visions when the time's right. Each time we learn something new, we—"

"Open the next level. Like a video game?" Jodi interrupted.

Graham beamed. "Yes, something like that."

"And the reality flip concerning the sword implies we've completed level number—whatever we're on."

As if on cue, one of the gamers at the next table raised his phone and cheered. He had achieved *his* current objective.

* * *

Darkness. Then a dim light surrounds her. Jodi is floating down a narrow corridor, at the end of which stands a woman. Middle-aged, her dark hair tied up in a bun, she wears a long black skirt and a white, high-collared blouse. Jodi slows as she approaches, hanging weightless in the air. The woman's face is pale, but her large eyes seem vibrant and astute. Jodi realizes she is in Biddulph's Egyptian temple, beside its bench alcove. Suddenly, a second figure appears from behind her. Graham, dressed in black pants and a black leather jacket with a couple of bags slung over his shoulder, emerges from the entrance passage to walk right past her and the mysterious woman, apparently oblivious to their presence. The woman, however, appears to see him, turning in his direction as he enters the main chamber and leaves through the Swiss cottage exit. Jodi watches as the woman moves into the bench alcove, where there is no bench. Instead, the recess forms the entrance to another chamber, in which stands a life-size marble statue of what seems to be a Greek or Roman goddess, and a round stone pedestal, decorated with the busts of two winged girls, upon which stands a large hourglass set in a golden frame. The woman places her hand on the hourglass and looks directly at Jodi, a faint, sad smile on her lips, before turning and disappearing into the darkness as she descends a flight of stone steps leading down behind the pedestal.

Sitting on a wooden bench in the small park surrounding Birmingham Cathedral, near her hotel the following day, Jodi told Graham of her previous night's vision.

"You're sure the woman wasn't Mary Heath?" Graham queried.

Jodi shook her head. "Mary only reached 28; this woman was much older. Approaching 50, I'd say. And the clothing was *late* nineteenth century."

"The 1890s. A middle-aged woman associated with Biddulph Grange." Graham did the math. "Laura Heath? She died in 1897, aged 47."

"Exactly what I thought. I feel certain it was her."

"You think it was *really* Laura?" Graham said. "Not an image created by whatever's behind all this?"

Jodi broke some bread left over from breakfast and tossed it to the pigeons gathered around them. "She seemed very real. Like a conscious being. It even felt, for a moment, like we shared minds."

"And you think there's something important about the bench alcove?"

Jodi nodded. "The woman was standing right beside it. That's where you said Jenny was standing when she gave you the message about the B Stone, and didn't Tara have the feeling there was something there? As I say, there was a further, now-bricked-up chamber beyond the alcove's back wall in the vision. It has something to do with that."

"Any idea what?"

"Not exactly. But I felt the woman wanted us to know what happened after the Meonia group disbanded. If we return to the alcove, we'll trigger something."

"And *I* was in the vision!" Graham said, bemused.

"Yes." Jodi looked Graham up and down. "You were wearing exactly the clothes you are now. And you had those." She pointed to the bag and camera case hanging from his shoulder.

Jodi opened her phone and showed Graham a picture of a white marble statue: a woman with braided hair in a long gown, holding a large drinking horn in one hand, from the top of which cascaded bunches of grapes and berries. "Fortuna, the Roman goddess of fortune, holding the Horn of Plenty, the symbol of good fortune and prosperity," she said. "I searched online this morning to find a statue resembling the one in my remote. They're identical."

"Interesting. The very ethereal being associated with the Roman shrine under the old Rhododendron House of Biddulph Grange. The celeste of fate and fortune," Graham watched the large flock of pigeons gathered around their feet, squabbling for bread. "Fortuna, Bride, Chang'e, and all the rest, attributed with the power to change reality! Exactly what we've been experiencing."

At that moment, Graham's phone chimed. It was a message from his friend Clark, who had randomly picked the tarot card depicting the tunnel like the one in Spring Wood. Since that time, he had been fascinated by what Graham and Jodi were doing and was texting to say that he would, for the first time, be visiting Biddulph Grange later that day. Would they like to meet up?

"One hell of a coincidence," Graham said loudly, scattering the pigeons. "If there still *is* such a thing." He showed Jodi the text. "We were discussing the possibility of a concealed room at Biddulph Grange. Clark will be there today—an *expert* on old buildings."

A few hours later, accompanied by his friend Tom, Clark met with them in the Biddulph Grange parking lot, and together they made their way to the Egyptian temple. It was dark, rainy, and heavily overcast, with few other visitors braving the elements to visit the place that day. The four of them sheltered in the main chamber of the mock tomb, Graham filming with his phone camera as he explained the Ape of Thoth statue to Tom while Jodi was in the bench alcove asking Clark if he thought there might have been another room behind its back wall.

Clark wrapped his knuckles against the red, plaster-covered brickwork. "It's a thick wall, but the reverberation indicates a hollow space beyond." He moved around the alcove knocking on separate surfaces to illustrate the different sounds. "This is wood," he said, banging on the architrave to one side of the recess. He then knocked on a side wall. "This is solid stone." Returning to the rear wall, he rapped it again. "And this—"

"Is hollow," Jodi intervened. They could all clearly hear how the sound differed from wood or unyielding brick.

Clark nodded in agreement. "It's hollow. They've paved over something."

As Graham continued filming, and Jodi and Tom looked on, Clark put his ear to the wall and knocked on it again, saying the word "Hello," hoping the resonance of his voice might reveal further evidence of a concealed chamber. Discussing what might be hidden beyond the alcove, Jodi continued to tap the walls to deduce the extent of what seemed once to have been an opening. At the same time, Clark stomped his heel against the floor tiles, deciding that there might have been a flight of steps beneath, as Jodi had seen in her vision.

"What's behind this building?" Tom asked.

"An embankment," Graham explained. "The shrine is built into it. The steps round here lead up to the higher ground at the rear." He led the way past the Ape of Thoth chamber, along the shorter corridor, and up the stone steps into the dull, misty daylight.

Directly over the central chamber was the séance room. The ground above the bench alcove and whatever lay beyond it, however, was a piece of flat, overgrown wasteland around a foot higher than the level of the temple ceiling below. Together, they moved aside some of the brambles to reveal a wall, some six inches wide, in the form of a rectangle, around 12 feet square, extending out from the back of the temple.

"I'd say that these are the top of the now bricked-up chamber walls," Clark said, stooping down to examine the stonework. "I imagine it was filled in at some point. Perhaps because it became unsafe; however, some of it must still be hollow to account for the resonance when we knocked on the alcove wall."

"I think you're right," said Tom, kneeling at the top of the steps. "This looks like a lintel stone that once supported the chamber roof." He showed them how the slab forming the top step extended under the earth. Just below it was a horizontal gap around half an inch wide.

Graham came over and shone his phone light into the crevice. "There's an open space in there. It goes down some way." He took out a penny and dropped it through the gap. A second later, it clinked on something solid. "Sounds like a stone floor." He turned to Jodi. "Seems like your vision was right.

There *was* another room."

After Clark and Tom had left, Jodi and Graham sat in the Biddulph Grange café. Messing with his phone, Graham said, "I guess, as your remote was right about the extra chamber, you may also be right about Laura wanting us to know about what happened to the Meonia group."

Jodi nodded thoughtfully. "What are you doing?" she asked, indicating his phone.

"Playing back the video I shot in the temple. If we were meant to be there, and Laura does have a message for us, there may be something on film."

They watched the fifteen minutes of footage showing the interior and rear of the mock Egyptian tomb but saw nothing unusual. "Play back the part where we examined the alcove," Jodi said. "Maybe the camera has picked up coloration differences in the plasterwork, suggesting a bricked-up entrance." Graham obliged. The footage showed Clark talking and knocking on various surfaces before rapping on the rear wall. But the resolution was insufficient to distinguish anything of significance in the plaster. Jodi, though, tilted her head to one side, placing an ear closer to the phone. "Play it again with the volume higher. I think I hear something."

They replayed the footage showing Clark knocking on the side wall and the architrave with nothing unusual occurring, but when he knocked on the rear alcove wall, something seemed to knock back. It was faint, but immediately after the three occasions he hammered on the plaster three times in quick succession, three equally-timed rapping sounds could be heard, seemingly copying his own.

"Is that an echo?" Graham said.

"It can't be," Jodi took the phone and played the footage again. "There's no echo when Clark knocks on the side wall and the architrave."

Graham leaned over the table, intrigued. "You're right. Play it further."

After three successive raps on the wall, Clark puts his ear to the wall and playfully says "Hello" to check the chamber's reverberation. Immediately, a woman's voice can be heard, as if replying, also saying "Hello."

"Wow!" Jodi put down the phone as if it was possesedcontaminated. Graham picked it up and played back the entire sequence.

"It sounds spooky; I grant you. But it might just be someone else in the building copying us. A few visitors passed through."

"But no one was there when we were in the alcove." Jodi was certain.

"The place does echo strangely," Graham offered. "Someone could have been on the rear steps, where the narrow opening to the bricked-up chamber seems to be, and heard the knockings and voices, then rapped and spoke back."

"Let's check it out."

Back in the Egyptian temple, Graham stood just outside the bench recess, filming as Jodi rapped on the wall as Clark had done. No echo was heard or caught on film. Jodi then climbed the rear steps to knock and speak by the narrow opening at the top.

Still in the central chamber, Graham heard nothing. Try as they might, they could not reproduce what had been recorded.

"Do you think only the camera picked it up?" Jodi asked. "That it wasn't audible to the naked ear?"

Graham grinned. "Naked ear? Is that a thing?"

Jodi shrugged. "Well, you can say 'naked eye.'"

Graham cocked his head. "Fair enough. To answer your question. Who knows? We didn't notice anything at the time. We've had to fully turn the camera volume up to hear the rapping and voice. We could well have missed it. One way or the other, I'll take it as a sign that we should try something here. Are you up to sitting in the alcove and attempting another remote?"

Almost at once, Jodi finds herself standing on a broad, lush-green lawn. Before her is a large two-story building with leaded bay windows, steep gables, and a gray slate roof from which rise tall, red-brick chimney stacks. The walls of the lower floor are red brick like the chimneys, but those of the upper floor are plastered white between aged, black timbers.

The vision was brief but piercing. The image of the old building almost burned into Jodi's mind. "That was intense," she said as she regained her senses.

Graham listened as Jodi described what she had seen. "It sounds like an Elizabethan manor house," he said. "Sixteenth century, like from Shakespeare's time. Any idea where?"

Jodi shook her head. "No, but I'd certainly recognize it. I had the strong impression we should go there. It holds the answers."

"To what?"

"To what the Order of Meonia were trying to achieve."

Jodi could add nothing further, even after sitting quietly in the alcove for some time, trying to get another vision. Before they left, Graham wanted to get some extra footage of the Egyptian temple for a short movie. Jodi filmed him from behind as he entered the building along the central passageway, narrating as he walked before entering the main chamber and exiting into the dim daylight of the Alpine path.

That evening at Graham's home, the pair searched online for an Elizabethan, half-timbered building that matched Jodi's vision. Firstly, in the Midlands, then further afield, but to no avail. Some were similar, but Jodi was adamant that no photograph they viewed showed the manor house she had seen so vividly in her mind. Before Graham drove Jodi back to her hotel, they decided to review all the film and photos they had taken at Biddulph Grange that day.

"What's that?" Jodi said as she played her video of Graham guiding the viewer through the Egyptian temple. He leaned over to see her phone screen as she replayed the footage.

Passing between the flanking sphinxes, Graham enters the shrine beneath the winged sun disk. The building has no lighting, and little daylight penetrates the corridor from heavily overcast skies. As the camera follows Graham along the passage, he can barely be seen in the gloom. Then, as he enters the central chamber, a dim, gray shape seems to move in the darkness to his left, just behind him.

"Isn't that just a faint light reflecting off the wooden pilaster beside the alcove?" Graham suggested.

"No, you can make out the pillar here," Jodi replayed the footage and pointed to the screen. The shape is in front of it, right behind you. And it moves!"

Graham peered closer, screwing up his eyes. "I don't remember anyone else being there,"

"There wasn't. It was just before closing time, and almost everyone had left the grounds."

Graham copied the video onto his desktop computer to get a better view. When he increased the brightness and slowed the film, they were astonished. For all the world, the misty grey image appeared to be a female figure standing in the darkness. It appeared out of nowhere to turn in Graham's direction as he passed before fading from view as the camera moved on. Only the upper part of the woman was visible; the rest was shrouded in darkness. As they altered the contrast, they could make out that she seemed to be wearing a high-collared blouse and had her hair tied back in a bun. Her face, however, was in deep shadow. She was visible for about three seconds when the film was played at normal speed. Experts who later examined the film were divided. Some thought it was simply a trick of the light in the low illumination, but others felt it resembled a person standing in the darkness. Interestingly, when Graham posted the footage online to gain different opinions, as with the photograph of what seemed to be a little girl in the Hoar Cross Hall library mirror, only about half the people who saw it could see anything unusual, Graham and Jodi, however, could see it clearly.

"The high-collared blouse and the hairstyle, it looks like the woman from my remote last night. And she's standing exactly where she was in my vision." Jodi was about to say more when she placed a hand over her mouth. "Oh my god! In my vision, you walked right past her, and she turned to look at you. Just like what's happening in the film."

Graham realized the implications. "You had a vision of the future."

"Far more than that." Jodi stared intently at her friend. "In my remote, I saw the place as it was before the adjoining chamber was closed off—the past. As the woman entered the now bricked-up chamber, she was *also* in the past. But although you were in the present, she saw you. Me last night, you today, and Laura in the nineteenth century. We seem to be confronted with an overlap of different times."

Graham took a moment for the connotations to sink in. "That beats everything. Laura's no ghost. She's somehow communicating through time."

-12-

Wightwick Manor

The pair searched online for an Elizabethan, half-timbered building matching Jodi's vision, but to no avail. Some were similar, but no images they found showed the manor house she had seen so vividly in her mind. It was some time before Jodi returned to England, and things resumed.

It was the morning of October 10, 2022. They had made an early start to visiting various sites in the Biddulph area, hoping that Jodi might get more information concerning the elusive manor house. First, they stopped off at a location they had yet to visit: Gawton's Well, the third site on the alignment that included Spring Wood Priory and the Bridestones. In a wooded valley on the Knypersley estate, once owned by the Batemans, the well was encompassed by a grove of ancient yew trees deep within an unspoiled forest. It wasn't a well in the usual sense—a deep hole in the ground—but a natural spring flowing from the hillside. The water emerged from a hole in a lichen-covered stone wall, into two successive troughs cut from solid rock, before flowing away as a tiny stream.

The adjoined rectangular basins, with other walls on each side, were both about 4 feet square and 2 feet deep, while lines of small boulders flanked the rivulet. Early mist hugged the ground, and the dappled light filtering through the overhanging branches gave the dell an unworldly feel. The air was still and filled with the rich scent of fall; the only sounds were birds singing and the soothing babble of the spring.

Graham stood on the hillside just above the well where the surrounding evergreens were tied with colored ribbons left by visitors, while the forest beyond was brown, red, and gold, with autumn leaves.

"During the Middle Ages, most sacred pagan springs were Christianized and consecrated to saints," he said. "Somehow, this one got forgotten. Gawton's Well derives its name from a hermit who supposedly lived here, but that's a relatively recent legend. The spring's guardian was originally said to be a ghostly Druid who offered help to travelers. Possibly a folk memory of a time the place had been a Celtic shrine."

Jodi stooped down to run her fingers through the water. "It's certainly a magical place. How old is it?"

"The surrounding stonework is more recent, but the basins are ancient. Maybe 2000 years or more."

Jodi looked around her at the trees. "The forest is deciduous, meaning these yews—conifers—aren't native. They were deliberately grown."

"True. And a long time ago." As Graham stepped forward, a piece of card tied to one of the ribbons brushed against his face. He briefly glimpsed what was written on it and moved it aside. "Yews live for centuries; they're not even considered old until they've been growing for a thousand years. They've been known to live for three times that long. The Romans record that the Druids venerated these long-lived trees and planted them around sacred sites, so they likely created this grove."

"So, the place looks much as it did in ancient times." Jodi cupped water in her hand and took a sip.

Graham frowned. "It's supposed to have curative properties, but I wouldn't drink it."

"It's clear spring water." Jodi shook her head despairingly when Graham refused to try it himself. "Anyway. The well, the cave, and the Bridestones formed a single complex of Celtic shrines," she said. "For what purpose?"

"We can only guess. But I wouldn't mind betting it had something to do with fate."

At that moment, the tranquility was disturbed by a breaking twig. They turned to see a bearded middle-aged man, wearing a hooded jacket, waterproof pants, and hiking boots, descending the woody hillside above the well; he had a pack on his back and held a walking staff.

"Morning." His red face beamed as he greeted them in what seemed like a Scottish accent.

They exchanged pleasantries before he continued down the slope, following the stream. Then he stopped and turned. "You don't have much time," he said, gazing upwards.

They assumed he was referring to imminent rainfall. "We've got umbrellas," Graham said with a wave.

The man continued to stare at the sky. "October the thirteenth is three days away. By sunset then, I'd say." The man smiled, turned, and walked away into the trees.

"What happens on October thirteenth?" Jodi said, bemused.

"Beats me."

"Maybe his words are important, like the red-haired lady and the old man in the museum."

"He's probably eccentric."

"What did he mean about sunset?"

"Perhaps we should ask him."

They followed the man into the trees but were quickly bogged down in a muddy quagmire. By the time they navigated their way around it, the stranger had gone. As they plodded back to the well, with Graham saying that he doubted the man's odd warning meant anything, Jodi abruptly slapped a hand on his shoulder.

"October thirteenth!" she said.

Graham jumped, then shrugged.

"The day Mary Heath died!"

Graham stopped and turned. "You're right, but I can't see how—"

"October thirteenth—1872," she interrupted. "150 years ago! Exactly!"

Graham was about to say that he thought it was probably a coincidence when he remembered something. "At the well, a piece of card tied to one of the ribbons brushed against my face. It had a number on it—150."

They returned to the well and found the card. There were dozens of ribbons tied to branches surrounding the spring, some with attached cards holding messages, wishes, and words of remembrance. The one that Graham had seen was different: a simple white piece of card, the size of a postcard, bearing nothing but the number 150 written in large red numerals.

"I can't imagine what it might have meant to someone," Graham said, "but I'd say that, like the Queen of Hearts at the Bridestones, it's another synchronicity. And the man is another unwitting guide."

"Do you think he fell into a temporary trance like Jenny did all those years ago?"

"No idea. But whatever happened to him, together with this piece of card, the message is clear. We have three days to do something."

Having no idea what it could be, Jodi decided to attempt a remote. Sitting on the wall beside the spring, she stared at the narrow lip where the water flowed from the upper to lower basins. She was suddenly reminded of an old-fashioned hourglass, like the one in her vision, where the sand falls through a stem between two glass bulbs to measure time.

Graham broke her thoughts. "I wonder why there are two troughs, one after the other. Sacred springs and holy wells are usually single basins." Jodi was surprised when he added, "It's like an ancient timer."

"Like an hourglass. I thought that myself."

"I was thinking a water clock," but it's the same principle.

Suddenly, Jodi's eyes closed, and her head slumped forward momentarily. Then she shook, opened her eyes, and turned to Graham. "For just a second, in my mind, I again saw a vision of the Egyptian temple with the woman, Laura. Once more, she had her hand on the hourglass. Then she pointed to the sand flowing through it. She seemed to be speaking, but I heard no words. Instead, in my mind, I knew what she was trying to say. We must find the Heart of the Rose by sunset in just over three days."

Graham sat down next to her. "Why?"

"All I know is that after that, the window of opportunity closes—and time runs out."

Jodi could offer no further explanation and, despite an hour or so of trying, could not achieve a remote or experience another vision. Nevertheless, they agreed that the man's cryptic warning, the synchronicity of the number on the card, and the well independently and simultaneously reminding them of a timer, signified that for some unimaginable reason they must find the mysterious relic by sunset precisely one and a half centuries after Mary's death.

* * *

"My phone's GPS is going haywire," Jodi complained the following morning as Graham drove them north from Birmingham along the M6 motorway. They were heading for the town of Stafford to reexamine its county historical records, hoping for a lead on the Elizabethan building in Jodi's vision. They exhausted all other avenues of inquiry, and her remotes had been of no further help. Still, she felt it was crucial to find it.

Graham indicated to the glove compartment. "Try *my* phone." Although his vehicle was nifty, it was anything but smart. It was an old, basic model with nothing fancy: no parking sensors, cameras, or GPS.

"Just as bad," Jodi said after a moment. "Must be a dead zone."

Graham frowned. "I drive this road all the time. Never had trouble before." He glanced briefly at Jodi. "Anyway, we don't need the GPS. It would have been useful to be warned of congestion, but I know the way."

Jodi returned Graham's phone to the glove compartment and placed her own in one of the cup holders between the seats.

"Leave the motorway at the next exit and take the first turning, A454 west," the pleasant female voice of Jodi's GPS announced.

Jodi picked up the device. "It seems to be working now."

Graham wasn't convinced. "Maybe, but it's suggesting a completely wrong direction. Is there a traffic jam ahead?"

Jodi zoomed in on the map. "Doesn't seem to be."

"Where's it taking us?"

"There's no route indicated."

"But it told us to take the next exit." Graham decided to ignore the GPS and drove straight on.

"Continue on M6 until the next exit. Then take M54 west."

Graham and Jodi exchanged confused glances. The GPS now had a deep male voice, sounding almost riled.

"Does the voice usually change?" Graham asked.

"No. And it never sounds insistent."

Graham shrugged. "Then we'd better do as it says."

"Really?"

"Another bizarre synchronicity? Maybe it wants to take us somewhere."

"You think my phone's possessed?" Jodi said with an uneasy laugh.

Graham raised an upturned palm. "Perhaps it's being used by the *whatever.*"

"Is that even possible?" Jodi said. "No, forget that. These days, impossible stuff's happening all the time."

Although the map had now frozen, remaining unchanged on the phone's screen, not indicating where they were or where they were heading, the creepy male voice continued to direct them. Graham and Jodi repeatedly questioned it to see if it would answer, but without success. It just kept up the instructions in a monotone timbre—unless they took a wrong turn, then it sounded positively vexed. Eventually, they found themselves in Wolverhampton, some 17 miles south of their intended location, and the familiar female voice returned.

"Take the next turn on the right, and you will arrive at your destination."

They swung into a driveway where a signboard

welcomed visitors to *Wightwick Manor and Gardens*. Graham was already familiar with the estate (pronounced "Wittick"), having visited before, some years earlier. It was owned by the National Trust and open to the public.

"Does this place mean anything to you?" Jodi asked as they pulled into the parking lot.

"Not really. I know it was built by a wealthy industrialist sometime in the late nineteenth century. It's famous for its interior design of the Aesthetic movement: an extravagant, romantic style popular at the time."

"But nothing to do with the Heaths or the Order of Meonia?"

"Not that I know of. There are Pre-Raphaelite paintings on display—some by Edward Burne-Jones, I think, and wallpaper by William Morris—but that's nothing unusual for Victorian mansions of this area. Pre-Raphaelite artists like Burne-Jones and William Morris had wealthy contacts in the West Midlands."

"Well, for whatever reason, I'd say we're meant to be here." Jodi checked her phone. The GPS was back to normal.

After they had paid to enter the grounds, they followed a bush-lined pathway to emerge before the manor.

Jodi came to an abrupt halt to remain motionless in stunned silence. "This is it!" she said eventually. "The house in my vision."

They stared up at the old, two-story building. With its black-and-white, half-timbered upper and red-brick lower levels, leaded bay windows, steep extending gables, gray-tiled roof, tall chimney stacks, and a broad, well-tended lawn spread out before it, the place did indeed match Jodi's description. Although Graham had been here before, he hadn't considered it while searching online for what Jodi had seen during her remote. They had been looking for an Elizabethan manor. Wightwick was a *mock* Elizabethan manor built in much later Victorian times—no wonder they hadn't found it.

Graham searched online with his phone, quickly reading up on the place. "It was built in 1887 by Theodore Mander for his wife Flora," he summarized. "Canadian by birth, she was a patron of the arts, a feminist, a women's rights campaigner, and had more than a passing interest in the unexplained, being a practicing spiritualist and member of the Theosophical Society. She was fascinated by Tudor history, the reason her husband used his considerable wealth to build her this Elizabethan-style manor. The couple continued to live at their mansion home nearby; Wightwick was mainly used to accommodate and entertain Flora's wide circle of friends."

On entering the building, they learned from a guide that this group of friends included not only people associated with the Order of Meonia, such as the artist Edward Burne-Jones, the writer A. E. Waite, the poet W. B. Yeats, the textile designer Jane Morris, and the actress Florence Farr but none other than Laura Heath. The Heath and Mander families were partners in several business ventures, while Flora and

Laura were close companions around the same age. As far as Jodi and Graham were concerned, Wightwick Manor was precisely where they were meant to be. And they had been directed there in the most extraordinary way.

A broad, wood-paneled corridor led to the large, elaborate hall. Known as the Great Parlor, it was a spacious room featuring a grand piano, richly embroidered sofas, hand-carved armchairs, a lofty, wood-vaulted ceiling, and a balcony that would once have served as a musicians' gallery. The upper walls were faced with original William Morris wallpaper. On the lower walls, which were interspersed with book-shelves, stained-glass windows, and niches displaying expensive tableware, there hung paintings by some of the leading Pre-Raphaelite artists of the time. Off the main hall, short passageways led to the various rooms on the first floor or the ground floor as it is called in England. They were all similarly ornamented, the floors spread with exotic hand-woven Turkish carpets or laid with bright, exotically-decorated tiles. Everything was almost as it had been in Flora Mander and Laura Heath's time.

Jodi and Graham moved into the drawing room, with a prominent snooker table center place, the scent of old-style potpourri filling the air. On an alcove wall beside a bay window, there hung a painting showing a group of four women dressed in tattered garments sitting dejected on the ground, the others with their arms raised in anguish. Behind them, in the sky, was a whirling vortex of color, like a portal to another realm, which contained a scene of ancient classical buildings. Here, a young man was depicted playing the flute while a group of Greek-or-Roman-clad men and women danced to his tune.

"It was painted by the late Pre-Raphaelite artist Evelyn de Morgan in 1915," said a woman standing nearby. She was one of the official guides. "It portrays the artist's distress over the First World War. Called *The Mourners*, it depicts grieving war widows haunted by visions of past happiness."

"If it's to do with the war, why a scene from ancient times?" Jodi asked as she and Graham examined the picture more closely.

"The important thing is that it illustrates Evelyn's belief in spiritualism and the afterlife," said a male voice behind them. The pair turned to see that the guide had wandered off, to be replaced by a short, elderly, white-haired man in a scruffy black suit. "She was fascinated by ancient Greek and Roman mysticism, which is why she rendered the scene in that era." His voice was high-pitched and throaty.

"The vision in the sky looks like a portal to another world," Jodi said, assuming the man was another guide, although he looked and sounded familiar.

"Indeed." A thin smile formed on the man's lips. "Evelyn had been a member of an occult society called the Sphere Group. They believed they could open portals to other realms—even other times. They took their name from a magical mirror ball they claimed to possess, which was said to reveal the future. They were into all kinds of mythology but particularly revered Fortuna, the Roman goddess of fortune, fate, and time." He pointed to one of the female figures standing behind the flute player. "See here; the artist has painted her into the scene, holding the cornucopia—the Horn of Plenty—her emblem."

Jodi was immediately reminded of her vision of two nights before, in which she had seen the statue they identified as Fortuna. The figure behind the flute player closely resembled depictions of the goddess they had found. She decided to say nothing but realized by Graham's expression that he was thinking the same.

"We're familiar with the Sphere Group," she said. "Founded by Florence Farr. She'd been a member of another group—"

"The Golden Dawn," the man interrupted.

"I was going to say the Order of Meonia. Have you heard of it?"

Oddly, the man ignored her question. "There is quite a collection of Evelyn's paintings in the gallery of the old malthouse behind the manor. You should have a look." And with that, he turned and left through the passage leading to the dining room.

To Jodi's surprise, Graham immediately took off after him, bumping into a visitor and sending her flying. After apologizing profusely, he moved on and out of sight.

Entering the dining room, Graham found it packed with people listening to a lecture by a tour guide. It took a while for him to push his way through the throng, not seeing the old guy amongst them, before leaving through the only other exit, a corridor that led to the kitchens and then out into the rear yard. The strange little man was nowhere to be seen.

"Who was he?" Jodi asked as she eventually caught up with Graham outside.

"Well, he wasn't a guide. I just asked one of them. Only two male volunteers are working today, and they're both students."

"You think he might know about the Meonia group?" Jodi said, assuming that was why Graham had followed.

"Yes, but didn't you recognize him?"

"He *did* seem familiar."

"He's the same guy from the Tudor House Museum. The one who told us it was once the home of John Dee."

Jodi gasped. "You're right! I knew I'd seen him before. And he had the same weird, crackly voice."

They searched the manor and its grounds, repeatedly asking visitors and guides if they had seen a strange, elderly little man in an ill-fitting black suit. He would be hard to miss. But they drew a blank. It was as if he had never been there at all. A ghost? A projection? An impossibility? Whoever or whatever he was, he seemed to have given them yet another strange message. Visit the old malthouse gallery to view the Evelyn de Morgan works.

"The red-haired lady, the guy at the well, and this odd character—twice." Graham shook his head.

"And they just seem to vanish."

"Weird beyond weird."

"Do you know anything about Evelyn de Morgan?" Jodi asked as they crossed the yard to climb the outside steps of the old malthouse, following signs to the gallery.

"Nothing at all."

The small gallery was filled with Evelyn's paintings and exhibits of tiles and ceramic works by her husband, William. A guide was at hand to provide an account of the artists and their connection to Wightwick Manor. Evelyn was born in 1855, they learned. Although she came from a wealthy London family, she spent much of her time in the West Midlands, exhibiting her work in the large industrial towns of Birmingham, Dudley, and Wolverhampton. Here, she met Flora Mander, with whom she shared many interests, including mythology, spiritualism, mysticism, social reform, and women's rights. The two became close friends. When work on Wightwick Manor commenced in the mid-1880s, Evelyn and her husband were invited to work on its interior design, which included layout, flooring, and general ornamentation. After completion, the de Morgans were regular visitors to the manor, Evelyn sometimes staying for weeks.

Many of Evelyn's paintings involved figures from classical mythology, particularly goddesses and female protagonists; others included Arthurian or romanticized medieval themes. They were highly colorful, almost photographic, and astonishingly vivid, considering they had been painted over a century ago.

A large landscape painting was on the wall, facing

the gallery entrance. About 3 feet high and over 5 feet wide, it depicted a castle on the left and a town with a mill and waterwheel on the right, separated by a river winding its way from the hills beyond. In the foreground were two young men dressed in medieval tunics and headgear. Behind them, in front of the town, a beautiful, somber young woman wearing a sleeveless, silky robe stood with her hands on her head as if in frustration. She stood before a rose-pink, decorated marble bench, upon which lay an old book. At her feet were strewn pieces of expensive jewelry: a golden crown, a bracelet, a brooch, and several scattered pearls. The two men in the center of the picture were looking toward a second young woman standing before the castle on the left. With a serious expression and dressed in a long, green-and-blue gown, she held out what appeared to be a palm-sized, shiny metal ball. A white dove was perched on a stone terrace in the immediate foreground, closest to the viewer.

"Painted in 1892, it's called *The Garden of Opportunity*," said the guide. The elderly lady was highly enthusiastic. This was, they were to learn, her first week working here as a volunteer. "The right-hand side of the picture showing the town represents the riches of Evelyn's contemporary society," she continued. "The female figure in that section symbolizes Wisdom. She is in despair as the two men, wearing the robes of medieval scholars, have turned their backs on her, enticed instead by Folly, represented by the female figure on the left. The castle behind her depicts the ignorance of past times. She offers these students a shiny silver ball with a skull reflected in it, signifying nostalgia for the flawed ancient beliefs in magic and the supernatural. In her other hand, she holds a branch of *henbane*, a poisonous plant, signifying her true nature, while behind her on the stairway to the castle, a little devil peeps out from behind the banister—a further warning to those tempted by her wiles." It was clear the woman was reciting from a script. "The 'opportunity' Evelyn is alluding to is the choice between the modern world of knowledge and learning and the old ways of ignorance and superstition—the kind of foolishness that intrigued so many people of Evelyn's time."

Jodi needed clarification. "Surely Evelyn was *one* of those people," she said with a frown. "You said earlier that she was a spiritualist interested in mysticism."

It was the guide's turn to look confused. After a few "ums" and "errs," she turned and left, heading for another group of visitors.

"The usual contradictory interpretation, I'm afraid," said a middle-aged lady standing beside them, listening to the guide. "Evelyn spoke little about her work, meaning that after her death, the conventional artistic establishment could interpret it as they saw fit. The orthodox interpretation of Evelyn's works was formulated by traditionalists who disapproved of her paranormal and occult interests. Although they knew of her fascination with such things, they refused to acknowledge that it influenced her art—except as pure symbolism. As far as they were concerned, Evelyn de Morgan held the same societal views as them."

Graham and Jodi stared at the woman, sharing the same thought. Was she another inexplicable guide, like the red-haired lady at the Leek Museum or the strange little man in the scruffy black suit?

The woman apologized for interrupting, introducing herself as Simone, an art historian working on a paper concerning Evelyn de Morgan's works. "It annoys me how these volunteers are given a script offering such a dogmatic interpretation of the artist's paintings," she continued. "Any historian worth their salt knows that Evelyn de Morgan was a political reformer, a feminist, and a social rebel. Why would she paint a picture supporting the establishment and decrying the mystical?"

"What do you think the painting *really* means?" Jodi asked.

Simone was clearly pleased to be sharing her knowledge. "Firstly, there's the castle," she said enthusiastically. "It's hardly the place of darkness described in the orthodox interpretation. If anything, it's a romantic scene—it has bright, sandy walls, and the sun shines directly above it. The imp on the castle steps isn't a devil, but a motif Evelyn often employed in her pictures to depict the mysteries of fate." She pointed to the mischievous-looking little figure with grey skin, pointed ears, and a tail. "A celestial trickster, neither good nor evil, but one who spins the wheel of fortune to initiate new, but sometimes perilous, adventures of enlightenment."

"Like the tarot Fool?" Graham suggested.

And the Ape of Thoth, Jodi thought.

"Exactly." Simone held out a hand, indicating the right part of the painting. "Conversely, the town on the other side of the picture is a claustrophobic cluster of industrial buildings—mills, factories, and warehouses—not exactly the utopia the conventionalists imagine the artist to be depicting. In Evelyn's philosophy, such buildings were places of exploitation." Simone's attention shifted to the figure on the left, the guide called Folly. "The young woman offering the silver ball is actually the Roman goddess Fortuna."

Graham and Jodi exchanged glances. Fortuna!

"How do you know?" Graham asked.

Simone smiled. "Evelyn seldom named her paintings," she said. "*The Garden of Opportunity* was simply a working title chosen by the art gallery where it was first exhibited after the artist's death. Her sister Anna was unhappy with the title, insisting that Evelyn referred to the work as *Fortuna's Gift*. Namely this." Simone pointed to the silver ball the figure was offering the students. "And over here," she motioned to the ornamentation depicted on the marble bench, "are two representations of the Horn of Plenty, Fortuna's symbol. The branch in her hand, henbane, may be toxic, but it doesn't symbolize evil. In measured amounts, it was a hallucinogenic widely used in ancient Greece and Rome. Believed to open portals to other realms, it represented Fortuna's power to alter fate. As does the skull reflection in the silver ball. To the Romans, the skull was a symbol of chance, fate, and fortune."

"The two students being offered the ball. It's difficult to tell if they're men or women at first glance," Graham observed.

"They're androgynous, both male and female. Evelyn often portrayed scholars in this way, opposing the contemporary concept that learning was an exclusively male right. A bold statement. In her day, many people still considered higher education inappropriate for women."

"And the figure on the right?" Jodi queried.

"The goddess Athena. We see her sacred bird, the owl, carved on the bench behind her. In ancient Greece, she was the deity of civilization and city life. In Evelyn's painting, she is in despair. Her riches—the crown, bracelet, and other jewelry cast off at her feet—symbolize her contemporary industrial society, which she regarded as corrupt, opulent, and failing. The book discarded on the bench behind Athena symbolizes the kind of strict, inflexible, Victorian learning the artist abhorred."

"So, the right-hand side of the painting, including the town, is the negative side, and the left side the positive?" Jodi was puzzled. "Isn't the left-hand path regarded as evil?"

"It's only the left-hand side from *our* perspective." Simone held her palms up as if they were balancing scales, then crossed them. "For the protagonists in the painting, the castle is on the right. To me, the meaning of the painting is clear: Leave the stringent path of nineteenth-century materialism and learn from ancient mystery—magic and the the esoteric."

Graham noticed that the guide was now standing sternly beside a glass cabinet displaying ceramic works close by, obviously listening to their conversation. She was noticeably unhappy with what she heard. "You're familiar with Evelyn's occult interests," he said to Simone.

"Indeed. She and her husband spent years in spiritualism, even writing a book, *The Result of an Experiment*, concerning their attempts to contact the spirit world. She was also involved in far more controversial aspects of the supernatural. In 1896 she joined the Sphere Group, an occult lodge founded that year by the actress Florence Farr, remaining a member until it disbanded in 1902."

The Sphere Group again!

"Have you heard of the Order of Meonia?" Jodi asked. She paused to stare at Graham, pointing at two phoenixes facing one another depicted on the rose-colored bench in the painting. "The Meonia group's emblem," she elucidated.

Simone thought, then shook her head. "The Order of Meonia? It doesn't ring a bell."

"It was another esoteric lodge, one which met at Biddulph Grange in North Staffordshire from the 1850s," Jodi explained. "Florence Farr seems to have been a member. Perhaps Evelyn was too."

"As a close friend of Florence Farr, she may have been a member of such a group. The Fortuna figure holds a silver sphere, and the Sphere Group claimed to possess such a talisman. Florence was given it in the 1880s by MacGregor Mathers, the head of the

Golden Dawn. As Evelyn depicted it in this picture, we can assume she was already involved in Florence's occult life when it was painted in 1892."

"What exactly *is* the sphere?" Jodi asked, moving closer to the painting.

Simone shook her head. "No idea. I'm no expert on the occult, I'm afraid."

The strange little man had mentioned a "mirror ball." He said the Sphere Group was named after it and that they believed it could reveal the future. The reflective silver sphere the Fortuna figure holds could be described as a mirror ball. Graham took out his phone and began browsing as Jodi gave Simone a potted history of the Order of Meonia—leaving out the weird parts.

"Does the painting depict a real place?" Graham asked, putting away his phone.

"Not entirely, but the castle is Castle Hautdesert, a mythical fortress in the Arthurian tale *Sir Gawain and the Green Knight*. It was written in the fourteenth century by an anonymous author who probably came from the Peak District in the North Midlands as that's where the story is set."

Graham was already familiar with the work and knew that it concerned the adventures of one of King Arthur's knights. He nodded. "Yes, Gawain's adventures take place in Dovedale, a region of the southern Peak District comprising a stretch of the River Dove and its tributary, the Manifold."

Simone agreed, gesturing to the picture. "In the painting, the river that winds between the hills and past the castle represents Dovedale, as implied by the white dove in the foreground."

"Evelyn was familiar with the Peak District?" Jodi asked.

"Yes, she visited several times."

"Any idea where she stayed?" Graham said. He and Jodi both had the same thought. A mansion on the very edge of the Peak District—Biddulph Grange!

"No. We only know of her visits from her sister's diaries, which provide little detail."

Jodi moved away, her attention drawn to another painting on the same wall, the other side of a glass cabinet displaying ceramic works by Evelyn's husband. Some 3.5 feet wide and close to 4 feet high, the oil painting depicted an aging woman with greying hair. Dressed in a splendid gown of yellow and russet hues, she sat in an old, embellished wooden armchair.

On the wall, immediately behind her on the left of the painting, there hung a tapestry depicting figures in medieval clothing. On the extreme right, there was an open doorway in which stood what appeared to be a young female angel dressed in a calf-length, light-blue, chiffon gown, playing a wind instrument resembling two pipes. The seated woman seemed deeply tired, staring forlornly down at a large hourglass set in a golden frame upon which she rested her right hand. The hourglass stood on a round stone pedestal, which appeared green jade, decorated with the busts of winged women, one to either side.

"An hourglass, exactly like the one in my vision!"

Jodi said excitedly as Graham joined her. "Even the pedestal's the same, with the winged girls."

"The painting's called *The Hourglass*—at least that's the name it's known by." Simone had joined them. "It's something of a mystery," she continued. "Evelyn revealed nothing about it. Even her sister thought merely that it depicted an aging woman close to death, the sand running through the timer counting down her remaining days."

"Who's the winged woman in the doorway?" Graham asked.

"I've often wondered that," Simone said. "She's playing a double-reed pipe known as an aulos, the instrument you often hear in medieval music with a modulated drone, something like bagpipes."

"And the winged women on the pedestal?"

"They're angels."

"But they have naked breasts," Jodi said, surprised.

"Evelyn often depicted angels naked." Simone smiled. "Probably to annoy the Church."

"When was it painted?" Graham asked.

"Between 1904 and 1905. The model was Jane Morris, the wife of textile designer and Pre-Raphaelite artist William Morris."

Jane Morris! Yet another person they'd linked to the Order of Meonia.

Jodi moved close to examine the face of the woman in the picture. "Who's the character she's portraying?"

"No one knows. That's the mystery. Time itself,

maybe." Simone glanced at her watch. "Talking of time, I should be going."

Having exchanged contact details and phone numbers, Simone left the gallery to descend the outside steps. After a few seconds, Graham and Jodi followed her to the top of the stairway to see where she was going. Was she another bizarre, disappearing specter like the old man and the red-headed woman? Evidentially not. In the courtyard, she met up with other women making their way toward the main house.

"Well, it's certainly another synchronicity," Jodi said as they returned to the gallery. "She just happened to be here to explain the paintings and offer invaluable information about the artist. Simone, together with the crazy GPS and the weird little man, Fortuna, and an hourglass depicted in the paintings! Way, way, beyond coincidence. We're meant to be here."

Graham agreed. Still looking at the painting, he said, "Simone reminded me that the Sphere Group was founded in 1896. It hadn't occurred to me before, but that was right after the Biddulph Grange fire. At least in the reality we now find ourselves in. Florence Farr was almost certainly a member of the Order of Meonia. Maybe she began the Sphere Group hoping to continue their work once the group ran into problems following the blaze." He turned to Jodi. "Perhaps that's what we've been led here to discover."

Jodi remained silent for a moment. "Possibly. But I think there's more."

Graham began pacing as he continued to speculate, eliciting a concerned expression from the official guide, who was watching them suspiciously from the gallery door. "I assume the answers lie with Evelyn de Morgan. From what we've learned, I reckon it's safe to say she was involved with the Order of Meonia. She spent time in the southern Peak District, close to Biddulph Grange. She was a friend of Florence Farr and Flora Paint and presumably knew Laura Heath by association. And she was engaged enough in their occult world to know of the silver sphere in 1892 when she depicted it in the Fortuna painting. That was well before the Sphere Group began, and the amulet became public knowledge. But it was during the period the Meonia group was still in existence."

Jodi's gaze turned to the Fortuna painting. "The silver sphere. I wonder what it is."

"It was called the Orbuculum," Graham said. "I looked it up when Simone was talking. It was a talisman for supposedly seeing the future, like a crystal ball, just like the old guy said. It once belonged to John Dee. Maybe we should try to find—"

Jodi suddenly seemed to have drifted off. She was now staring at *The Hourglass* painting with a strange expression as if she was looking right through it, at something far beyond.

"Jodi." Graham gently shook her shoulder. "Jodi!"

After a few anxious moments, she blinked as if clearing her vision.

"Are you okay?"

"Er, yes." She looked at Graham, seemingly still dazed. "That was weird. I was looking at the picture… Suddenly, an image from the other night's remote of the Egyptian temple was superimposed over it." Jodi was speaking in staccato statements as if not fully awake. "The woman from my vision … I'm sure it was Laura … and the figure in the painting … both had their right hands resting on the hourglass…"

Jodi's eyes refocused as she snapped from her reverie. Graham suggested she sit, leading her to a bench against the opposite wall.

"Do you know what it means?" he asked when Jodi had recomposed herself.

Jodi explained that during the vision, impressions had formed in her mind. "I can't explain it, but I know something about what happened when the Order of Meonia disbanded. Laura handed leadership over to someone else."

"Florence Farr?" Graham said when Jodi stopped talking.

"No, she was just a figurehead." She seemed deep in thought.

"Evelyn?" Graham suggested.

Still seated, Jodi looked up at Graham and then at *The Hourglass* painting. "The woman in the picture," she said. "That's why their hands were superimposed. She was the one that Laura handed it on to and who eventually hid it after the Sphere Group disbanded in 1902."

"'It!' You mean the Orbuculum?" Graham asked.

"No. *The Heart of the Rose.*"

Graham was not expecting that. "I thought Laura hid it."

"The memorial pamphlet said only that she 'assured its safety.' My strong impression is that she handed it on to her successor, the woman in the painting. That's why their hands were superimposed."

"The woman in the painting? Simone said that no one knows whom she's supposed to be," Graham recalled.

Jodi leaned forward, half-covering her face with one hand as if immersed in contemplation. After a while, she said, "I think the reason why Evelyn never revealed whom it was *supposed* to be, was that it wasn't *supposed* to be anyone."

Graham held out his hands. "Sorry. You've lost me."

"It wasn't *supposed* to be anyone because it depicted the model herself."

Graham thought back to what Simone told them. "Jane Morris?"

"Yes."

It made sense. She was Laura's close friend and almost certainly a member of the Order of Meonia.

"So, you think Jane Morris eventually hid it once the Sphere Group disbanded."

Jodi nodded firmly. "Definitely. That's what I feel."

"Any idea where?"

"No. But I think that's why we're here." Jodi stood up and walked over to *The Hourglass* painting. Graham followed. "Seeing this picture triggered the vision and then—what would you call them? Impressions. I think this is what we're meant to see. Evelyn knew Jane Morris. She was one of her closest companions. She knew what became of the Heart. I'm certain of it. And she left a cryptic message in this painting. Don't ask me how I know, but I'm sure *The Hourglass* reveals the secret location of the Heart of the Rose."

-13-
The First Wave

Next morning, October 12. Just a short walk from Jodi's hotel, the Birmingham Art Gallery housed one of the world's largest collections of Pre-Raphaelite paintings. Most of the museum was closed for renovations, but the restaurant, gift store, and a few galleries remained open. Its core exhibition area was the Round Room, built in 1885, a large circular gallery with an ornate domed ceiling and an 11-foot bronze statue of an angel at its center. Here, an exhibition of photographs celebrating the people of modern Birmingham was presented on display boards set against the lower walls, in front of which were viewing benches where Jodi and Graham sat, leafing through books bought in the gallery gift store to learn more about the extraordinary life of Jane Morris.

Born into a low-income family in 1839, Jane Morris started life with nothing. Her father, Robert Burden, was a lowly stableman, and her mother, Ann, was a domestic servant working for a wealthy family in Oxford. Jane became a humble lady's maid, but everything changed in October 1857, when she was 18.

While attending a play with her sister at a local theater, she was approached by the Pre-Raphaelite artists Edward Burne-Jones and Gabriel Rossetti. Having been commissioned to work on murals at the Oxford Union debating society, they needed new models and, struck by her appearance, offered Jane a job. Jane, or Janey as she was known to her friends, soon became the most famous and sought-after artist model of the time. Considered to embody the Pre-Raphaelite ideal of beauty, she modeled for numerous contemporary painters, her image adorning the walls of galleries, public places, and stately homes throughout the land. In 1859 she married the wealthy Pre-Raphaelite William Morris, whose tapestries, textiles, and wallpaper designs epitomized the late nineteenth-century Arts and Crafts interior design movement.

Jane and her husband seemed to have enjoyed an open relationship. Having two homes—one in London and the other at Kelmscott Manor in the Cotswold Hills of the southern Midlands—the couple spent much of their time apart. Jane would later admit that, although she loved her husband, she was never *in* love with him. As for William, he was married to his work. He pretty much had to be. As well as being an artist and designer, he was a poet, novelist, printer, translator, publisher, architect, and social activist. The Morris' marriage was one of convenience: Jane made William the envy of his peers—she was a supermodel of the time—while his wealth and influence helped to change her life beyond belief.

Having had no formal education, Jane decided to

educate herself. She filled Kelmscott Manor with books and manuscripts and read profusely. She also used her fame and her husband's sway to access colleges and centers of learning, usually inaccessible to women. Jane was highly intelligent and seemed to have a photographic memory. She absorbed the subjects of history, philosophy, and the classics to the remarkable extent that within a few years, she could impress—even outargue—university professors. She became fluent in French and Italian, as well as the ancient languages of Greek and Latin. And to top it all, she became an accomplished pianist.

Moreover, she reinvented herself to pass in contemporary high society. It was said that her acquired graceful manners and erudite speech were those of a queen, allowing her to move freely in aristocratic circles. Her almost miraculous transformation inspired the playwright George Bernard Shaw to write *Pygmalion*, later adapted into the musical *My Fair Lady*. Jane Morris inspired Eliza Doolittle, the poor working girl who was taught to pass for royalty. Jane, though, was so much more. Unlike Shaw's protagonist, for the most part, she taught herself.

Ultimately, Jane found her calling as a celebrated textile artist and interior designer, creating furnishings to rival those of her famous husband. In 1875, when Jane was 36, William started the textile and decorative arts business Morris & Co. The "Co" being Jane. However, although William wanted his wife's artistic and design talents acknowledged, influential corporate buyers insisted that her work be credited to her husband. It was considered better for business. Although she was eventually recognized for her work, during much of her life, Jane was known chiefly as an "embroiderer," even though she designed hangings, furnishings, tapestries, prints, stained-glass windows, and decorative paneling. In truth, she was one of the leading British designers of the late nineteenth century.

"Embroiderer! Makes her sound like a humble seamstress," Jodi said, irritated by the all-too-familiar Victorian misogyny.

Graham agreed, pointing to a passage in the book on his lap. "It says here that many of her works are *still* attributed to William Morris."

Jodi shook her head. "Anyway, how was she associated with Evelyn de Morgan?"

Graham opened another book he'd been flicking through earlier. "According to this, even though Evelyn was sixteen years Jane's junior, the two were firm friends. Evelyn was the favorite niece of Pre-Raphaelite artist John Roddam Spencer Stanhope— apparently, he insisted people use his full name— indeed, he taught her. And Stanhope was bosom buddies with painters Rossetti and Burne-Jones. He was involved in the Oxford Union murals project for which Jane first modeled. Evelyn had therefore known Jane virtually as an aunt since she was a child. Jane was Evelyn's confidant, mentor, and friend. As expected, they shared interests, passions, and pursuits. Like Jane, Evelyn mixed with progressives, women's rights campaigners, suffragists, political activists, and those fascinated by mysticism and the supernatural. It seemed that Evelyn de Morgan was Jane's protégé."

"Remind me again how Jane Morris was connected to the Order of Meonia," Jodi said.

The previous night's online research and that day's reading revealed many new details concerning the life of Jane Morris. However, Graham was already familiar with how she likely became involved with the Meonia group. "It started in the mid-1870s," he said. "In that year, Morris & Co formed a commercial partnership with Wardle & Co, a dye-manufacturing and textile-printing company in Leek. As you know, that's only seven miles from Biddulph Grange. Jane and William Morris spent much time staying in the town, at the home of the owner Sir Thomas Wardle and his wife, Lady Elizabeth. Like Jane, Elizabeth was a businesswoman and designer. She managed her own company, one of England's leading producers of fashionable fabrics, supplying some of the country's major department stores. She even had a store in London's classy Bond Street. Thomas Wardle was a business associate of his close neighbors, the Heaths, and Elizabeth was a member of a local suffragist movement to which Laura Heath belonged. Therefore, through Lady Elizabeth, Jane knew Laura Heath and probably joined the Order of Meonia."

"So, you think both Jane *and* Elizabeth were involved with the Meonia group," Jodi said.

"That's right."

"With their husbands?"

"Unlikely. They must have known of the group, but it's doubtful either Sir Thomas or William Morris was actively part of it. The pair were engrossed in commercial projects, developing new dying techniques for fabrics and wallpaper. Jane and Elizabeth would stay at Biddulph Grange while their husbands were busy at the Wardle factory in Leek. Nearly all the husbands of the Meonia women were absent from the scene. Flora Mander's husband, Theodore, was absorbed in his paint manufacturing business. Indeed, he specifically built Wightwick Manor for his wife to pursue her interests and mix with her friends. While the husbands of three of them weren't even in the country: Barbara Bodichon was married to a French physician from Algiers, with whom she only spent the winter months; Mary Heath's surgeon husband James spent nearly all his time in India; and Florence Farr was married to fellow actor Edward Emery who spent virtually their entire marriage in America."

"What men *were* involved with the Order of Meonia?" Jodi asked.

"We know from the memorial pamphlet that Laura Heath's husband Robert was. As was Bateman's son Robert. Edward Burne-Jones was almost certainly involved, as were the author A. E. Waite and the poet W. B. Yeats. Apart from them, Evelyn's husband William probably was too. The Morgans worked closely on interior design projects and shared a common interest in women's rights, spiritualism, and the supernatural. That's about it."

Jodi stood up to take a panoramic view of the nineteenth-century paintings adorning the walls around them. "You say they were 'suffragists,' not 'suffragettes.'" Is there a difference?"

Graham smiled. "That confused *me* at first. Suf-fragists were the early votes-for-women campaigners. The more militant activists, like the Women's Social and Political Union founded in 1903, those engaged in direct action and civil disobedience, were known as suffragettes. I didn't discover this until last night, but Flora Mander of Wightwick Manor was president of the Staffordshire Suffragist Alliance, of which Eliza-beth Wardle and Laura Heath were members. Yet an-other link between Wightwick Manor and Biddulph Grange."

Jodi continued to gaze at the paintings around her, many depicting women as angels, warriors, and classical goddesses. "All the women we know, or sus-pect, to have been involved with the Order of Meonia shared more than simply a fascination with the mysti-cal." She turned to Graham. "They all had the same freethinking, feminist views. They were strong, inde-pendent women with commercial interests, managed businesses, ran estates, and were political campaign-ers."

Graham nodded. "They were what have been termed 'first-wave feminists.' An informal but wide-spread movement advocating women's rights. By the end of the nineteenth century, they were more for-mally established as international organizations that campaigned for female suffrage. They were remark-ably successful. From the 1890s, many countries inde-pendently began granting women the right to vote." Graham looked at his phone and read through a list on a website he'd found. "Australia 1902, Finland 1906, Norway 1907, Denmark 1915, Canada 1917. And immediately after the First World War, the UK, Germany, the USA, Jamaica, Belgium, Armenia, and even the newly-formed Soviet Union, gave women the vote. By the early 1920s, countries as far and wide as India and Mongolia in Asia, El Salvador and Guatemala in Central America, and Hunan and Guangdong provinces in China gave women the vote. And that's only a partial list."

Like Graham, Jodi had been unaware of how widely and concurrently women had secured the right to vote in the early twentieth century. "Did any women get into power?" she asked.

Graham scrolled through the site. "They did," he said after a moment. "Some of the most influential countries in the world saw women entering government. Just a few examples: In the USA, in 1916, Jeannette Rankin of Montana became the first woman elected to Congress, four years before women even got the vote; in 1918, in the UK, a law was passed to allow women to stand for election, and in 1919 the first women MP, Nancy Astor, took her seat in the House of Commons; and in Germany, in 1919, only a month after female suffrage became law, no less than 36 women were elected to the National Assembly."

Jodi and Graham continued searching online to learn of other remarkable achievements of the first-wave feminists in the late nineteenth century. There had been feminists before, they discovered, writers and activists working independently or within other organizations, such as the missionary, anti-slavery, and social-reform groups. However, the first truly structured feminist organizations were founded in the mid-1880s. It began in 1865 with the German Association of Female Citizens in Germany. The American Equal Rights Association was founded in the USA the following year. In 1868, the global women's movement, the International Association of Women, began in Switzerland. And in Scandinavia, the women's movement, the Danish Women's Society, started in 1871. Other countries throughout the world followed suit. The first was the Langham Place Circle in 1857, named after their headquarters in central London. They not only advocated female suffrage but campaigned for women's property rights and changes regarding their access to employment and education. They even started the world's first feminist magazine, *The English Woman's Journal*, to advocate female rights and highlight equality issues.

"Tracing it right back, it all seems to have begun when the Langham Place Circle's founder, Barbara Bodichon, published her extremely influential *Brief Summary of the Laws of England Concerning Women* in 1854," Graham said, reading from the site on his phone. Suddenly, he raised his eyebrows and opened his mouth in stunned silence.

Jodi didn't notice, as something had abruptly occurred to her. "When did she start work on the book?" she asked.

"Err, sorry." Graham was deep in thought. "1851."

"The same year the Meonia group began."

Graham finally voiced his revelation. "Barbara Bodichon! She was in the Order of Meonia. Remember, along with Maria Bateman, she was one of its founders. She was the Pre-Raphaelite artist and teacher, the friend of Edward Burne-Jones, who tutored Robert Bateman at Biddulph Grange. She painted the only known picture of what might have been the Order of Meonia. The one showing them gathered in a valley wearing white, hooded robes."

Jodi jumped to her feet. "For some time," she said excitedly, "I've felt that there was a link between the Meonia group and early feminism. And not only the campaign for voting rights." She began picking up their books. "We should find somewhere better to study. We need to know more about how things began changing for women at the time."

They found a quiet, empty reading room in the art gallery, set themselves up at a table, opened their laptops, and spent the rest of the morning researching and making notes. They were astonished to discover how much *had* changed for women in the late nineteenth century. Before this time—except for a few notable exceptions—women worldwide had virtually no rights. They could not govern, had no say in who ruled, and all they possessed belonged to their father, husband, or a male guardian. In most countries, it was legal and acceptable for a man to beat his wife. And outside the home, few women had any role in contemporary culture. Although there were occasional women writers, most under pseudo names, the work of female artists hardly ever got commissioned, bought, or exhibited. Women's involvement in business and academia was virtually unheard of, while working-class women didn't enjoy the meager rights granted to their male counterparts. Then—after the activities of Barbara Bodichon and the Langham Place Circle—things began to change.

In 1867 the first suffragist organization was founded in London; after that, the women's rights movement expanded rapidly. In 1870 the British parliament passed the first-ever act allowing women to legally keep the money they earned rather than hand it over to their husbands or male guardians. Furthermore, it enabled them to own property and assets and directly inherit wealth. From then, a woman was legally entitled to run her own company and retain business interests. In 1888, the TUC, the federation of trade unions in England and Wales, accepted that women had the right to equal pay; there was to be a long road ahead, but it was an astonishing U-turn by the male representatives of working people at the time. And in 1891, it was finally outlawed for a husband to beat his wife. The occasional female artist had previously been recognized in the arts, but by the late 1800s, there were over twenty famous, regularly-exhibited female painters in the Pre-Raphaelite movement alone. As for businesswomen: by the First World War, around twenty-five percent of all companies registered in England were owned by women, and many more held management positions. Education rapidly opened for girls. Boys' boarding schools had long existed, but in the mid-1800s, similar girls' schools began to appear. The second half of the nineteenth century saw not only the establishment of schools open to girls but universities began to accept women. The first university in the UK to award degrees to women was the University of London in 1878. After that, nearly all new universities founded in late Victorian times were co-educational. By 1920, virtually every university in the UK accepted women and awarded them degrees. And all this was by no means just a British phenomenon. Similar dramatic changes were happening concurrently in the USA, Europe, and other areas of the world.

Such fundamental liberties may not sound much by today's standards, but considering what existed before, they were revolutionary. Throughout history, throughout most of the world, women had never attained such rights. Even in the early, so-called democracies, like the Greek states and the Roman Republic, women had no say and no representation; they received no education and were utterly subject to the authority of a man, be it a father, husband, master, or brother. In the later kingdoms of medieval Europe, women of every class were, for all intents and purposes, as much possessions as cattle, tools, and land. The Renaissance and the supposed Age of Enlightenment that followed the Middle Ages brought little change. As for the following alleged Age of Reason: after successful revolutions, the US Constitution of 1788 and the French Constitution of 1791 both failed to address female rights, while in the United Kingdom, in the radical Great Reform Bill of 1832, women were only explicitly included to *deny* them rights (for the first time, they were formally and legally *excludea* from any right to vote or participate in politics; before this time there were rare instances where certain privileged women *coula* vote).

"It's astonishing just how rapid and widespread all this was." Graham stretched his fingers, sore from so much typing and scrolling. "It went on hold for a while during the upheavals following First World War: The Russian Revolution, the social turmoil of the 1920s, the Great Depression, the Spanish Civil War, the rise of dictators like Hitler, Mussolini, and Stalin, and of course World War Two. Nevertheless, the wartime years made it abundantly clear that women were just as capable of working in and managing industry as the men who'd gone off to fight. It took the 1950s for things to stabilize, but the 1960s saw the birth of what's known as 'second-wave feminism' and the gradual improvement for women in many parts of the world that followed. There's still a long way to go. However, the point is this second wave was essentially a resumption of the first. And the entire feminist revolution, from Victorian times to the present day, all began in 1851—with a member of the Meonia group."

"Not just one!" Jodi intervened animatedly, pointing to a webpage she'd found. "Besides Barbara Bodichon, Maria Bateman was also involved in establishing the Langham Place Circle. It seems that founding members of the first feminist organization and the

Order of Meonia, the first Victorian occult society, were the same."

Graham was taken aback. "That can't be a coincidence. The Order of Meonia began following little Mary Heath's revelations after she entered the Bridestones' tomb. But it was Maria and Barbara who seemed to have started the group. Both events occurred in May 1851." There was a pause while Graham consulted the webpage concerning Barbara Bodichon. "Then in August that year—incidentally, the same time Mary met Lewis Carol—Barbara began work on her influential treatise."

"I don't know if Mary Heath's revelations helped inspire feminism," Jodi said, "but the activities of the Order of Meonia might have been responsible for the rapid rise and widespread success of the feminist cause around the world. It all happened so astonishingly fast and was so widespread. We always wondered about the primary purpose of the Meonia group. Okay, they did magic, sought to control fate or whatever, but what for? Why were they doing it?" Jodi stopped for a moment to think the scenario through. "What if their mystical activities prepared the ground for feminism? Altering fate so the world would be more receptive to change. Think about it. To get any changes to the law would require—certainly to begin with—the support of men. Powerful men. Why did enough men in government in so many countries suddenly support women's rights? Undoubtedly, some were swayed by the arguments of the new feminist organizations. But for it to happen so quickly and simultaneously in so many places worldwide, it needed a revolutionary shift in attitude, not of everyone, but still an extraordinary number of men in positions of power."

"You're saying that, in some unbelievable, mystical way, the Order of Meonia influenced the world on a cognitive level?" Graham said.

"Not so unbelievable. Just think what we've witnessed—bizarre changes to reality. Their ceremonies, or whatever they did, might have awakened certain people and maybe even selectively changed reality here and there to bring about a desired goal they all shared—women's rights. Activism and mysticism, a two-pronged approach."

"You think they could control the weird stuff we've been experiencing? That would be beyond extraordinary." Graham blew out a long breath as he considered the possibilities. "So, how come reality seems to be shifting, seemingly randomly, around us now?"

Jodi shrugged. "I imagine we've somehow attracted the attention of whatever force empowered the Meonia group."

Graham leaned forward, his head resting on one hand. "Whatever it was that little Mary awakened at the Bridestones?"

Jodi nodded. "The person buried there seems to have been a Druid priestess who died around the year 500—a priestess of Bride. Someone believed to have channeled the celeste's power. At least the power she represented. What if, like that Druidess, Mary Heath

channeled the same power? The influence, energy—
the whatever—that the Celts referred to as Bride?"

"We can't keep calling it the whatever." Graham
thought for a moment, recalling an earlier discussion.
"Then again, maybe it's best we don't give it a name.
Remember what we discussed about labeling it or
conceiving of it in a particular way, limiting, negating,
or changing its nature."

"Anyway," Jodi said. "What do you think the
Meonia group would have done in the belief they
could alter fate?"

Graham made an educated guess. "Certain incantations, rituals, meditations, performed at specific
times. The same as occultists like John Dee and the
Rosicrucians—the earlier Order of Meonia—did in
the late sixteen and early seventeenth centuries. If
they found the Rosicrucian vault as we suspect—
which contained Kabbalistic talismans and inscriptions—the Victorian Meonia group had ready access
to such esoteric knowledge at hand."

"We've already concluded that they used the mystical beliefs of various ancient cultures to supplement
their incomplete knowledge of Celtic mysticism. So,
do you think they also incorporated whatever Kabbalistic wisdom they discovered in the vault?"

"That would be my guess."

Jodi leaned back in her chair. "If the Meonia
group was recreating, in their way, what the ancient
Druids had done, wouldn't Biddulph Grange itself
have to have been on a sacred Celtic site?"

Graham thought it through. "You're right. Maybe

Biddulph Grange just 'so happened...'" He used his fingers to form air quotes, "to be on an already existing ancient power grid, so to speak. The Cloud, the hill of the double-setting sun, one of Britain's most sacred Druidic sites, rose above the Bridestones. The line—call it a ley line if you like, although 'geomantic alignment' is probably better—linking the Bridestones, and Gawton's Well passes right through the Spring Wood Chapel site, possibly once a sacred cave, halfway between the two. Which is where the Templars 'just so happened...'" air quotes again, "to have built their secret vault. And finally, there's the line formed by the Wellingtonia Avenue, which leads directly to Biddulph Grange along the alignment of the midsummer sunset."

On her laptop, Jodi opened a satellite view over the Biddulph countryside, imagining the arrangement of the ancient monuments. "So, if the other sites—the Cloud, the Bridestones, Gawton's Well, and the location of Spring Wood Chapel—were all venerated by the ancient Celts, so probably was whatever once stood at Biddulph Grange."

"Perhaps a huge stone circle or something like that," Graham suggested.

"And this grid or complex of ancient monuments could tap into the power of Bride." Jodi clapped her hands together in conclusion. "And the shrines, perhaps even the layout of the grounds, were all constructed to utilize, influence, or channel this force."

"Exactly," Graham agreed. "Which explains why their principal shrine, the underground Roman Fortuna chamber, was constructed at the house. A particular part of the house—at the very end of the Wellingtonia Avenue. Remember how the catacomb is thought to have stretched from the Rhododendron House to under where the tea terrace is now? That is smack bang at the end of the Wellingtonia line, which started at the priory and ran across the front of the house to terminate at the tea terrace. Directly below it is probably where the focal point, perhaps an altar, was located."

"Where we think the Heart of the Rose was kept." Jodi tilted her head to one side. "But how would they have known about an old stone circle or something similar, having been there, to build the Grange on that spot?"

"Maybe Mary Heath told them."

"But Biddulph Grange was already built when little Mary entered the tomb."

Graham ran a hand through his hair. "Good point. Then perhaps the Batemans had been drawn to that location, as might Mary Biddulph two and a half centuries before, by something that wanted them involved. Just like we've been drawn to places by synchronicities, weird circumstances, and quirks of fate."

Something still bothered Jodi. "We speculated that little Mary's gifts resulted from her entering the Bridestones tomb and that the power of Bride was directed by whatever activities the Meonia group conducted. What was the purpose of the all-important Heart of the Rose?"

"Maybe we're soon to know." Graham closed a

book he was holding with a thwack. A man who had just entered the room jumped, turned, and left. "Perhaps now we finally know the purpose of the Meonia group—if we're right, to mystically adjust fate in favor of women's rights—we might be ready to find it."

"And we only have a day and a half."

-14-
Morgana

They decided to have lunch in Jodi's hotel restaurant. Set beneath a huge glass ceiling, it was a plush, elegant space with white tablecloths, velvet-covered chairs, and a grand piano in one corner. As breakfast was served in another part of the hotel and Jodi had been eating out, this was the first time they had seen this splendid room. They were, therefore, surprised to find the walls decorated with copies of Pre-Raphaelite paintings, which they learned from their waiter, were all either in the Birmingham Art Gallery or by artists associated with the industrial Midlands. He showed them to a table set against one wall, upon which one of the colorful Victorian pictures hung directly over where they were seated. It depicted a young woman with flowing red hair, green and yellow robes, a purple cloak, and a leopard-skin apron, surrounded by bottles, manuscripts, a flaming brazier, and magical signs. She stood holding out a burning lamp shaped like a golden dragon; her head thrust back in anguish.

After they ordered, Jodi continued their discussion. "Just to clarify: The Meonia group was inher-

277

ently linked with the power or influence the Celts associated with Bride. As presumably are we," she added. "Bride must have been associated with dozens of sacred places throughout the British Isles, so why the Bridestones?"

Graham thought for a while. "I assume it's because of the person once buried there. Not just *any* high priestess of Bride, but the *last* of them. If these ancient Celtic women did have the gift to channel some inconceivable power, then maybe it would have been handed on through the ages until the last Druidess was laid to rest at the Bridestones, and the power buried with her."

"And it remained there until Mary Heath came along?" Jodi offered.

"I assume that's what the Meonia group believed."

Jodi took a sip of wine. "So, the last high priestess of Bride, the last Druidess, was buried in the Bridestones tomb around 1500 years ago. Remind me again, what was happening in Britain at that time?"

Graham poured himself a glass of sparkling water. "It was the start of the Dark Ages, the period following the collapse of the Roman Empire of which Britain had been part when the country divided into dozens of feuding kingdoms. Within a few years, the Anglo-Saxons from Germany and Denmark invaded the East of Britain, establishing their own kingdoms, while the Irish raided the West and the Scottish the North. Amongst this turmoil, Druidism died out."

"Then what were the Druids to which James

Bateman and Edward Burne-Jones later belonged?"

"They originated with the eighteenth-century Romanticist movement. Masonic-like groups that reenacted Druidic rituals recorded by the Romans."

"So, the true Druids became extinct around the year 500," Jodi reiterated. "Would the name of their last high priestess have been recorded?"

"Unlikely. It's called the Dark Ages because it's a 'dark' period from the historian's perspective, a time from which few records survive. Consequently, there's probably no way to know who she was…" Graham fell silent to stare intently at the painting on the wall beside them. "Maybe there is," he said slowly.

Jodi turned to look at the picture of the girl with the lantern. "What is it?"

"I think I know who the Bridestones priestess might have been." Graham looked back to Jodi. "Some historical events and important people of the period *were* remembered in oral accounts, handed down the centuries to become myths and legends recorded in medieval Welsh manuscripts."

"Why Welsh?" Jodi asked.

"Wales, in the west of Britain, was where the Celts were driven after the Anglo-Saxons conquered what is now England during the sixth and seventh centuries. Amongst these manuscripts are stories of King Arthur, supposedly the last Celtic leader to unite Britain and defend the country from the invaders." Having written several books regarding the Arthurian mystery, Graham could elaborate. "In the romantic Arthurian tales of the later Middle Ages, Arthur was transformed into a medieval-style king, living in a world of jousting knights and huge Gothic castles. However, the earlier Welsh legends based on these stories concerned an early Dark Age chieftain in a land of crumbling Roman cities where warriors looked more like Romans. Although the king in shining armor, whose knights fought dragons and rescued damsels in distress, was pure literary invention, the Welsh narratives seem to have been based on a historical figure. A few surviving Dark Age manuscripts include historical references to a British leader, Arthur, who fought a successful series of battles against the Anglo-Saxons around AD 500. Arthur and other characters in medieval Arthurian romances seem to have been based on contemporary figures who lived at the time. For example, the sorceress Morgana."

"Morgan le Fey?"

"Yes, that was her name in the later romances of the Middle Ages. In these, she was portrayed as Arthur's half-sister, a malicious witch who conspired against him to seize the throne for her son Mordred. However, in the earliest medieval tales and the Welsh legends, Morgana was portrayed as a kindly enchantress. She is not Arthur's relative but his councilor—a powerful mystic who uses her intelligence, knowledge, and supernatural powers to support his reign."

Jodi had seen Morgana portrayed in the movies and on TV but had never considered that she may have been based on a real person. "Why do you think she might have existed?"

"Because the oldest references don't refer to her as a fanciful sorceress but as a real-life Druidess, and British chieftains around AD 500 often had such female advisors."

Jodi turned to glance up at the picture Graham had been staring at. "You keep looking at this. Does it mean something?"

"The original is in the Birmingham Art Gallery. It depicts Morgan le Fay as the hate-filled sorceress of the medieval Arthurian tales. It suddenly got me thinking about the *historical* Morgana. Just like the person believed to have been interred in the Bridestones tomb, she is recorded in the oldest accounts not merely as a Druidess but the *last* of them. Furthermore, she was said to have been a priestess of Bride. And she seemingly lived at the very time the tomb was built."

Jodi raised her eyebrows. "You think the Bridestones tomb was hers?"

"At least, the historical figure upon whom she was based."

Jodi looked back up at the picture. "Was this by one of the artists involved with the Meonia group?"

Graham browsed his phone. "No. It was painted by Frederick Sandys in 1864. A loner." He shook his head, still amazed by the remarkable synchronicities that kept happening. "A picture that inspires a train of thought 'just so happens' to hang where we 'just so happen' to be sitting."

"Divination by location." Jodi quipped. But she

wasn't joking. They both realized that something along those lines had to be occurring. "So, in the early stories, Morgana was like a female Merlin?" she said.

"Only more powerful. Amongst other things, she's a shapeshifter and can fly."

Jodi sighed. "I guess that *had* to be removed from the stories by the sexist male authors of the Middle Ages."

"Sadly. Some even depicted her as Merlin's wayward student." Graham paused as their food was brought and set down. "The point is, if, like Arthur, the original Morgana was based on a historical figure who lived around AD 500, then she's a good candidate for the person buried at the Bridestones. Not only is the dating right, but the tomb is also thought to have been the final resting place of Britain's last Druidess, which Morgana is said to have been.

"Moreover, the southern Peak District, where the tomb is located, has many legends involving her. For instance, she is said to have spent time as a recluse in the woodland of Wolf Dale, a valley in Wolfside, just two and a half miles east of the Bridestones. Apart from the gifts of shapeshifting and flight, Morgana is also accredited with the powers of a water nymph and, in the form of a mermaid, is associated with several lakes in the Peak District, including Black Mere Pool a few miles north of Leek. In some accounts, she becomes queen of the fairies—the name Morgan le Fay means Morgan the Fairy—and in this guise, she is said to have held court in the Peak District, at the Nine Ladies stone circle near Matlock. In the

Arthurian stories, Morgana leads a group of nine magical sisters who, in local legend, are said to have been transformed by Merlin into the megaliths of the site. Then there's the anonymous medieval tale of *Sir Gawain and the Green Knight*—the story Simone mentioned—concerning Morgana sending one of Arthur's knights on a quest for enlightenment, which is set in the southern Peak District and the region of Dovedale, not far from Leek.

"I've seen the movie. I thought Gawain was tested by the Green Knight," Jodi said.

"True. But in the original tale, the quest is set by Morgana, the Green Knight having been enchanted to do her bidding. Her role in the story is only revealed at the end. She resides in a fortress called Castle Hautdesert—interestingly, the one in Evelyn de Morgan's *Fortuna's Gift* painting. As its surrounding landscape matches the topographical features described in the story, some scholars believe its location was somewhere around the village of Alstonefield, on a 900-foot hill overlooking the River Dove.

Jodi summarized. "Morgana was associated with the area around the Bridestones and Biddulph Grange, she was believed to have been the last Druidess and a priestess of Bride, and she is thought to have lived around the year 500. She fits perfectly. I'd say she must have been the person buried in the Bridestones tomb." She paused. "Have you considered this before?"

"Oddly, no. It only occurred to me just now." Graham shook his head in self-reproach.

Jodi smiled. "It's fitting that an ancient Celtic *feminine* energy should have been involved with establishing female emancipation. The Celts were among the few historical cultures where women enjoyed equality."

"That's right. The eldest child held the right of inheritance—male or female—including royal succession. Celtic warrior women fought alongside, even commanded, their male counterparts, the most famous being Queen Boudicca who led the Britons to defeat an entire Roman legion."

Already aware of this, Jodi had returned her gaze to the Morgan le Fey painting. "If Morgana was buried at the Bridestones, then her bones may long since have gone, but the ancient power she wielded might remain, waiting for the right person to come along."

Graham nodded thoughtfully. "Mary Heath."

"Now us."

"Really?"

Jodi shrugged. "Well, we've certainly attracted its attention."

At that moment, Graham's phone pinged. It was a text from a friend who had been interested in Jodi and Graham's research. In the message, the man, Darren, said he had visited one of the many properties owned by the Heath family in the 1800s—a seventeenth-century farmhouse called Ford Green Hall in Stoke-on-Trent—where a pentacle was carved into wood paneling above the fireplace of the old drawing room. The place was now a museum and opened to the public, and the curator suggested that the symbol had been put there in the 1600s to ward off evil. As the pentacle was a sign widely used in magic, Darren wondered if it might be significant to Graham's investigation. Graham replied that he knew of the place, and as the Heaths had rented it out, and none of the family lived there, it was probably unimportant.

"I wonder if it *is* important," Jodi said after Graham explained the message.

"Go on."

"Well, I've lost count of the times you get a text or message from someone regarding something that ties up with what we're doing. Maybe we should visit Ford Green Hall."

Graham shrugged. "We can. But I don't see a connection."

The waiter arrived and left their check. As Jodi leaned down to grab her bag, she made a muffled sound of surprise. "I don't believe it!" she said as she picked something up off the floor beneath the table and showed it to Graham.

It was a small, metal, five-pointed star set in a circle around three-quarters of an inch in diameter, made of dull silver.

"A pentacle! We were talking about—"

"It was just there, beside my bag. It *must* mean something."

"Yet another synchronicity. It must have fallen off someone's neck chain or bracelet," Jodi suggested. She felt the item between her fingers. "Maybe not. The outer ring is completely smooth. There's no loop where it could have been attached as a pendant or a charm."

"You're right," Graham said as he examined it himself. "It must be some kind of amulet. Whoever dropped it was probably a Wiccan or something."

"The probability of a pentacle being on the floor right here—just when you get a text from someone *about* a pentacle! We're being told something."

"But what?"

"I suppose we should go to Ford Green Hall."

After finishing their meal and leaving the restaurant through an adjoining bar, Jodi halted in her tracks, staring at yet another Pre-Raphaelite print. They had not seen it on entering, but in an alcove beside the exit was a full-size copy of Evelyn de Morgan's picture, *The Hourglass*.

"That's it!" Jodi said, placing her bag and coat on the upholstered bench in the recess facing the picture. "It's time to solve the message in this painting. Divination by location. Fate wants us to figure it out—now."

"You still think this painting might lead us to the Heart of the Rose?" Graham asked as they waited to order drinks.

"Absolutely. Seeing it again, I have the same feeling I had when I first saw the original at Wightwick Manor."

Sitting in the alcove, looking at the painting just a few feet away, Graham reiterated what they knew. "Featuring Jane Morris, Laura Heath's successor and the last head of the Meonia group, it was painted between 1904 and 1905."

Jodi added what she felt had occurred. "The last vestige of the Order of Meonia, the Sphere Group, disbanded in 1902, after which Jane hid the Heart of the Rose and her close friend Evelyn knew where. Evelyn then painted this picture that somehow reveals its location."

Graham looked into the eyes of the figure in the picture, who seemed to be gazing despondently down at the hourglass. "So, who was the painting intended for?" he said. "Who was meant to solve it?"

Jodi stared at the picture for quite a while before answering. "Perhaps someone they hoped might re-form the group."

Graham thought it through. "I doubt there was anyone left *to* re-form it. Although it fails to reveal what—maybe manuscripts, talismans, occult para-phernalia—the memorial pamphlet says that so much was lost in the fire that the Order of Meonia could not continue. Led by Jane Morris and Florence Farr, some of them tried to resume work with the Sphere Group, but that failed. Although she lived until 1914, Jane was in her mid-sixties in 1904, a reasonable age for the time. She probably felt she was no longer up to whatever the group's leadership entailed. Assuming it needed a woman as leader, of the last female mem-bers, Barbara Bodichon had died thirteen years earlier, Elizabeth Wardle had died in 1902, Flora Mander spent the last part of her life bed-ridden before dying in 1905, and from 1902 Florence Farr returned to working full time as a theatrical producer."

"Then perhaps they felt they had done enough," Jodi suggested. "The feminist cause had gained enough momentum to continue. Maybe *The Hourglass* was Evelyn's epitaph to the Meonia group, painted for posterity."

"So, it wasn't meant for anyone in particular?"

Jodi considered her following words carefully. "Us, maybe?"

"Really?"

"Who knows? Perhaps … Evelyn saw us in the future. We've no idea *how* it all works. But we *do* seem to have witnessed time shifts ourselves."

Graham pulled an uncertain face. "Well, it's no weirder than all the rest. But you're convinced the location of the Heart of the Rose is somehow revealed in the painting?"

"Absolutely. That was the overwhelming feeling I experienced yesterday and again just now."

Graham had a nagging question. "If you can get such a message, then why doesn't it just tell us where it is?"

Jodi thought for a while before answering. "As we've speculated, the quest might be as important as where it leads. We learn things along the way." She cocked her head to one side and furrowed her brow. "No, it's more than that. By following the clues, we open doorways of opportunity."

"What sort of opportunities?"

"No idea. Sorry. Again, it's just a feeling."

Graham leaned forward, examining the painting. "Ok, then, let's solve the picture. Presumably, it contains some cryptic message. A code, maybe."

"The important feature must be the hourglass. Jane is looking at it, and I saw that very item in my remote of the Egyptian temple, even the pedestal it's standing on." Jodi pointed to the circular stone plinth decorated with the busts of two angels, one to either side. "And Laura rested her hand on it, just like the figure in the painting, as she did again in my vision yesterday."

Graham looked pensive. "You're sure it was Laura?"

"Although we've found no pictures of her, as you said, the woman *was* around the same age Laura was when she died."

"But she died in 1897, well before the Heart of the Rose was hidden. How would she have known of the painting?"

Jodi closed her eyes and sat motionless momentarily before looking at Graham. "Remember how we thought that my vision of her appearing on film when you were at the Egyptian temple, and the fact that she seemed to see you implied that she had somehow projected through time? Maybe she had already seen the future and knew the picture would be painted."

Graham considered it. "I suppose."

"Or—and this, in my opinion, is more likely—the specter was not Laura. Not her ghost or projection, but an acceptable conduit for whatever power is behind it all. It morphed into something familiar that we expected. You said it yourself when we were in Upton-upon-Severn; the way the phenomenon manifests itself is determined by what the observer already believes."

Graham leaned back in his seat. "I see what you mean. Others might have seen something else. Fortuna. Bride. Chang'e, for instance. Even Morgana."

"And because we're not into goddesses or ghosts but are familiar with reality shifts, it appeared as a time-traveling human." Jodi played with the silver pentacle between her fingers. "Previously, it may have appeared as the weird red-haired lady and the strange old man. Even little Mary in the Alice mirror might not so much be a tulpa but another aspect of the *whatever*. Phantasms and other ethereal beings we encounter might all be the same thing."

"Ok, so the *whatever*." Graham smiled and shook his head. "We really can't keep calling it that. The *it*, manifesting as Laura, specifically drew attention to the hourglass and the pedestal it's standing on. If there are clues in the painting, they are likely to be in that part of the picture."

They stood and walked over to the print and examined it closely. Their attention immediately focused on the two items depicted lying on the floor at the foot of the pedestal. One was a rose.

"A rose. Perhaps to draw attention to the Heart of the Rose," Jodi proposed.

And right next to it, also on the floor directly in front of the pedestal beside the rose, there was depicted an old, closed book; it was light beige and looked to be leather bound with dark metal clasps. There was something written on the cover in capitals.

It was an inscription in Latin. Three enigmatic words:

MORS JANUA VITAE

Graham ran it through a translator on his phone. "'Death is the Door of Life.'" He browsed the adage. "That's the literal translation, but its meaning is, 'Death is the Gateway to Eternal Life.' Referring to the promise of life after death, it's often found over the gates to cemeteries and on gravestones."

"And what does *this* mean?" Jodi pointed to the spine of the book, where there was a further inscription:

OPUS II V

Graham again translated. "*Opus* is Latin for 'Work,' and the letters are the Roman numerals 2 and 5."

Jodi consulted a website concerning the painting. "Evelyn never explained what any of it meant, but after her death, her sister Anna thought the spine inscription might refer to a piece of music by Beethoven." She explained how the word 'opus' was a musical term to denote a movement in a composition. "In this case, Beethoven's *Sonatina in F Major, Opus 2, Number 5*."

They found it on YouTube. It was a relatively short, lively piece for piano that neither of them could relate with anything associated with the Order of Meonia or the seemingly forlorn nature of *The Hourglass* painting. Maybe Anna had been wrong.

"I think I can explain it," Jodi said, having found

a relevant website. Remember how Jane Morris was an accomplished pianist? Well, that piece of music was her favorite; she often played it when seeking artistic inspiration. I think the inscription on the spine alludes to Jane, specifically that she had been *inspired* where to hide the Heart of the Rose."

Graham nodded. "I like it. And the words on the cover somehow reveal where?"

Graham had been scrolling through website links while listening to the music. "Other than the grave-yard inscriptions," he said, "there's an early twentieth-century book about spiritualism called *Mors Janua Vitae* by one Helen Dallas. Although she was a British psychical researcher, as far as I can tell, she had no connection with the Order of Meonia or anyone re-lated to it. Besides, the book wasn't published until 1910. The only thing I can find that might be relevant and titled *Mors Janua Vitae* is a funerary monument commemorating a doctor named Percy Macloghlin from Liverpool. He died the same year Evelyn started work on *The Hourglass* painting in 1904."

They examined a photograph of the seven-foot-high memorial. On top of a marble altar, inlaid with representations of Anteros and Eros, Greek gods of love, there rested the bronze busts of Percy and his wife Eliza, embracing and gazing down at a casket they cradled between them: evidentially the actual cas-ket containing their mingled ashes. The finished work was in the Royal College of Surgeons in London, but the original template, made from colored plaster, was in the Walker Art Gallery in Liverpool. Neither Graham nor Jodi had heard of the Macloghlins before, and, as far as they knew, they had nothing to do with the Order of Meonia. But, with nothing else to go on, and as Liverpool was only about 50 miles from Biddulph, they decided to look at it. It was after 2 p.m., and as the gallery closed at 4, they agreed to visit it the next day.

Because of the pentacle connection, they considered visiting Ford Green Hall on the way, but something quite extraordinary made them decide against it. As they passed the hotel reception, Jodi decided to hand in the item so it could be claimed. After explaining that she had found it on the floor under their table, she showed it to the receptionist, who immediately recoiled in horror.

"No! Keep it," she said, backing away.

Assuming the tiny pentacle conflicted with the lady's religious beliefs, Jodi asked if she should hand it to someone else. The woman mumbled something and left the counter.

"O-kay," said Jodi hesitantly. She turned to Graham. "What should we do?"

Graham smiled. "I'd say fate wants us to keep it."

-15-
The Secret Vale

Next morning, Jodi awoke with a start. And the overwhelming feeling they should get an early start. Not only because they only had until sunset to find the Heart of the Rose, but because they would be led to find a vital clue to its whereabouts.

Shortly after 8, they were heading north along the M6 motorway. With time running out, they had decided to ignore Ford Green Hall and head directly to Liverpool to see the Mors Janua Vitae memorial. However, about a third of the way there, the rush-hour traffic reached a standstill. The GPS, which seemed to be working perfectly, informed them that there was congestion for miles and suggested they take the next turnoff and follow the A500 road around Stoke-on-Trent to rejoin the motorway about 20 miles further on. The road was clear for a while until the traffic stopped again. Once more, the GPS recommended another route, telling them to take the next turn, the A527. The detour suggested was to join the A50 a couple of miles to the east, a major highway leading almost to Liverpool. When they reached the roundabout where they were to join the A50, a police car blocked the way, and an officer informed them there had been a burst water main, and the road was closed. All they could do was carry on to the east, getting further from their intended destination, and loop back around through a heavily built-up area.

"I think fate is directing us again," Jodi said, pointing to a road sign. "We are only four miles from Biddulph. I'd say we're being led back there."

Graham pulled over and studied the GPS. "We've been taken well out of our way by three separate diversions. I reckon you're right."

They drove on to reach Biddulph about ten minutes later and were only a few hundred yards from the entrance to the Grange when a truck traveling a few cars in front of them stopped abruptly. Simultaneously, on the other side of the road, a large van pulled up, and its driver leaned out of the window and started shouting at the truck driver. A fierce argument had erupted, and with both lanes wholly blocked and vehicles backing up in both directions, no one was going anywhere.

As angry horns blazed, Jodi noticed a driveway on their right that led to the parish church. "Pull in here," she directed. No sooner had they parked than the drivers' quarrel ceased, and both vehicles drove on. "I'd say this is where we're meant to be," she said.

Jodi seemed right. They have virtually been *herded* to Biddulph's St. Lawrence Church.

They had been here before. It was the church surrounded by the Templars' coffin lids, moved there by James Bateman in 1851; its graveyard, the last resting place for members of the Heath family—apart from Mary. Her burial site remained a mystery. They walked up the gravel pathway and tried the church door. It was locked.

"Perhaps we should revisit Laura's grave," Graham suggested. "You've recently experienced two visions of her—or maybe her facsimile—and she even appeared on film. Perhaps we're meant to go *there*."

Jodi and Graham stood silently by Laura's grave for a while, but nothing unusual happened until they heard singing from the church.

"Seems like it's now open," Graham reasoned, suggesting they go inside and look at Laura's commemorative plaque that he had seen on a previous visit to the church. "Perhaps there's something about it I overlooked."

They returned to the church door to find it wide open. The singing had stopped, and they were surprised to find the place empty. Neither was there any sign of a device that could have been playing music.

"Weird!" said Graham. "It's also strange that the door's suddenly open when no one's around."

"Maybe a warden or the vicar just opened it, and they had a radio on." Jodi proposed.

They went outside and searched the graveyard but found no one. "I suppose someone only came to open the church," Graham mused.

"Would they have left the door wide open?"

"I doubt it."

"Then I say we're *meant* to be in the church," Jodi said.

They re-entered the building that now seemed ominous, despite bright sunlight streaming in multi-color beams through the stained-glass windows of the south wall. It was unusually cold, and the musty smell of age and mold was more potent than before.

There was a sudden loud bang, which echoed through the empty church. They both jumped, turning to find the door slammed shut behind them.

"I hope they're not locking us in," Jodi said as they hurriedly made their way to the exit. But the door was still unlocked, and there was no one outside.

"Must have been the wind," Graham suggested.

Jodi left the porch and peered around at the empty churchyard. "It's dead calm."

Graham opened and closed the creaky door, seeing if there was any way it could have flung shut on its own. Seemingly not.

As they reentered the building, Graham explained how, in one corner of the church, to the right of the chancel housing the high altar, was a large recess separated from the south transept by an arch and low wrought iron railings and a gate. A kind of open mausoleum, it was installed by the Heaths above their family vault in the nineteenth century to display commemorative wall plaques and cremation urns. There were marble memorial tablets in memory of Robert Heath Sr., his wife Anne, and their children, Robert Jr., and his wife Laura, and virtually every other member of the Heath family in the nineteenth and twentieth centuries—but nothing to commemorate Mary. Over the years, Graham and fellow researchers had scoured the church and the surrounding cemetery, but, although they had located the graves and tombs of others of interest, they found nothing bearing the name of Mary Heath. Churchwardens, members of the congregation, and local historians had no idea where she was buried. As she died in London, it was assumed that she was interred or cremated there. But that still didn't explain why there was absolutely nothing in the church in her memory.

Graham led the way to the corner of the building that contained the memorial tablets. Perhaps they imagined it, but the temperature suddenly seemed to drop.

"They've installed a new feature." Graham said with surprised as he looked up at the huge, twenty-foot high, white marble monument, set against the back wall of the Heath memorial recess, where he remembered there had been a small altar. The memorial was shaped like a church doorway: a decorated, pointed arch supported by pillars. Within it were three figures in bass relief: Christ looking down at two winged female angels, kneeling with eyes closed as if praying. Above Christ's head was a flying dove.

Jodi was examining the plaque in memory of Laura on the wall when Graham took a shocked step back to lean against the railings. "That's impossible!" he gasped. She saw what had disturbed him. At the bottom of the monument, beneath the kneeling angels, was a marble plinth or base divided into three panels. Two were blank, but the middle panel was inscribed:

> In Loving Remembrance of William and Mary, Eldest Son and Daughter of Robert and Anne Heath of Biddulph Grange.

After recording that William had died on November 11, 1872, aged 25 years, it was further inscribed:

> Mary, the Wife of James Joseph Heffernan, died in London on October 13th, 1872, Aged 28 Years. Their Remains Rest in The Family Vault in this Church.

And at the bottom, it revealed:

> This monument is erected by their affectionate and sorrowing parents.

Graham shook his head in disbelief. "It's not a new monument at all. It's been here for 150 years." A fact supported by the brown stains covering parts of the memorial.

"The universe has changed again!" he said in awe.

"Or it's the same universe we swapped into when the fire date changed," Jodi suggested. "We haven't been inside the church since."

"Or the one where the Meonia sword had been in the Tudor House Museum for decades."

"Or yet another patch from an alternate reality."

Graham rubbed his eyes and blew out a long breath. "It does your head in."

"One way or the other, there's no way you and your friends could have missed it." Jodi stared up at the monument. "It's massive—pride of place in this corner of the church. All the other memorials are simply plaques. Besides, you say you've spoken to churchwardens and congregation members. They knew nothing of it. Bottom line: reality's shifted." Jodi pointed to a tablet on the wall to the right of the monument. "Look, a plaque commemorating the same Mary Heath, confirming when and where she died and that she was interred here in the family vault."

Graham let out a long sigh and held up his hands. "That wasn't here either."

"Well, whatever's going on, it seems she was buried here and has been all along," Jodi said, adding, "In *this* world anyway. Have you heard of William before?"

"Yes, he also contracted typhoid at the same time as Mary on their trip to London, if I remember right."

"Was he involved with the Meonia group?"

"Possibly, but I've found nothing to confirm it." Graham was still in shock.

The corner of the church was in deep shadow until a light, set on the inside of the open archway that separated the memorial area from the rest of the church, abruptly came on to fully illuminate the monument. Jodi and Graham jerked their heads involuntarily upwards to see the electric lamp that had ominously turned on—seemingly by itself.

"Must be on a sensor," Jodi proposed.

Graham examined the lamp. "No sensor," he said, following the cable to a switch on the wall. It was in the down position. He flicked it up, and the light went off. "Someone had to have switched it on manually."

"Impossible. No one's here. There must be another switch."

Graham further examined the wiring. "There's not."

Jodi fell silent momentarily, looking at the light and then at what it was illuminating—the Mary Heath monument. "Then I guess we've been brought here to examine this," she said.

The figure of Christ, holding up his right hand in blessing, with his left over his heart, looked down at the two kneeling angels below him. Above his head, at the top of the monument, was a dove. Facing one another, the winged angels had their heads bowed in prayer, one with her hands clasped to her breast, the other with her hands in her lap. Below them was the panel inscribed with the epitaphs for Mary and her brother William.

"The monument must be a clue to lead us to the Heart of the Rose," Jodi said.

Graham scratched his head. "I know you felt we would find a vital lead to its whereabouts today, and we appear to have been led to this church—to this monument—but it's just what you'd expect to find in a church. Jesus, angels, and the dove at the top representing the holy spirit."

Apart from the references to those buried here and those who commissioned the work, there was a single Bible verse near the bottom of the inscription panel. It read:

> I am the resurrection and the life: He that believeth in Me, though he were dead, yet shall he live. John. 11:25.

"Standard stuff for a tomb," Graham concluded.

Jodi knelt and ran a finger across the black lettering. "Maybe. But it reminds me of the translation of the book title in *The Hourglass*: 'Death is the Gateway to Eternal Life.' You said yourself that it refers to the promise of life after death."

"I suppose, but the monument dates from 1872, over thirty years before the Heart of the Rose was hidden."

Jodi stood up, stepped back, and gazed silently up at the memorial, deep in contemplation. After what seemed like ages, her eyes widened, and a knowing smile formed on her lips. She took out her phone and searched online as Graham waited, and silence filled the church. Then she burst out laughing. "Yay! I'm right!"

"What?" Graham held up his palms impatiently.

"Robert and Anne Heath commissioned the monument," she said. "They had to have been involved with the Meonia group, or at least sympathetic to it. Otherwise, they would never have permitted their little girl to be involved. Nor, I doubt, would they have bought Biddulph Grange from the Batemans and left Mary to run it. They must have known, and fully accepted, that their daughter was special. Very special. This is a vastly more impressive memorial than anything else in the church. The Order of Meonia might have been nominally Christian, but they were hardly religious. Not in the conventional sense. So why the huge representation of Jesus and the angels? There's nothing like it on the plaques commemorating the other family members."

"So, what are you saying?"

"What if the monument represents something of extreme importance to Mary?"

"Like what?"

"A place. A secret, special, maybe venerated location that the Order of Meonia had long revered— well before the group disbanded. Maybe that's where the Heart of the Rose was taken. Jane Morris wouldn't have hidden it just anywhere."

Graham was puzzled. "Go on."

Jodi beamed. "What paintings were we led to at Wightwick Manor?"

"*Fortuna's Gift* and *The Hourglass*."

"I think they both contain clues. *Fortuna's Gift* was painted in 1892 before the Heart of the Rose was hidden—but maybe when the secret location was already important to the Meonia group. What if the painting alluded to this venerated place? Simone told us that the picture's landscape represented Dovedale in the Peak District, symbolized by the dove in the foreground. In *The Hourglass,* the sand timer rests on a plinth bearing the busts of two winged angels." Jodi pointed to the Mary Heath monument. "At the top, there is a dove, and at the bottom, there are the two angels, just like in the paintings. I'm convinced that all three works allude to Dovedale. I looked it up just now. Dovedale has two towering rock formations, Ilam Rock, and Pickering Tor, on either side of the river. Because they stand like guardians to the valley, they are known locally as the Angels."

Graham was impressed but frowned. "But what about the Christ figure?"

"That fits, too," Jodi said with a broad grin. "Look at his feet. He's not just standing; he's floating in the air. The only time he does that, according to the Bible, is when he rises to heaven. The image of Jesus here represents that specific occasion known as the Ascension. Dovedale and its surrounding district are associated with that same event."

Jodi went on to explain what she had just read. Ascension Day, the 39th day after Easter Sunday, commemorates the Christian belief that Christ ascended to heaven at that time. Churches worldwide celebrate that biblical episode on that date, but villages around Dovedale do so in a big way. Each year, in the week leading up to Ascension Day, holy wells in the area—like you said, ancient sacred springs later venerated by the Church and consecrated to saints—are lavishly decorated by the villagers with elaborate flower designs, while the local communities host fairs, fetes, carnivals, and other events, attracting thousands of tourists. It is thought to have originated in pre-Christian times as a ceremony to honor the gods of the afterlife; later Christianized as a festival to celebrate Jesus' ascension to heaven and Christ's promise of resurrection.

"The dove, the ascending Christ, and the two angels all fit with Dovedale," Jodi concluded, "as do Evelyn's two paintings."

"Which would explain why we've been guided to Wightwick Manor and now here," Graham said excitedly. He agreed that it was way beyond coincidence. "We were only talking about Dovedale yesterday; it's association with Morgana, the person we reasoned was buried in the Bridestones tomb."

"Where the Heart of the Rose was discovered," Jodi added. "It makes sense that the relic would be hidden at another location connected with her."

"Then Dovedale is where we should go," Graham said.

Just as they reached the church door, it creaked slowly open before they could reach for the handle. They expected someone to enter, but they could see nobody there once it was fully ajar.

"How on Earth! I latched it." Graham closed the door, finding no way to explain how the latch could have risen on its own. When he raised it, the door stayed put. It was not hanging in such a way that it could swing open by itself.

Jodi left the porch and looked around. "No one

about," she said, mystified. "And still no wind."

Graham glanced around. "After all we've witnessed," he said, shaking his head, "it still astonishes me just how any of this can happen."

"Well, however, it happened; I think we're being told it's time to leave." Jodi beamed.

"Which means we're on the right track."

* * *

Today, Dovedale is a three-mile stretch of the river Dove winding through a steep-sided scenic valley in the extreme south of the Peak District, between a hill called Thorpe Cloud in the south and the tiny hamlet of Milldale in the north. Before the National Trust acquired the land in 1934, however, the region known as Dovedale also included some four miles of the adjacent, equally picturesque valley of the Dove's tributary, the Manifold, the rivers converging close to Thorpe Cloud. As two angels featured in *The Hourglass* and Mary Heath's memorial monument, Jodi and Graham decided to head for Dovedale's twin rock formations, the Angels. Later in the morning, after driving from Biddulph, they parked in Milldale and crossed a medieval stone footbridge. Known as Viator's (Traveler's) Bridge, it is one of the landmarks believed to feature in *Sir Gawain and the Green Knight*, and, as they crossed it to follow the pathway that hugged the eastern bank of the Dove, Graham related what he knew about the area's association with the story.

"According to the seventeenth-century English writer Charles Cotton, who lived in the district, the

Milldale bridge was where Gawain was said to have slayed a monster. In the tale, the knight is on a quest to find a secret place called the Green Chapel, where he is to meet the Green Knight for a final confrontation. After many adventures, Gawain arrives at Castle Hautdesert—which Cotton inferred to be in the vicinity of Alstonefield, less than a mile to the northwest of Milldale—where Bernlak, the lord of the manor, makes him welcome, and together they hunt down the monster in the form of a giant boar. Interestingly, Cotton recorded a local tradition that after killing the monster at the Milldale bridge, Gawain rode a mile downriver to the Angels rock pinnacles to thank God. So, presumably, it was considered a holy site."

"When I was searching online on the way here, I found a reference to a painting inspired by that legend." Jodi couldn't get reception in the deep valley, so she read from the webpage she'd downloaded onto her phone. "Interestingly, it was depicted by the American Pre-Raphaelite artist Robert Van Vorst Sewell, somewhere around 1900, in a painting known simply as *Knight and Two Angels*. Does it ring any bells?"

Graham examined the picture depicting a mounted Sir Gawain flanked by a winged angel, one to either side. "As far as I know, Sewell wasn't associated with the Order of Meonia. But I know of him through my Arthurian research. He was familiar with Charles Cotton's work, which inspired him to depict several Arthurian themes. I've seen this painting before but didn't realize what it represented."

They followed the crystal-clear river, which glistened in the sunshine as it wound its way through the lush, verdant slopes of the vale, interspersed with patches of woodland and craggy outcrops of rock, until the awesome work of nature stood imposingly before them. The Angels: the giant, 80-foot fingers of rough grey stone towered high above them like sentinels on opposite banks of the Dove—Ilam Rock, right beside the water's edge to the west, and Pickering Tor, a few yards downstream beside the path to the east. A relatively modern wooden footbridge crossed the river between them. There were a few smaller limestone pinnacles higher up the hillsides; like The Angels, they were left stranded as free-standing pillars when the relentless glaciers of the last ice age wore away the softer rock around them.

As hawks circled above and smaller birds shrilled warning cries in the branches below, Graham scoured the area on both sides of the river, searching for anything that might indicate the Heart of the Rose's hiding place. Meanwhile, Jodi sat in the mouth of a shallow cave at the foot of Pickering Tor, hoping for a vision or impression to guide them. But after about an hour, they gave up.

"Okay," Graham said, clapping his hands together in determination. "Let's assume there's nothing here. Like the Christ figure and the dove, the angels on the memorial and the painting were merely indicators of Dovedale. Then what are we left with?"

"The castle in the *Fortuna's Gift* painting," Jodi

said. "Castle Hautdesert. That's where Morgana lived, right?"

"The *Green Knight* story relates how she was old at the time and close to death, and Castle Hautdesert is where she had chosen to live out her remaining days."

Jodi stood and left the cave. "The place that Charles Cotton thought it was. You said it's nearby."

"Yes, a hill called Steep Low just outside the village of Alstonefield where he was born. It's about a mile from where we parked."

"We should try there," Jodi suggested. "What do we know about it?"

Sir Gawain and the Green Knight was written in Middle English, which differs considerably from today's language, but Graham had already downloaded a modern translation onto his phone. He perused it on their walk back to Milldale, providing Jodi with an outline of the narrative.

The tale is somewhat complicated and full of symbolism, but the gist is that Sir Gawain, a young knight at King Arthur's court, is challenged by a giant of a man dressed all in green to find a secret, mysterious place called the Green Chapel. Referred to only as the Green Knight, the giant gives Gawain a year to fulfill the task. The young knight travels the land having various adventures, following clues to the chapel's whereabouts until, as the year ends, he finds himself at Castle Hautdesert, where the lord, Bertilak de Hautdesert, makes him welcome. Amongst the nobles and ladies residing in the castle is a strange, sinister-looking older woman who seems to be silently observing everything. Everyone treats her with great respect; even the lord of the castle behaves as if she is his superior. Yet, despite his curiosity, Gawain fails to discover her identity. She is eventually revealed to be none other than Morgana, who charged the Green Knight to test Sir Gawain and devised the search as a quest during which he would gain enlightenment and become a brave and noble hero.

"Morgana, the very person we believe was buried in the Bridestones tomb," Jodi said as they reached the Milldale bridge. "The one whose power Mary Heath seems to have inherited. The same power that may be guiding us. We *must* go to the site of Castle Hautdesert." She spread her hands as if it was a no-brainer.

Driving out of the valley, they returned to the world of modern communication. The internet was back, and they could read up on their destination. Steep Low was a relatively flat-topped, 1000-foot hill about half a mile northeast of Alstonefield, with an artificial mound at its summit. Believed to have been erected during the Dark Ages as a fortified earthwork used successively by the post-Roman Celts and the Anglo-Saxons, it was the site that Charles Cotton reasoned the author of the *Green Knight* had in mind for Castle Hautdesert. There was no evidence that a stone castle, such as the one imagined by the writer, had ever been there, but archaeology has revealed that a wooden fortification had once stood on the mound. Indeed, it is possible that the fourteenth-century author had access to earlier material referring to the fort's association with the Arthurian saga, which has since been lost to time.

"Early legends might have linked Morgana with this site," Graham said as they climbed the grassy hillside toward the artificial hillock, now covered with trees. "It's known as a 'motte.' Even now, after centuries of erosion, it's well over fifty feet high; it may have been eighty feet or more when it was built. Its steep sides would have left attackers vulnerable to the spears, arrows, and projectiles flung from the high timber ramparts above them. Within the stockade was the keep, a large wooden tower where chieftains, their families, and their entourage resided. This privileged elite and their guard would hole up here in times of danger."

"And the ordinary folk?"

"Left to fend for themselves, I guess. Or flee."

After climbing the sharp slope to reach the top, Graham was covered in mud, having repeatedly slipped, while Jodi somehow remained immaculate. The sun was still shining in a clear blue sky, and there was hardly a breath of wind. The trees prevented them from enjoying the panoramic view of the surrounding landscape once afforded to the fort's inhabitants. However, the rich scent of wood smoke from bonfires in the valley below pleasantly filled the air.

"So, you think the *historical* Morgana lived here?" Jodi asked.

"It's possible. But the important point is that the author of *Sir Gawain and the Green Knight* seems to have located her here so that the site may have been important to the Meonia group."

"Important enough for them to have hidden the Heart of the Rose here?"

"Perhaps."

Jodi looked around at the trees rising from long wild grass, hearing nothing but the haunting echoes of sheep bleating in the neighboring hillsides. "But where? There's nothing here."

"I suppose they could only have buried it," Graham proposed, scratching his head.

Jodi made a sweeping gesture with her hand. "We can't dig up the entire mound."

Their only hope was for some serendipitous sign or for either of them to experience a vision or an intuition. But nothing happened. Jodi sat against a tree and tried again to achieve one of her remotes, but half an hour passed without success. Eventually, she said, "There *is* one potentially relevant location we haven't tried: The Green Chapel. What does the *Green Knight* story say about it?"

Consulting his phone, Graham summarized the end of the story. "It turns out to be a shallow cave in a hillside mound overlooking a stream. During the Middle Ages, caves were sometimes used as religious shrines. It's described as more of a rocky hollow than a true cave, as it is short and has an opening at either end. Above and to the sides, it is covered with vegetation, hence the name 'Green Chapel.'"

"And where was it?"

"We're not told exactly, but the author relates how it lies two miles from Castle Hautdesert."

"Where do literary scholars think it was?"

Graham browsed his phone. "There seem to be two locations that match the description. One at a gorge called Lud's Church." He checked an online map. "That's about ten miles away. The other is called Wetton Mill Cave." He again consulted the map. "And that is almost exactly two miles west of here."

"That must be it," said Jodi enthusiastically.

"I'd say so. Most experts propose Wetton Mill Cave as the most likely location the author had in mind."

It was decided. They were heading for the Green Chapel—and the experience of a lifetime.

-16-

The Green Chapel

As Jodi and Graham left the mound and crossed the fields back to the car, they noticed that low clouds had descended over the hills to the immediate west—the direction they intended to go. It was still sunny where they were, but it seemed they were in for bad weather. Strangely, the weather app on Jodi's phone said it would be fine all day. "Now we know where we're going, I can tell you what time sunset is," she said. "The app says 6:16 p.m. precisely."

Graham glanced at his watch. "Which leaves us just over six hours. What do you think will happen if we don't find the Heart of the Rose by then?" he added.

Jodi stopped at a stile overhung by trees; grazing cows watched them in the open field on the other side with curiosity. She sat on the wooden step and concentrated, head in hand. "I have no idea what the stone does," she said eventually. "But the overwhelming feeling I still have is that finding it somehow starts a completely new cycle for us. Maybe a new quest."

Graham looked weary. "There's more to do?"

Jodi smiled. "Not immediately. At least, that's the impression I get."

"Any idea what it involves?"

"Absolutely none," she said after a few moments of concentration. "Although I don't think it will be for a while. Maybe there are more artifacts to find—possibly other secrets to discover. I can't say. What I get very clearly, though, is that it's the end of our interaction with the—*whatever*—for good if we don't find it by sundown today."

"We'll be out of the loop?"

"Exactly."

"It could have revealed this months ago!"

"I don't think that's how it works. Remember, we considered our quest to be like a computer game. We're being tested, I suppose. Last level: A race against time."

"And this information, these impressions; where are they coming from?"

"As I said before, it feels like Laura. But it might be the *whatever* itself. Either way, the window closes in six hours."

"Then we'd better get a move on."

Back in the car, before departing, they examined their detailed map of the area, noting that they would be passing through the village of Wetton en route to their destination. Here, a pub was marked, which they discovered online was called The Mermaid. Popular with rock climbers, hikers, and ramblers, it was open all the year round and served lunch between noon and 3 p.m. They decided to stop there to eat and discuss what they should do once they reached the cave. Even though time was of the essence, reception was patchy, and the inn's website said it had Wi-Fi.

"The Mermaid!" Jodi said. "Morgana could transform into a mermaid. Perhaps she's connected with the village."

They consulted various sites concerning the inn, discovering that it catered for bed and breakfast, was highly rated for food and drink, and dated from the 1700s. However, they were unable to find out how it got its name. Various photographs showed the old building with a traditional pub sign hanging outside, depicting a mermaid sitting on a rocky beach and combing her long red hair. Graham recognized the image.

"It's a copy of a Pre-Raphaelite work," he said, checking it online. "It was painted in 1900 by the artist John Waterhouse."

"Was he involved with the Meonia group?"

"Not that I know of. Neither has the picture anything to do with Morgana. It was inspired by a Tennyson poem about a sea siren." Graham started the engine.

As they drove along the narrow country road that wound its way across the moorlands towards the village of Wetton, they abruptly hit a sheer bank of mist. Graham braked to a crawl and turned on the fog lights, visibility down to just a few feet. Jodi consulted the map, indicating a road coming up on the left. But, peering through the enveloping cloud, watching the drystone wall move slowly by at the side of the road, she could see nowhere to turn.

"We obviously missed it," Graham leaned forward, his face close to the windscreen, hoping to gain a better view through the almost impenetrable murk.

Jodi narrowed her eyes. "But I was looking out for it all the way."

"It's pretty foggy."

"I never lost sight of the wall. There were a few gates, but no side road as marked on the map."

"Then we can't have reached it yet."

They drove on at a snail's pace until they came to a crossroads with a signpost pointing left to the village of Wetton. Jodi was perplexed. "We should have passed the correct turnoff a couple of hundred yards back. Anyway, take *this* turn."

Graham did as instructed but almost drove off the road when Jodi shouted.

"That's impossible!" she cried.

"What? For god's sake! We nearly ended up in a ditch."

"On the map. The original road we should have taken. It's gone." Jodi shook her head in disbelief.

"Gone?"

"Yes, it was clearly shown on the map. I took my eyes off it; now it just shows fields."

Graham suggested Jodi had misread the map, but she was adamant the road had been there. As so often occurs between driver and navigator, an argument almost erupted. But then, as suddenly as they had entered it, they left the mist, and a signboard welcomed them to Wetton. The quiet little village was picture-perfect, a collection of grey-stone farm buildings and cottages with a small, fourteenth-century church and a population of around 150. Now in bright sunlight, with no sign of clouds, not even the one from which they had just emerged, they pulled into the pub parking area and left the car.

"Oh, they've changed the name," Graham remarked, pointing to a black wooden panel attached to the pub wall. It was painted with an image of a tree with a crown above it and, in gold, the words *Ye Olde Royal Oak*. There was no sign of the board decorated with the Waterhouse picture and the lettering *The Mermaid* beneath it or even the tall, L-shaped beam from which it hung.

Once inside, they were shown to a table in the dining area, where the waiter gave them menus, politely asking if they could order quickly as the kitchen would soon be closing.

"I thought you served food until three," Graham queried.

The man frowned. "We do."

"But it's only…" Graham trailed off as he stared incredulously at his watch."

"What is it?" Jodi asked when the waiter had left, without them ordering.

"It's 2:45! Impossible!"

Jodi checked the time on her phone, and gasped. "It should only be around 12.30," she said in disbelief.

"We've just lost two and a half hours!"

Jodi put her hands together and pressed her fingers tightly to her lips. After deep thought, she said,

"It's that weird mist. I'd say we've just gone through a time warp!"

Graham pulled a "now what?" expression and checked his phone. "Well, it's the same day and year. Is this *supposed* to be happening?"

Jodi's expression was, "How should I know?"

They agreed that as they now had far less time—only three hours—they could not afford to dwell on how such a thing was possible. They must act fast. There was no time to hang around this inn, but there was a question Graham needed to answer before they left. Its old name might be some clue. On the table next to them, six people sat in hiking gear, listening to a woman who seemed to be their guide talking about the pub's history. "Excuse me," he said, leaning over. "Do you know why this place was called The Mermaid?"

The woman frowned. "You must have the wrong pub," she said pleasantly. "It's always been called The Royal Oak, or more recently, Ye Olde Royal Oak."

Graham opened his phone to show her pictures of the pub and its Pre-Raphaelite sign. "We were just looking it up online, and it was called…" He trailed off and began rapidly consulting several sites. To his surprise, all the websites that had previously referred to the pub as The Mermaid now called it the names the woman had told them, while photographs, even old ones, revealed no trace of the distinctive mermaid sign.

"We've swapped universes again!" Graham exclaimed loudly.

"I beg your pardon?" the woman said with raised eyebrows while her group looked on in confusion.

Jodi grabbed her friend's arm. "He's…" She made a twirling gesture with a finger beside her temple.

Having finished their meals, the hiking party hastily left.

"Great, they think I'm nuts," Graham said, folding his arms.

"At least we can speak freely now they've gone."

Graham stared at his phone. "Well, we've certainly had a universe swap or something. There's nothing online about this place ever being called The Mermaid. The photographs are of the same building, but there's no pub sign outside, only the plaque."

"And the map *did* change. I knew it! That road vanished. I told you something was weird."

"Well, we're not only in a different universe but a different *time*—if only by a few hours."

They both shared the same anxious concern. Just how weird were things going to get? Would they end up lost in space and time?

Searching online for anything else that might have changed, they found nothing obvious. Everything concerning Biddulph Grange, the Bridestones, people associated with the Meonia group, and even the daily news was all the same.

"In the *Green Knight* story, did Gawain find himself in another world when he was heading for the Green Chapel?" Jodi asked.

Graham checked the story translation. "Not that

I can tell… But *that's* interesting. As Gawain rode over the hillsides between Castle Hautdesert and the Green Chapel, a mysterious mist settled over the moor."

Jodi's eyes widened. "Just like with us. Then again, I supposed it's common enough around here."

As Graham continued to read the Gawain story, Jodi typed away on her phone, entering various key phrases into the browser. "Here's something else that wasn't there before," she said.

Graham looked up. "Another change?"

"I typed in 'Mors Janua Vitae,' the words on the book cover in *The Hourglass*, and I got this." Jodi handed over her phone.

It was a painting of a knight in silver armor and a red cloak, his sword and helmet by his side, kneeling before a beautiful female angel with feathered wings and wearing a white gown. The two figures were in a cave where the angel held back a dark veil to reveal a door-sized opening leading outside from where the bright daylight shone in. There was a second opening some distance behind the figures, seemingly the mouth of the cave, which led out onto a paradoxical scene where a crescent moon and a single bright star shone in a twilight sky.

Graham read the description below the image. "The cave mouth leads to early dawn, with the moon and Venus in the sky, while the secret exit revealed by the angel leads to full daylight." He turned to Jodi. "It presumably holds symbolic meaning, but how does it tie up with those Latin words?"

"*Mors Janua Vitae*—it's the name of the painting."

"Really!" After typing the Latin words into the browser, Graham was astonished that several websites concerning the same painting appeared among the first few search results. "How come we didn't find them before? We searched for 'Mors Janua Vitae' countless times."

"Another universe. Or a patchwork from one." Jodi said, casually taking back her phone. These bizarre changes to reality were becoming almost commonplace.

"On his phone, Graham read more about the picture. "It was painted by the Scottish Pre-Raphaelite artist Joseph Noel Paton in 1866. I've not come across him in connection with the Meonia group. He lived in Edinburgh, but… Wow! But the painting is relevant." He slapped a palm to his forehead. "It depicts Sir Gawain in the Green Chapel."

"You're joking!" Jodi found the same reference. "This picture has *got* to be what Evelyn's Latin phrase was referring to, not the Liverpool memorial." She frowned. "But why the angel?"

Graham checked a few more sites. "I can hazard a guess. It says here that Paton was an expert on folklore, particularly Celtic mythology and Arthurian literature. He was familiar with *Sir Gawain and the Green Knight* and its Celtic undertones."

Jodi waited patiently as Graham reread the end of the *Green Knight* story, where Gawain finally discovers the Green Chapel.

He continued. "When Gawain enters the cave, the Green Knight reveals that he is Lord Bernlak, the man who had been his host at Castle Hautdesert. He tells Gawain that on this, and the first occasion they met, he had been temporarily transformed into the green-clad giant by Morgana. Indeed, Morgana herself was the creepy old woman treated with such respect at the castle. Bernlak reveals that Morgana has the power of a goddess, which Gawain has been chosen to inherit as the sorceress is dying. In completing his quest to find the Green Chapel, he has proved himself worthy."

"So, how does the angel come into it?"

"She represents the power that Gawain is offered. As an authority on Celtic mythology, Joseph Paton knew that Morgana's power was represented by Bride. It's even symbolized in the painting. The cave has one entrance where dawn is breaking, with the moon and Venus in the sky, and the other has sunlight streaming in—Bride was associated with the four celestial lights: the dawn, the moon, Venus, and the sun. Remember also how in Celtic mythology, she was represented with wings."

Jodi considered the implications. "You think Evelyn de Morgan is directing us—or at least whomever she thought might one day search for the Heart of the Rose—to this picture because it depicts Bride manifesting in the Green Chapel?" She thought momentarily, playing with a beer mat on the table. "Would Evelyn have known of the painting?"

"Like Paton, she was a Pre-Raphaelite painter," Graham said. "Even if she hadn't seen the original, by the end of the nineteenth-century, color prints of such works were widely available. Evelyn de Morgan was almost certainly familiar with it."

"So, the title of the book shown in her painting —*Mors Janua Vitae*, referring to Paton's picture—was her final clue to confirm the whereabouts of the Heart of the Rose, namely the Green Chapel." Jodi exhaled. "Well, as the world is now, anyway."

"Maybe the painting already existed in our world —at least, the one we were in before the mist—but its significant online presence has changed." Graham leaned back and stared at the ceiling. "Geez! Universe paradoxes make your head spin."

Jodi laughed. "So, the 'Mors Janua Vitae' reference in Evelyn's picture was the clue to lead the seeker to Paton's painting of that name."

Graham nodded. "For anyone who knew of the relic and was actively seeking it. Remember, Evelyn also depicted a winged, angelic woman barring a doorway behind the seated Jane Morris in *The Hourglass*. A further allusion to Paton's painting, I'd say. Wetton Mill Cave has long been regarded as the *Green Knight* poet's setting for the Green Chapel. It's bizarre how, once again, something just so happens to appear to confirm what we're onto. We're heading for the Green Chapel, and suddenly there are web links concerning this painting of the Green Chapel where none existed before. Bottom line—Evelyn de Morgan *and* fate are directing us to Wetton Mill Cave."

Jodi weighed the evidence. "We've already concluded that it would make sense for Jane to hide the Heart of the Rose somewhere important to the Meonia group. And a place associated with Bride's power would make perfect sense. After all, a location believed to be where Bride's power emanated—the Bridestones—was where it was found." She paused for a moment. "I don't know if it's relevant, but what power *did* Gawain inherit?"

"He doesn't. He refuses it and returns to Camelot."

Jodi pulled a face. "That's a letdown."

"I assume it was the author's way of portraying a true hero—someone who rejects power. Anyway, the important thing, as far as we're concerned, is the clues left by Evelyn de Morgan. Her paintings allude to Dovedale and the Gawain story; the Latin words refer to Paton's painting. I'd say she's telling us quite clearly that Jane Morris hid the Heart of the Rose somewhere in this area that was believed to be the Green Chapel—Wetton Mill Cave."

Concern etched its way across Jodi's face. "It's a bit ominous," she said. "The translated title of the painting, *Death is the Gateway of Life!*"

Graham checked his phone, then smiled. "The title refers to Morgana's death releasing her power for Gawain to inherit. I don't think it has anything to do with the Heart of the Rose."

Something was still nagging in Jodi's mind. "We still don't know what the relic does."

A new party of hikers sat at the table next to them, the pair taking it as their cue to leave. Graham stood, slinging his bag over one shoulder. "I guess we're about to find out."

Once again, they were thankful for Graham's tiny car as they drove down a perilously steep, single-track, winding lane that led through thick woodland of gnarled trees before emerging onto the open valley floor. They continued for a while, following the River Manifold, which meandered its way between grassy hills, dotted with further woodland here and there and the occasional outcrop of grey limestone and rugged cliffs, until they crossed an old stone bridge to arrive at a parking area signposted *Wetton Mill Tea Rooms*.

The café, until the 1850s, had been a watermill for grinding corn. A few hikers in high-visibility, out-door clothing, and heavy boots were enjoying tea and sandwiches around the wooden tables in front of the building, some throwing bread to the ducks that bobbed along the babbling little river.

It was just after 4 p.m.; the sky was clear, and the autumn sun dropped ever closer to the horizon.

Finding the cave was no problem; it was visible around fifty yards up the steep hillside behind the old mill. Set in a sheer, craggy outcrop of rock, some 30 feet high and 90 feet wide, the distinctive, irregular-shaped mouth was about 12 feet tall and 10 feet across at its widest point. It was indeed a mound rising from the hillside, just as described in the *Green Knight* tale. To either side of the rock face were sharp slopes covered in wild grasses, brambles, small trees, and undergrowth, as were the flat area directly above the cave and the incline on the hillock's rear. This was indeed the Green Chapel, as described in the poem.

As it was on public land, there was no problem

gaining access. And surprisingly, no one was anywhere around it. Jodi and Graham stood at the cave mouth in the bright sunshine, peering inside. It couldn't have been much more than 50 feet deep, its floor sloping upwards to widen into a relatively flat area illuminated by daylight shining down from a gaping hole in the roof, around 20 feet above, presumably where the ceiling of the cavern had long ago collapsed.

"The second entrance described in the story," Graham observed as he sat down on a rocky ledge to recover from the arduous climb.

They both shared the same thought. Could this, at last, really be where the Heart of the Rose was hidden? They considered the circumstances that had led them here. Initially, there was only one thing they could discover that Evelyn's Mors Janua Vitae reference might refer to: the funerary monument in Liverpool. They had set out to go there, but fate had repeatedly steered them to Biddulph church, where they had found the inexplicably-appearing Mary Heath monument, alerting them to Dovedale and the *Green Knight* story. Then, when they ultimately decided that the relic might be hidden in Wetton Mill Cave, Paton's painting bizarrely appeared on the web. They *had* to be in the right place. The Heart of the Rose must be here. But exactly where?

As Jodi sat on a rock, hoping to receive a remote vision, Graham left the cave and wandered outside the mound. It consisted of a vertical rock face where the cave entrance was and heavily overgrown slopes on all other sides. He managed to clamber to the top but not without injury—slipping and falling face first into a patch of stinging nettles and tearing his hands on thistles—only to find it even more overgrown with brambles, vines, and ivy, which entwined and throttled stunted trees. In the middle of this tangle of foliage was a gaping hole, around 15 feet across, the collapsed cavern roof that opened into the cave below.

"If anything's buried on the mound, it won't be fun trying to find it," Graham said as he rejoined Jodi in the cave. "It's covered with brutal vegetation."

Jodi flinched on seeing the proof: a red rash with painful-looking hives on Graham's face. "Are you okay?"

"It's not as bad as poison ivy, so I hear," he said dismissively. "Anyway, on second thoughts, I doubt we need to dig up the mound. It's doubtful that Jane Morris would have buried their most precious relic in the steep ground that would erode with rainfall and be disturbed by roots."

"Then where?" Jodi said as she walked back to the mouth of the cave. She let out a cry.

"What?" Graham ran to join her, almost falling again.

"The sun's going down," she said anxiously, pointing across the valley to where the reddening solar disc was dropping behind the hills.

Graham let out a sigh of relief. "I thought you were hurt."

Jodi ignored his concern. "But it's sundown."

Graham smiled. "It's not sunset yet. Not in the true sense. It's falling behind the hills, but won't drop below the true horizon for…" he checked his watch, "another half hour." But that was no real comfort. They still had no idea where to search.

Back inside the cave, Graham looked around at the stone walls, pockmarked with hollows caused by the gradual dissolving of the limestone by rainwater filtering through the rock over thousands of years. "It could have been hidden in one of these," he suggested, gesturing to the holes. "Then, plugged with calcium carbonate cement. It might look no different from the surrounding rock if done right."

Jodi grinned. "How do you even know that?"

"Limestone is a common form of calcium carbonate and—"

"I believe you," Jodi interrupted, holding up a hand. "Thirty minutes and counting."

"Anyway, somehow, I can't see an elderly Victorian lady mixing cement," Graham said.

"She may have had help."

Graham screwed up his face, reconsidering the scenario. "No. There would be too much risk of the plug falling out."

"Well, we seem exactly where we're supposed to be."

"I agree. But I really can't think of a feasible hiding place. Not one that's unlikely to erode, crumble, or be accidentally found."

"Well, I've had no luck getting any kind of vision or even a feeling," Jodi said, looking at the Paton painting she'd downloaded to her phone. "Maybe there's…" She cut off mid-sentence. "Oh my god!"

Jodi held up her phone, comparing the scene around them with the image. "Paton's picture not only depicts the Green Chapel—it was painted here."

Graham joined Jodi to look at her phone. She was right. The distinctive, mushroom-shaped outline of the cavern's entrance and the unique profile of the protruding rocks to either side exactly matched the cave mouth in Paton's painting. "It's the same place, all right," he said. "Joseph Paton would surely have known that this cave was popularly identified as the Green Chapel and deliberately chose it as the setting for his picture. Although he was Scottish, he spent several years in England. He even studied here."

"We've been thinking that Evelyn de Morgan alluded to Paton's painting because it happened to represent the location where the Heart of the Rose was hidden," Jodi said. "What if Paton's picture gave Jane Morris the idea for where to hide it?"

Graham screwed up one eye. "What makes you think that?"

"The book that lies at Jane's feet in *The Hourglass*. As the 'opus' reference on the book's spine referred to a piece of music that inspired Jane, and the title of the book alludes to Paton's painting, Evelyn might be saying that it was Paton's painting that inspired her friend as to where to take the Heart of the Rose."

"But Mary Heath memorial, which helped to lead us here, was made three decades before the Heart seems to have been hidden."

"Yes, but that only reveals that Dovedale was important to the Meonia group, not this particular cave."

"You could be right. But it doesn't help us find what we're looking for."

"It might," Jodi smiled. "In the painting, the angel figure reveals a secret opening. The portal to life. There is no such opening in this cave, just the mouth and the collapsed roof above us." Graham watched as she moved to the back of the cavern and maneuvered her position while repeatedly looking at her phone until she said, "This is the spot where the picture was painted. Meaning that the hidden portal is depicted as being there." She pointed to her left, where a long, narrow, V-shaped cleft, around 3 feet wide and 2 feet deep, ran from floor to roof in a gentle, inwards-leaning arch running up the rock wall to meet the roots and vines hanging down from outside. Whereas the other walls were grey or appeared beige in the daylight from above, the cleft was darker, stained with green algae, and streaked with moss. "Maybe, in Jane's mind, this was the right place to hide the Meonia group's prized possession. Somewhere that Joseph Paton depicted as a portal to supernatural power."

Graham examined the crevice, noticing how it was covered with thin cracks—fissures in the stone that ran like veins up the rockface, branching here and there to resemble a photograph of a river system from space. Such formations could be seen nowhere else in the cavern. "If the Heart of the Rose is anything like the stone heart found at Cock Low, then it might fit into one of these cracks," he said. "With a rope hanging from above, someone could climb down and wedge it in, where it was well out of reach." He placed a finger in one of the cracks. "They're deep. If high up, I doubt it would be found by chance."

The light filtering in from above was beginning to dim—true sunset was only minutes away.

Just as Graham was about to suggest that they somehow find a rope and one of them abseil down from the top, Jodi said, "Maybe we can use something to call upon Bride to reveal exactly where we should look."

"Like what?"

"Something like this." She took out the tiny pentacle they had found beneath the table in the hotel restaurant. "The way we found it right after your friend messaged you about just such a symbol. Then the weird reaction of the receptionist led us to keep it. Surely, it's relevant."

Graham felt something stir in his memory, but it was just beyond reach. "In occult tradition, the five points of the pentacle symbolize the four mystical elements, earth, air, fire, and water, plus the transcendent fifth element, spirit or quintessence," he said. "It was used as a talisman of protection. It was only recently that it became associated with Devil worship. Originally it was the precise opposite. It is said to have been the symbol on a ring possessed by King Solomon with which he could summon angels."

"Angels! The figure guarding the portal in Paton's painting looks like an angel..." Jodi cut off as Graham examined his phone animatedly. "What is it?"

"Of course!" The memory had been accessed. "According to the *Green Knight* story, the pentacle was painted on Gawain's shield. The author specifically says that the sign held power once wielded by Solomon."

Jodi felt her grip involuntarily tighten around the silver trinket in her hand. At that moment, a strange sound came, like the buzzing of bees. Graham looked around but could see nothing to account for the noise. Jodi backed away from the cavern wall. "It's coming from here." She pointed to the crevice. Graham moved forward and tilted his head to where Jodi had indicated. She was right. It was louder in the crevice—and growing in volume. It was as if a swarm of angry hornets had gathered in the cleft, but nothing could be seen. The pair stared at one another in alarm, moving a few steps back from the rockface.

Then it got darker.

There were heavy clouds above. The droning continued, now accompanied by the noise of rain suddenly falling heavily on the greenery surrounding the opening in the cavern roof. A brilliant flash of lightning was followed by a deafening thunder boom as the rain began to fall like a tropical monsoon. Like the storm at the Bridestones, the squall had appeared abruptly, as if from nowhere, and was directly overhead. This time, however, there was also the swarming sound, rising in pitch to become like the painful shriek of a dentist's drill. Outside, the wind was howling, buffeting the bushes and small trees on the mound. In moments, rainwater was gushing from rocky channels around the sinkhole to fall around them and swell about their feet.

Then the ground shook.

A deep rumbling reverberated through the cave, and a tremor shuddered the rock. As Graham leaned against the wall to steady himself, he noticed that Jodi, still managing to stand, was transfixed by something above. He followed her gaze, astonished to find himself staring into a vertical tunnel of swirling debris. Above them, leaves, twigs, and dirt whipped around the hole in the cave roof. They were directly under a whirlwind. More lightning, another clap of thunder, and the ground shook again, sending Graham and Jodi stumbling into one another. Pieces of moss, broken roots, stones, and soil fell around them as they retreated to the cave's center. Looking back to the crevice from where the shrill sound still came, they saw it was now covered by a miniature waterfall, flood water cascading down before it like a translucent curtain of finely corrugated glass.

Then it happened.

An intense flash of lightning illuminated the cave wall surrounding the crevice. An explosion of thunder; the brilliance flickered for a few missed heartbeats as the discharge of enormous energy forked its way earthward somewhere outside. In what seemed like a moment frozen in time, Jodi stared at the silvery cascade falling before the crevice. Briefly, a silhouette appeared behind this watery veil, a shadow created by the overhead vegetation pummeled by the gale. It seemed like a human profile, around six feet tall, just inside the fissure. Then, a further discharge from the raging storm strobed the rock in further light. Shielding her ears from the thunder that blasted through the cavern, and with water gushing around her feet, Jodi watched, transfixed, as the silhouette seemed to shift, as if turning towards her, and other shadows unfolded above it—like wings.

Then all was calm.

Simultaneously, the wind fell, the rain stopped, and the vibrating of the cavern ceased. Water spouting from the edges of the hole in the roof was reduced to trickles, the cascade that had covered the crevice ran dry, and the torrent that had been the floor flowed out through the mouth of the cave. All was silent except the sound of echoing dripping and a dog barking somewhere across the valley. There was a smell of freshness in the air as early evening light again illuminated the cavern. It was 6:15.

They saw it together. As the water flowed away down the sloping ground of the cave, pieces of vegetation and rock were left, littering the area around the crevice. Here, amongst the detritus, something pebble-sized and pink was lying on the floor. Jodi bent down to examine it. It seemed to be a smooth stone, partly masked by a wet leaf. But when she picked it up and cleaned off the mud, she gasped. "It's…"

Graham couldn't believe what Jodi was holding. It was a small stone about an inch and a half long and wide, three-quarters of an inch thick, fashioned into the shape of a heart.

"The Heart of the Rose!" Jodi said, awestruck, holding out the item for her friend to see.

Graham took it, expecting it to be warm. But it

was just an ordinary piece of wet, cool stone, neither heavier nor lighter than it looked. It was slightly coarse, opaque, and a dull shade of pink. "It must have fallen with the other debris from above," he said. "It certainly wasn't there before. I guess it was washed out from the ground above or maybe dislodged from a fissure."

"How it got there aside, we came here looking for a stone heart and found one." Jodi turned to Graham. "Just like at the Bridestones, another freak storm. And the ground—the whole cave—everything was shaking. You don't get earthquakes here!"

"Earth tremors, occasionally," Graham said. They had experienced so many weird things since their investigation began, but it was still human nature to consider an alternative explanation, even for this new level of weirdness.

Jodi knew Graham was playing the devil's advocate and played her part. "And whirlwinds?"

"Sometimes."

"At the same time?"

Graham remained silent.

"It began exactly when we considered using the pentacle," Jodi realized she was still holding it.

Graham had been staring at the pink stone heart when his head jerked up. "The five elements! That's what the pentacle represents."

"Yes, you said."

"And that's what we got. The four mystic elements: water—rain, air—wind, fire—lightning, and earth—the tremor."

"And the fifth element—spirit," Jodi said, remembering what she had seen behind the cascade.

Graham nodded. "The figure in the crevice."

Jodi's eyes widened. "You saw it too? I thought it was a vision."

"I saw it all right. Formed from light and shadow, a human figure with unfolding wings. The falling water distorted it, but for all the world, it looked like—"

"An angel!"

-Epilogue-
Meonia

Over the days that followed, Jodi and Graham expected something astonishing to happen. But nothing did. No meaningful dreams, remote visions, synchronicities, or reality changes. Nothing. They took the stone heart to a professional geologist who told them it was made from simple rose quartz: a common, inexpensive, pale pink rock found worldwide. It was undoubtedly an artifact, something artificially shaped at some point, but how long ago and where was impossible to tell. However, the geologist thought it was unlikely to have been made recently as the polishing was somewhat crude. It could be Greek, Roman, or Celtic; from almost any culture or time they cared to name. They were disappointed.

As the land on which it was found belonged to the National Trust, they took their find to the organization's head office in Swindon, southern England, hoping that the organization might offer their services and subject it to scientific analysis. The pair explained how the item had been found on the cave floor after a storm had washed it from the land or rocks surrounding the hole in the cavern roof but left out the more bizarre events. A National Trust Collections team expert confirmed that the artifact was common rose quartz. However, as it had not been found during an archeological dig and wasn't made of organic material, such as bone or wood, there was no way to date it. As for its place of origin: as many cultures made stylized hearts from colorful stones, it could have come from just about anywhere. The most likely reason the artifact was in the cave, as far as the National Trust was concerned, was that it had been left there recently by someone with a New Age leaning. The bottom line: it was of no historical, scientific, or financial interest, at least not to them. So, the pair could keep it.

From the everyday perspective, the expert was right. The item could have been left there by anyone, for any reason, at any time. But for Jodi and Graham, the extraordinary circumstances surrounding its discovery confirmed that they had found what they had been seeking—the very item that Jane Morris had hidden well over a century before. They had followed a trail of historical clues leading to Wetton Mill Cave while fate had repeatedly, almost forcibly, guided them there. Furthermore, they would never have found it without the timely storm and accompanying quakes. It had, quite literally, landed at their feet. As far as Jodi and Graham were concerned, they had found— rather, been given—the Heart of the Rose. Yet, despite all the astonishing events they had witnessed, what they had found seemed to be just a typical ornament made from ordinary material, that did nothing unusual. They may have discovered the Heart of the Rose, the prize possession of the Order of Meonia, but they had no more idea as to its purpose than they had when their remarkable quest first began.

They had to accept that it might be some time before anything new occurred or things began to make sense. However, before Jodi's return to the States, some insightful new ideas seem to have been mysteriously imprinted on their minds. Graham was taking Jodi to Manchester Airport, where she would stay overnight before catching an early flight the following day. On the way, they visited the Bridestones. Perhaps, if this was where it all began for the Victorian Order of Meonia, something might occur now that they had the Heart of the Rose. But they were in for a disappointment. No strange weather, visions, synchronicities, mysterious guides, or anything. They decided instead to go to nearby Biddulph Grange, making for the Celtic glen where megaliths from the Bridestones circle were moved to in 1851. Maybe something would happen there.

Jodi was stooping down next to the little pool into which the spring flowed. "What *dia* we see in the cave?" she said, referring to the winged, humanoid shadow that had briefly appeared on the wall. They had asked themselves this question repeatedly.

Graham made his best guess. "The fifth element. What the ancient Celts called Bride. What we've been calling the *whatever*."

"But why an angel?" Jodi asked.

"Because we had Paton's painting on our minds?" Graham suggested, reminding Jodi of their discussion in the pub garden at Upton-upon-Severn. "Preconception determines how it manifests."

Jodi agreed. "I wonder if it has a *true* form."

"I doubt it. A Chinese lady from the moon, a Celtic celeste, what *we* saw, are just ways for the mind to ascribe a form to something that has no form. At least, not in three dimensions."

"An unimaginable being? An intelligence made by unimaginable beings. A computer in the sky?" Jodi mused.

Graham considered the possibilities. "Sacred stones," he said, pointing to the Bridestones monoliths. "Holy wells." He gestured to the pool. "Just two ways, perhaps, to envisage concepts without form."

"What would have happened had we not found the Heart by sunset on October thirteenth?" Jodi said, still mystified at the impression that overwhelmed her at Gawton's Well."

"You said you thought the window of opportunity would close."

"I did. But why?" Jodi stood and surveyed the glen, trying to focus on a notion that seemed to be forming just beyond conscious thought. "I think it was the end of a cycle." She said eventually.

Graham climbed the steps to the tunnel that led to the Chinese pagoda, then turned. "I can't help feeling it was the other way around," he said slowly. "This *whatever* seems to control fate and time, or at least has a higher perception of it. Like the finding of the B

Stone started our quest, what if we were always *meant* to find the Heart of the Rose 150 years after Mary's death? It's more than coincidental that we found it at exactly sunset on that very day."

Jodi frowned. "But why?"

"You said it yourself while sitting on the stile at Steep Low. To begin another."

Jodi had been holding the stone heart in her hand. Suddenly, she felt impelled to hold it under the pool's crystal-clear water. "Wow!" She pulled back her hand and turned to Graham. "That was strange."

"A vision?" Graham walked over to the pool to join her.

"No." Jodi shook her head. "I felt the abrupt need to hold the artifact under the water. Then, without warning, it was like an idea flooded my mind. I was thinking of what you said about material things giving form to abstract ideas when I suddenly thought: *that's what the Heart of the Rose is*. It's a physical embodiment of our quest. We've witnessed things that don't seem possible. We may not know *how* it works, but we know it *can*. Our adventure has given us an entirely new perspective on existence. Like Gawain's quest, what happened along the way may be more important than where it led.

"And the stone heart represents the quest."

"That's the feeling I had." Jodi again put her hand holding the heart into the pool. "Nothing now," she said after a while.

"So, it's not the one Mary Heath found?"

"It might be. Or it might have just appeared."

"Appeared from nowhere!"

"For something that can alter reality, creating a small stone heart would be child's play."

Graham raised his eyebrows. "I guess so. So, the Heart of the Rose can be anything to anyone?"

Jodi stood up and shook her head. "I don't know. Maybe."

They moved on to the Egyptian temple, where, for Graham, the strange adventure had begun all those years before when Jenny had told him he would one day be involved in a quest to find the Heart of the Rose. Inside the mock tomb built by Maria Bateman well over a century and a half ago, Jodi stood in the doorway leading out onto the Alpine path while Graham sat in the bench alcove.

"During our quest, we got the answers we wanted concerning the Order of Meonia," Graham said. "What they did, and why they were doing it, even if we don't understand the *whatever* behind it all." He was now holding the stone heart and turned to place it against the wall behind him—the division that sealed what may once have been a further chamber—in the nonchalant hope that something might happen.

"We really can't keep calling it the *whatever*," Jodi said.

"I wonder what the Meonia group called…" Abruptly, Graham fell silent. After a moment, he said, "Like what happened to you, an idea suddenly filled my mind. The answer to the question I was posing."

Graham began pacing as he explained. "I've always thought that the Order of Meonia—both the

Victorian and Elizabethan groups—got their name from the birthplace of Western occultism, the land now called Lydia. That may be so, but there might be more to it. Years ago, someone, maybe Jenny, I don't remember, remarked that the word 'Meonia' is an anagram for 'I am one.' Even in Elizabethan spelling, the words 'I,' 'am,' and 'one' are spelled as they are today. I checked it out in the original text of a Shakespeare play. I assumed this was just a coincidence. But when I placed the Heart against the wall just now, it was as if different parts of my memory were suddenly accessed and pieced together to form a coherent picture." He explained that, apart from the two Meonia groups, everyone else spelled the ancient land that became Lydia as 'Maeonia,' with the extra 'A.' "The two orders of Meonia may have deliberately left out the first 'A' so that the word had a dual meaning. The name of the ancient land *ana* the anagram."

"Fascinating, but you already knew that."

Graham nodded. "I did. But I never considered what 'I am one'—Meonia—meant. Bride, Chang'e, all the rest. Even that little critter in there." He pointed to the Aani chamber beside where Jodi was standing. As far as people like the Meonia groups were concerned, they were all one. All different aspects of—"

"The *whatever*."

A broad grin formed on Graham's face. "They called it Meonia."

"That's it!" Jodi suddenly knew what finding the stone to open a new level of the celestial game was all about. "We now know what the strange guiding force was called and at least some of what it can do. But what exactly is it?"

"No idea."

"I think that will be the next quest. Finding out what Meonia really is."

"And *we* must do it?"

"Or others. But, either way, we've now made it possible."

* * *

For quite some time, Jodi and Graham wandered the grounds of Biddulph Grange, taking turns holding the stone heart, placing it against various features in the shrines, and asking questions. They hoped that new answers would form in their minds. But nothing did.

"Maybe it only works in certain places at certain times," Jodi said when they returned to the Egyptian temple.

"I guess we have to be patient," Graham suggested. "Besides, we need a rest."

"There is one thing I would love to know before I leave," Jodi said as she stood in the doorway to the Ape of Thoth chamber, holding the stone and looking back down the long corridor to the entrance. "Was it Meonia that spoke through Jenny all those years ago?"

Graham came over to stand next to his friend. "Those words have certainty etched themselves into my memory."

"Mine too, even though I never heard them in person."

Together—for reasons they could not explain—they recited Jenny's message.

Find the stone carved with the letter B. Only then will your quest to understand the Order of Meonia and your search to discover the Heart of the Rose truly begin.

"It's quite strange," said Graham as the tomb fell silent. "When we were just reciting Jenny's words, I suddenly realized that we were standing exactly where she had been when she said them. At that moment, I had the vivid mental image of—"

"Your younger self standing before you."

Graham turned to Jodi, shocked. "We're telepathic now?"

Jodi shook her head. "I don't think so."

"Then how do you know what I was about to say?"

"Because I saw it too."

"Oh my god!" Graham said when the full implications sunk in. "I think you just got the answer to your question."

"About what spoke through Jenny?"

"Yes."

"Who?"

"*We* did."

As they stared at each other—the notion of time loops, now added to the concepts of altered timelines, parallel worlds, and patchwork universes, making their heads spin—the sound of children's laughter echoed through the building. A young girl and boy ran down the long corridor, passed them without a glance, and charged out into the Alpine pathway in the bright afternoon sun.

"Follow me," the girl cried as she skipped ahead.

* * *

This may be just the beginning. For updates, further research, and new adventures, remember to visit our website StrangeFate.Net.

Printed in Great Britain
by Amazon